WORD, SACRAMENT, CHARISM

MARC CARDINAL OUELLET

Word, Sacrament, Charism

Risks and Opportunities of a Synodal Church

Translated by Michael J. Miller

IGNATIUS PRESS   SAN FRANCISCO

Original French edition:
Parole Sacrement Charisme. Église synodale—Risques et opportunités
Published by Parole et Silence, 2024

Cover design by Roxanne Mei Lum

CONTENTS

ABBREVIATIONS

AG   Vatican Council II, Decree on the Missionary Activity of the Church *Ad Gentes* (December 7, 1965)

CFL   John Paul II, Post-Synodal Apostolic Exhortation on the Vocation and Mission of the Laity in the Church and in the World *Christifideles Laici* (December 30, 1988)

DCE   Benedict XVI, encyclical *Deus Caritas Est* (December 25, 2005)

DV   Vatican Council II, Dogmatic Constitution on Divine Revelation *Dei Verbum* (November 18, 1965)

EG   Francis, apostolic exhortation *Evangelii Gaudium* (November 24, 2013)

EN   Paul VI, apostolic exhortation *Evangelii Nuntiandi* (December 8, 1975)

GS   Vatican Council II, Pastoral Constitution on the Church in the Modern World *Gaudium et Spes* (December 7, 1965)

IE   Congregation for the Doctrine of the Faith, Letter *Iuvenescit Ecclesia* to the Bishops of the Catholic Church regarding the Relationship between Hierarchical and Charismatic Gifts in the Life and Mission of the Church (May 15, 2016)

IL   *Instrumentum Laboris* for the 2008 Synod of Bishops

ITC   International Theological Commission

LG   Vatican Council II, Dogmatic Constitution on the Church *Lumen Gentium* (November 21, 1964)

PE   Francis, Apostolic Constitution on the Roman Curia and Its Service to the Church in the World *Praedicate Evangelium* (March 19, 2022)

INTRODUCTION

Prolegomena for a Synodal Ecclesiology

Whatever you may say to complain or rejoice, you have to thank Pope Francis for having the audacity to go back to the drawing board with Catholic ecclesiology along the lines traced out by Vatican II, the Second Ecumenical Council of the Vatican. Some on the right are scandalized by the "revolutionary" elements that have been introduced by his gestures and initiatives; others on the left complain that decisions which long since have been deemed unavoidable for the modernization of the Church have still not been made. The pope has found the way to avoid favoring either extreme and to move the Church forward and *outward* based on a vast project of listening and dialogue with a view to building together a more synodal Church. Participation, communion, and mission are the fundamental themes of this synodal research.

This enterprise challenges theology to articulate the newness of the synodal concept in terms of the perennial data of tradition, so as to avoid developments that may be "creative" yet are "disconnected" from the ecclesial soil because they lack roots in the Church's previous discernments of the Holy Spirit—hence the need for a fundamental reflection so as to accompany the research and to keep it on the track of Catholic ecclesiology, which is duty-bound to be ecumenical at the same time. Some contemporary infatuations with democratic culture, with the human sciences, with innovative methods of inculturation, and with the use of artificial intelligence involve risks that must be incurred, but not without basing our discernment on the fundamental data of Sacred Scripture, Sacred Tradition, and Christian spirituality.

In the following pages, I propose some prolegomena with a view to elaborating a synodal ecclesiology. "Prolegomena" means preliminary materials that revolve around a central theme but do not yet offer a systematic overview. For that, it will be necessary to listen still more to the People of God, to consult with the authorities for the discernment of the synodal process, and to develop adequate theological and canonical hypotheses, while having a more refined sensitivity to cultural differences and historical conditioning. We are talking then about an initial stage of reflection, a perspective that is still a work in progress, which has not yet reached the point of maturity yet offers nonetheless the sketch of a tripartite system that is meant to become permanent.

This is because Catholic ecclesiology suffers from a pneumatological deficiency that is rather widely acknowledged now but has not yet been sufficiently explained theoretically and corrected in practice. Habits of thinking acquired centuries ago almost always reduce the Holy Spirit's mission to the categories of the Incarnate Logos, leaving only a smattering for him personally, weighed down by a Christomonist tradition that has increased the place and importance of the ordained ministry and the ecclesiastical hierarchy at the expense of the common priesthood of the baptized. And the result? Little missionary awareness among the baptized, and even among the ordained ministers, for in the context of Christendom, they spent their energies governing territorial communities and making sure that Christian values prevailed in the surrounding society. Only some communities of consecrated life—charismatics before the contemporary expansion of the term—had explicitly missionary objectives and consciously mobilized their resources for this purpose.

Vatican Council II changed the deal. It universalized the concept of mission, explained more precisely the sacramental nature of the Church, officially declared the universal call to holiness, completed the study of the sacramentality of the episcopate, and gave charisms the right of citizenship. This was an extraordinary advance, and more than sixty years later, we are still gauging its unexplored potentialities. What do we still need in order to make out of all this a synodal success? How can we articulate these gains in such a way that the ecclesiology of communion is transformed into concrete missionary communities that are aware of being sent to the world to bring to it the joy of the Gospel? This is the dream of Pope Francis.

The following essays are another contribution to this dream, in the form of prolegomena for a synodal ecclesiology. Catholic ecclesiology is still articulated in too binary a fashion: nature-grace, word-sacrament, clergy-laity, holy orders-jurisdiction, whereas the Council initiated us into a Trinitarian structure, starting with the introductory paragraphs of the dogmatic constitution *Lumen Gentium*. The third Trinitarian dimension in particular, so beautifully described in paragraph 4 on the mission of the Holy Spirit, still awaits a full acknowledgment despite the postconciliar liberalization of the charisms, the extraordinary rise of the Renewal in the Spirit movement, of ecclesial movements, and of new communities, which have succeeded in making evangelization central again, despite the postconciliar crisis of the traditional institutions. Unfortunately, the limits and defects of this charismatic wave have been recognized and pointed out more forcefully than the positive contribution they make to the Church's evangelizing mission. The weak pneumatological tradition of the Latin Church is not drawn to see and discern the gifts and charisms of the Holy Spirit, to the point where it sometimes too quickly discredits positive growth that could be pruned patiently and bear much fruit in the long run.

In saying these things, I am advocating no one; I am simply noting the meager recognition that is given to the Church's charismatic dimension, which is nevertheless acknowledged to be coessential, of equal dignity with the institutional dimension. I maintain that Catholic ecclesiology has not yet reflected enough on the charisms and integrated them systematically into its formal structure. This is a challenge that remains to be taken up for the building of a synodal Church. The experience of the coessentiality of the charisms is not new; it shaped ecclesial tradition, particularly by its contribution of major religious orders, saints, and mystics; since the Council we have had a new experience of it in these movements and communities, but also at the parochial and diocesan levels; the task still remains, however, of articulating a systematic ecclesiology in which their membership in the very structure of the Church is clearly established and not relegated to the margins and stifled by a clerical mentality.

Word, sacrament, charism: this is the tripartite division that seems to me to lie at the foundation of a synodal Church. A three-part division founded on revelation, rooted in tradition, and articulated in order to make participation in the mission more dynamic. For "in His goodness and wisdom God chose to reveal Himself and to make known to us the hidden purpose of His will (see Eph 1:9) by which through Christ, the Word made flesh, man might in the Holy Spirit have access to the Father and come to share in the divine nature (see Eph 2:18; 2 Peter 1:4)."[1] This summary of revelation expressed by the dogmatic constitution *Dei Verbum* is reflected in the mystery of the Church-communion, the sacrament of mankind's union with God and of the unity of the human race.[2] Charisms are given in abundance for the service of this sacramental and missionary vocation of the Church: multiple and varied charisms, from the Marian charism (which is a special issue and extraordinary), the Petrine charism, the Pauline and Johannine charisms, the institutionalized religious charisms, the emergent charisms, the charisms listed in the New Testament, not to mention the highest: the charism of charity that believes all things and endures all things, which forgives all things and integrates all things in the light of God, who is love and mercy.

A synodal Church cannot exist without a synodal ecclesiology in which the charisms are recognized and integrated. It is founded in the first place on the Word of God, kerygma proclamation, which leads to the sacraments, that is, to Baptism and to the Eucharist via the Sacrament of Holy Orders. With the Word and the sacraments, we have the foundation and the vital framework; with the charisms, we have the freedom of the Spirit, his gratuitous gifts, the particular vocations, missionary daring, and all sorts of creativity. How can missionary communities be built without their contribution? The priesthood of the baptized is essential; it is nourished by the sacraments, but it lives also by the Holy Spirit's gratuitous and generous impulses, which run through all states of life without exception.

This book then is a reading guide for these prolegomena that should lead to a synodal ecclesiology at the conclusion of a journey that has yet to be defined, although we already have the main lines of it at the Council:

> The Spirit dwells in the Church and in the hearts of the faithful, as in a temple (cf. 1 Cor 3:16; 6:19). In them He prays on their behalf and bears witness to the fact that they are adopted sons (cf. Gal 4:6;

---

[1] Vatican Council II, Dogmatic Constitution on Divine Revelation *Dei Verbum* (November 18, 1965), no. 2 (hereinafter *DV*).

[2] Vatican Council II, Dogmatic Constitution on the Church *Lumen Gentium* (November 21, 1964), no. 1 (hereinafter *LG*).

Rom 8:15–16 and 26). The Church, which the Spirit guides in way of all truth (cf. Jn 16:13) and which He unified in communion and in works of ministry, He both equips and directs with hierarchical and charismatic gifts and adorns with His fruits (cf. Eph 1:11–12; 1 Cor 12:4; Gal 5:22).[3]

---

[3] Ibid., no. 4.

Part I

Word

Chapter 1

The Word of God in the
Life and Mission of the Church

And to the angel of the Church in Smyrna write: "The words of the first and the last, who died and came to life.... Be faithful unto death, and I will give you the crown of life. He who has an ear, let him hear what the Spirit says to the churches."

—Revelation 2:8, 10–11

We have gathered in Synod to listen to what the Spirit is saying to the churches today concerning *the Word of God in the life and mission of the Church*. We share the conviction of the Fathers of the Church, expressed by Saint Caesarius of Arles, that "the light and eternal food of the soul is nothing else but the word of God, without which the soul can neither see nor live. Just as our body dies if it does not receive food, so, too, our soul is killed if it does not receive the word of God."[1]

The purpose of the Synod is eminently pastoral and missionary. It consists of listening together to the Word of God so as to discern how the Spirit and the Church are aspiring to respond to the gift of the Incarnate Word through the love of Sacred Scriptures and the proclamation of the Kingdom of God to all humanity. Let us make

"The Word of God in the Life and Mission of the Church" was the theme of the 12th Ordinary General Assembly of the Synod of Bishops, convoked by Pope Benedict XVI, October 5–26, 2008. The following is based on the opening conference, October 5, 2008.

[1] Caesarius of Arles, Sermon VI, in *Sermons*, trans. Sister Mary Magdeleine Mueller, O.S.F. (New York: Fathers of the Church, 1956), 40.

our own the prayer of Saint Paul that immerses us into the heart of
the mystery of revelation:

> For this reason I bow my knees before the Father, from whom every
> family in heaven and on earth is named, that according to the riches
> of his glory he may grant you to be strengthened with might through
> his Spirit in the inner man, and that Christ may dwell in your hearts
> through faith; that you, being rooted and grounded in love, may have
> power to comprehend with all the saints what is the breadth and
> length and height and depth, and to know the love of Christ which
> surpasses knowledge, that you may be filled with all the fulness of
> God. Now to him who by the power at work within us is able to do
> far more abundantly than all that we ask or think, to him be glory in
> the Church and in Christ Jesus to all generations, for ever and ever.
> Amen. (Eph 3:14–21)

The Synod will propose pastoral orientations to "strengthen the
practice of encountering the Word of God as the source of life",[2] by
taking stock of the reception of Vatican Council II concerning the
Word of God in its relation to the ecclesiological renewal, to ecumenism, and to the dialogue with nations and the world religions.

Beyond the theoretical discussions, we are invited to espouse the
Council's attitude: "Hearing the word of God with reverence and
proclaiming it with faith, the sacred synod takes its direction from
these words of St. John: 'We announce to you the eternal life which
dwelt with the Father and was made visible to us. What we have seen
and heard we announce to you, so that you may have fellowship with
us and our common fellowship be with the Father and His Son Jesus
Christ' (1 Jn 1:2–3)."[3]

Thanks to the Trinitarian and Christocentric vision of Vatican
Council II, the Church has renewed her awareness of her own mystery and mission. The dogmatic constitution *Lumen Gentium* and the
pastoral constitution *Gaudium et Spes* develop an ecclesiology of communion that is based on a renewed concept of revelation. Indeed, the
dogmatic constitution *Dei Verbum* marked a genuine turning point
in our way of dealing with divine revelation. Instead of privileging,

---

[2] *Instrumentum Laboris* for the 2008 Synod of Bishops, no. 4 (hereinafter *IL*).
[3] *DV*, no. 1.

as in the past, the noetic [intellectual] dimension of the truths that are to be believed, the Council Fathers accentuated the dynamic and dialogical[4] dimension of revelation as God's personal communication of himself. In this way they laid the foundations for a livelier encounter and dialogue between God, who calls, and his people, who respond.

This turning point has been greeted widely as a decisive fact by theologians, exegetes, and pastors.[5] However, it is rather generally acknowledged that the constitution *Dei Verbum* had an insufficient reception and that the turning point that it inaugurated has not yet produced all its desired and expected fruits in the life and mission of the Church.[6] Taking into account some progress that has been made, we must ask ourselves why the model of personal communication[7] has not made its way more into the consciousness of the Church, her prayer and pastoral practices, as well as into her theological and exegetical methods. The Synod must propose concrete solutions to fill in the gaps and to remedy the ignorance of the Scriptures, which adds to the current difficulties of evangelization.

Let us acknowledge, indeed, that the life of faith and the missionary impetus of Christians are profoundly affected by various sociocultural phenomena such as secularization, religious pluralism, and the globalization and explosion of the means of communication, with the multiple consequences of these phenomena, particularly the growing disparity between rich and poor, the proliferation of esoteric

---

[4] The adjective *dialogical* is a neologism. It is used here to express the personal and responsorial dimension of the faith as a dialogue with God. It corresponds to some extent to the distinction between *theological* and *theologal*, where the first expresses the noetic aspect, and the second, the personal aspect.

[5] See Joseph Ratzinger, "Commentary on *Dei Verbum*", in *Lexikon für Theologie und Kirche (LThK)* (Freiburg: Verlag Herder, 1967); Aloys Grillmeier, in *LThK* Vat. II, vol. 2 (Freiburg: Verlag Herder, 1967); Henri de Lubac, *La Révélation divine* (Paris: Éditions du Cerf, 1983); Albert Vanhoye, "La réception dans l'Église de la constitution *Dei Verbum*: Du Concile Vatican II à aujourd'hui", *Esprit et Vie* 107 (June 2004): 3–13; Helmut Hoping, "Theologischer Kommentar zur Dogmatischen Konstitution über die göttliche Offenbarung, *Dei Verbum*", in *Herders theologischer Kommentar zum Zweiten Vatikanischen Konzil*, ed. Peter Hünermann and Bernd J. Hilberath (Freiburg-Basel-Vienna: Herder, 2005), 695–831; Christoph Théobald, "La Révélation: Quarante ans après *Dei Verbum*", *Revue théologique de Louvain* 36 (2005): 145–65.

[6] *IL*, no. 6.

[7] Max Seckler, "Der Begriff der Offenbarung", in *Handbuch der Fundamentaltheologie*, vol. 2, ed. Walter Kern et al. (Freiburg: Herder, 1985), 64–67.

sects, and threats to peace, not to mention the current attacks against human life and the family.[8]

To these socio-cultural phenomena we should add the Church's internal difficulties concerning the transmission of the faith in the family, the deficiencies in catechetical formation, the tensions between the ecclesial Magisterium and theology at the universities, the internal crisis of exegesis and its relation to theology, and more generally "a certain gap between scholars and pastors, as well as between scholars and the ordinary people of the Christian communities".[9]

The Synod must confront the major challenge of transmitting faith in the Word of God today. In a pluralistic world, marked by relativism and esoterism,[10] the very notion of revelation raises a question[11] and calls for clarifications.

Convocatio, communio, missio. Around these three key words that express the threefold dimension—dynamic, personal, and dialogical—of Christian revelation, we will explain the thematic structure of the *Instrumentum Laboris.* The Word of God convokes or calls together; it makes us commune or share in God's plan through the obedience of faith, and it sends the chosen people out into the nations. This Word of the Covenant culminates in Mary, who welcomes in faith the Incarnate Word, the Desired of All Nations (see Hag 2:7, KJV). We will take up the three dimensions of the Word of the Covenant as the Holy Spirit incarnated them in salvation history, the Sacred Scriptures, and ecclesial tradition.

Let us ask the Holy Spirit to increase this desire to rediscover the Word of God, which is always contemporary and never outmoded. This Word has the power to "put the Church back into the world", to rejuvenate her, and to inspire a new hope with a view to her mission work. Benedict XVI reminded us that this great hope rests on the certainty that "God is love"[12] and that "in Christ, God has revealed himself"[13] for the salvation of all.

---

[8] Ibid.

[9] *IL*, no. 7a (translated by Ignatius Press).

[10] Jean Rigal, "Le phénomène gnostique", *Esprit et Vie* 192 (avril 2008, 2ᵉ quinzaine): 1–10.

[11] Philippe Bordeyne and Laurent Villemin, eds., *L'herméneutique théologique de Vatican II*, Collection "Cogitatio Fidei" (Paris: Éditions du Cerf, 2006).

[12] Benedict XVI, encyclical letter *Deus Caritas Est* (December 25, 2005).

[13] Benedict XVI, encyclical letter *Spe Salvi* (November 30, 2007), no. 9.

Convocatio: Identity of the Word of God

God Speaks

In principio erat Verbum, et Verbum erat apud Deum, et Deus erat Verbum. "In the beginning was the Word, and the Word was with God, and the Word was God" (Jn 1:1). From the outset we must start with the mystery of God as he revealed himself to us in Sacred Scripture. The God of revelation is a God who speaks, a God who is in himself a Word and gives himself to humanity to be known in various ways (Heb 1:1). Thanks to the Bible, mankind knows that it is addressed by God; the Spirit allows us to listen to and receive the Word of God, thus becoming the *Ecclesia*, the community gathered by the Word. This believing community receives its identity and mission from the Word of God that founds it, feeds it, and employs it in the service of the Kingdom of God.[14]

Let us clarify at the outset the many meanings of "the Word of God". The prologue to John's Gospel offers the most exalted and most comprehensive perspective from which to make these clarifications. With the term *Logos* the evangelist designates a transcendent reality that was with God and which is God himself. This Logos is *with God and turned toward God*—πρὸς τὸν θεόν (Jn 1:1)— in the *beginning*, that is to say, before all things, in *God* himself (ἐν ἀρχῇ). The end of the prologue specifies the personal divine nature of the Logos in these words: "No one has ever seen God; the only-begotten Son, who is in the bosom of the Father, he has made him known" (Jn 1:18).

In his Letters to the Colossians and to the Ephesians, Saint Paul expresses in more or less equivalent way the mystery of Christ, the Word of God: "He is the image of the invisible God, the first-born of all creation, for in him all things were created, in heaven and on earth, visible and invisible.... All things were created through him and for him" (Col 1:15–16). In his plan for salvation, God willed "to unite all things in [Christ], things in heaven and things on earth. In him, according to the purpose of him who accomplishes all things according to the counsel of his will, we who first hoped in Christ

---

[14] See Jn 19:25–27; 20:21–22; 1 Pet 2:9–10.

have been destined and appointed to live for the praise of his glory"
(Eph 1:10–12).

The Word of the New and Eternal Covenant, Jesus Christ

The Word of God therefore signifies first of all God himself, who
speaks, who expresses in himself a Divine Word belonging to his
interior mystery. This Divine Word gives to all things their origin,
for "without him was not anything made that was made" (Jn 1:3).
He speaks in many languages, particularly the language of material
creation, of life, and of the human being. "In him was life, and the
life was the light of men" (Jn 1:4). He speaks moreover in a special
and even dramatic way in human history, particularly by choosing a
people, through the law of Moses and the prophets.

Finally, after having spoken in many ways (Heb 1:1), he recapitulates and crowns it all in a unique, perfect, and definitive way in Jesus
Christ: *Et Verbum caro factum est et habitavit in nobis.* "And the Word
became flesh and dwelt among us" (Jn 1:14). The mystery of the
Incarnate Divine Word holds the central place in the prologue and
in the New Testament as a whole. To see Jesus is to see his Father
(Jn 14:9). "For this reason Jesus perfected revelation by fulfilling it
through His whole work of making Himself present and manifesting
Himself: through His words and deeds, His signs and wonders, but
especially through His death and glorious resurrection from the dead
and final sending of the Spirit of truth. Moreover He confirmed with
divine testimony what revelation proclaimed, that God is with us
to free us from the darkness of sin and death, and to raise us up to
life eternal."[15]

The "Word of God" to which Scripture testifies consequently
assumes different forms and contains different levels of meaning. It
designates God himself, who speaks; his Divine Word; his creating
and saving Word; and finally his Word made flesh in Jesus Christ,
"the mediator and the fullness of all revelation".[16] For Luke, the
Word of God is identified even with the oral teaching of Jesus (Lk
5:1–3), or to the paschal message, the kerygma, which through the

---

[15] *DV*, no. 4.
[16] *DV*, no. 2.

preaching of the Apostles "grows and multiplies" like a living organism (see Acts 12:24). This Word of God, which is one and many, dynamic and eschatological, personal and filial, dwells in the Church and enlivens her by faith; it is recorded in the Sacred Scriptures as a historical and literary testimony, as a sacred deposit destined for all humanity—hence this new and decisive modality of the Word of God, the sacred text, the written form that the people of Israel kept as a testimony of the first Covenant; hence, too, the Scriptures of the New Testament, which the Church received in turn from the Holy Spirit and from the apostolic tradition: Scriptures that she considers normative and definitive for her life and mission.

In short, the Word of God, whether written or transmitted orally, is a dialogical, even Trinitarian, Word. It is offered to humanity in Jesus Christ so as to introduce it into the Trinitarian communion, where it will find its full identity. According to John's prologue, this personal Word of God calls out to humanity and immediately poses the question about his reception: "He came to his own home, and his own people received him not. But to all who received him, who believed in his name, he gave power to become children of God" (Jn 1:11–12).

God speaks, and by that very fact, man is constituted as a being who is called. This anthropological dimension of revelation is expressed laconically in the constitution Dei Verbum: "Through Christ, the Word made flesh, man ... in the Holy Spirit [has] access to the Father and come[s] to share in the divine nature (see Eph 2:18; 2 Pet 1:4)."[17] On this anthropological theme, the Fathers of the Church unfolded the traditional doctrine of the Imago Dei. Saint Irenaeus of Lyons, for example, commenting on Saint Paul, speaks about the Son and the Spirit as "the Father's hands", which fashion man in "the image and likeness of God".[18]

It is important to keep in mind this anthropological dimension of revelation, because it plays a very important role today in the interpretation of biblical texts. Vatican Council II redefined man's dialogical identity in terms of the Word of God in Christ: "The truth is that only in the mystery of the incarnate Word does the mystery of man take on light. For Adam, the first man, was a figure of Him

---

[17] DV, no. 2.
[18] Irenaeus of Lyons, Contra Haereses I, 3.

Who was to come (cf. Rom. 5:14), namely Christ the Lord. Christ, the final Adam, by the revelation of the mystery of the Father and His love, fully reveals man to man himself and makes his supreme calling clear."[19] Thus, it appears, in this Christological light, that by accepting this sublime vocation through faith and love, man attains his full personal identity in the Church, a mystery of communion, "a people assembled in the unity of the Father and of the Son and of the Holy Spirit".[20]

On the pastoral level, shouldn't we verify whether this dialogical and filial theo-anthropology founded on Christ actually holds the place that belongs to it in the Liturgy, catechesis, and theological instruction? "For in the sacred books," the constitution *Dei Verbum* recalls, "the Father who is in heaven meets His children with great love and speaks with them; and the force and power in the word of God is so great that it stands as the support and energy of the Church, the strength of faith for her sons, the food of the soul, the pure and everlasting source of spiritual life."[21]

Man's divine vocation, as we said, is clarified in the mystery of the Incarnate Word, the New Adam. This vocation confers on him his transcendental dynamism in the form of a deep desire for God that is inscribed on his very being. Man is a being of desire who aspires to the infinite, but he is also a being of service who obeys the Word of God: "I am the handmaid of the Lord" (Lk 1:38). All of anthropology is at stake in this passage from desire to service that makes man an ecclesial being, an *anima ecclesiastica*.

The Bride of the Incarnate Word

The Daughter of Sion and the Ecclesia

"In communion with those whose memory we venerate, especially the glorious ever-Virgin Mary, Mother of our God and Lord, Jesus Christ."[22]

---

[19] Vatican Council II, Pastoral Constitution on the Church in the Modern World *Gaudium et Spes* (December 7, 1965), no. 22 (hereinafter GS).

[20] Cyprian of Carthage, *De Oratione Dominica* 23 (PL 4, 553).

[21] *DV*, no. 21.

[22] Roman Canon [Eucharistic Prayer I].

A woman, Mary, perfectly fulfilled the divine vocation of humanity by her Yes to the Word of the Covenant and to his mission.
Through her divine maternity and her spiritual motherhood, Mary
appears as the model and the permanent form of the Church, as the
first Church. Let us dwell for a moment on the pivotal figure of
Mary, between the Old and the New Covenants, who completed
the passage from the faith of Israel to the faith of the Church. Let us
meditate on the account of the Annunciation, which is the origin
and the unsurpassable model of God's self-communication and of the
Church's experience of faith. It will serve as our paradigm for understanding the dialogical identity of the Word of God in the Church.
On the part of God who speaks, the Trinitarian dimension of revelation appears quite clearly. The angel of the Annunciation speaks
in the name of God the Father, who takes the initiative to address
his creature so as to make her vocation and mission known to her.
This is a grace-filled event, the content of which is communicated
despite the fear and astonishment of his creature: "You will conceive
in your womb and bear a son, and you shall call his name Jesus. He
... will be called the Son of the Most High." In the lively dialogue
that follows, Mary asks: "How can this be, since I [do not know
man]?" The angel replies: "The Holy Spirit will come upon you ...;
therefore the child to be born will be called ... the Son of God" (Lk
1:31–32, 35). Besides this Trinitarian dimension of the account of the
event, Mary's dialogue with the angel instructs us at the same time
concerning the vital reaction of the woman who is called on: her fear,
her perplexity, and her demand for an explanation. God respects the
freedom of his creature; this is why he adds the sign of Elizabeth's
fruitfulness, which enables Mary to give her consent in a way that is
simultaneously supernatural and fully human. "I am the handmaid
of the Lord; let it be to me according to your word" (Lk 1:38). As
Spouse of the living God, Mary becomes Mother of the Son through
the grace of the Spirit.

As soon as Mary gives her unconditional consent to the angel's
announcement, the life of the Trinity enters her soul, her heart, and
her womb, inaugurating the mystery of the Church. For the Church
of the New Testament begins to exist at the place where the Incarnate Word is welcomed, cherished, and served in complete availability to the Holy Spirit. This life of communion with the Word in the
Spirit begins with the *announcement* of the angel and extends to Mary's

entire existence. This life includes all the stages of the growth and mission of the Incarnate Word, particularly the eschatological scene at the Cross where Mary receives from Jesus himself *the announcement* of the fullness of her spiritual motherhood: "Woman, behold, your son" (Jn 19:26). At all these stages, through her "uninterrupted response of 'yes' ",[23] Mary communes in the life of God, who gives himself, and she collaborates whole-heartedly in his plan of salvation for all humanity. She is the New Eve, whose praises are sung by Saint Irenaeus, who as the Bride of the Lamb participates in the universal fruitfulness of the Incarnate Word.

The scene of the Annunciation and the life of Mary illustrate and recapitulate the covenantal structure of the Word of God and the responsorial attitude of faith. They highlight the personal and Trinitarian nature of faith, which consists of a gift of the person to God, who gives himself by revealing himself.[24] "This attitude is the attitude of the saints. It is the same attitude as that of the Church which does not cease to be converted to her Lord in response to the voice that He addresses to her."[25] This is why attention to the figure of Mary, as model and even archetype of the Church's faith,[26] seems to us to be of capital importance in order to bring about concretely a paradigm shift in our relation to the Word of God. This paradigm shift does not comply with the philosophy of the day, but rather with the rediscovery of the original place of the Word, the vital dialogue of the Triune God with the Church, his Bride, which is carried out in the Sacred Liturgy. "Christ indeed always associates the Church with Himself in this great work wherein God is perfectly glorified and men are sanctified. The Church is His beloved

---

[23] *IL*, no. 25.

[24] See *Catechism of the Catholic Church*, no. 170: "We do not believe in formulas, but in those realities they express, which faith allows us to touch. 'The believer's act [of faith] does not terminate in the propositions, but in the realities [which they express].' (St. Thomas Aquinas, *STh* [*Summa Theologica*] II-II, q. 1, art. 2 ad 2)." The formal object of faith is the Person who utters and gives himself in his supreme utterance, Jesus Christ, whom the Holy Spirit authorizes us to profess. Faith is essentially Trinitarian; it is an act of personal giving in response to the Tri-Personal gift of God. We sense in the text of *Dei Verbum* a balance that has yet to be found between the personal or dynamic aspect of faith and the noetic (intellectual) aspect.

[25] Henri de Lubac, *L'Écriture dans la tradition* (Paris: Aubier, 1966), 100.

[26] In other words, Mary's life of faith is more than an example for the Church; she is her Mother, that is, the permanent source of life for the Church.

Bride who calls to her Lord, and through Him offers worship to the Eternal Father."[27]

Tradition, Scripture, and Magisterium

To speak about the Liturgy as a living dialogue of the Church with God is to speak about tradition in the first sense of the term, that is, the living transmission of the mystery of the New Covenant. Tradition is established by the apostolic preaching; it precedes the Scriptures, elaborates them, and always accompanies them. The Word of God, when preached, gives rise to faith, which is expressed at its summit by Baptism and the Eucharist. This indeed is the place where God, in Christ, offers his life to men "that He may invite and take them into fellowship with Himself".[28] This is also where the Church, in the name of all humanity, responds to the God of the Covenant by offering herself with Christ for his glory and for the salvation of the world.

In the living tradition of the Church, the Word of God holds the first place: it is the living Christ. The written Word bears witness to him. Scripture, in fact, is a historical proof and a canonical reference that is indispensable for the prayer, the life, and the doctrine of the Church. However, Scripture is not the whole Word; it is not totally identified with it—hence the importance of the distinction between the Word and the book, just like the one between the letter and the Spirit. Saint Paul forcefully declares that we are the "ministers of a new covenant, not in a written code [i.e., the 'letter'] but in the Spirit; for the written code kills, but the Spirit gives life" (2 Cor 3:6). It is clear that the letter of Scripture plays a primordial and normative role in the Church, but "Christianity, strictly speaking, is not a 'religion of the book': it is the religion of the Word [de la Parole]—but neither uniquely nor principally of the Word in its written form. It is the religion of the Word

---

[27] Vatican Council II, Constitution on the Sacred Liturgy Sacrosanctum Concilium (December 4, 1963), no. 7 (hereinafter SC). Compare Council of Trent, Session XXII (September 17, 1562), Decree De Sanctissima Eucharistia, c. 1: "He willed to leave to the Church, His beloved Spouse, a sacrifice that is visible"; LG, no. 4; DV, nos. 8 and 23. See also Eph 5:21–32; Rev 22:17; cf. Jn 2:1–12; 19:25–27.

[28] DV, no. 2.

[*du Verbe*]—and 'not of a written, mute word, but of an incarnate, living Word.' "[29] This religion of the Word, however, remains inseparable from the written Word, maintaining a complex but essential relation with it.

The unity of living tradition with Sacred Scripture is based on the assistance of the Holy Spirit to those who perform pastoral ministry. "But the task of authentically interpreting the word of God, whether written or handed on, has been entrusted exclusively to the living teaching office of the Church, whose authority is exercised in the name of Jesus Christ. This teaching office [Magisterium] is not above the word of God, but serves it, teaching only what has been handed on, listening to it devoutly, guarding it scrupulously and explaining it faithfully in accord with a divine commission and with the help of the Holy Spirit, it draws from this one deposit of faith everything which it presents for belief as divinely revealed."[30]

The assistance that the Holy Spirit gives to the Magisterium (2 Tim 1:14) completes the action that he performs in creation and salvation history. Indeed, the Holy Spirit is at work in history, stirring up *actions* and *words* that interpreted the events and were set down in writing in the sacred books.[31] Historical-critical exegesis has made us more aware of the complex human mediations that occurred in elaborating the sacred texts, but nonetheless the Holy Spirit guided all salvation history, he inspired its verbal and written interpretation, and he fashioned its culmination in Christ and the Church. Saint Paul poetically describes the Word of God as "the sword of the Spirit" (Eph 6:17). He excels in highlighting the Spirit's role in God's plan, particularly in the magisterial synthesis of the Letter to the Ephesians (see 1:13; 2:22; 3:5). Note, however, that the action of the Holy Spirit does not oppose the dialogical dimension and the doctrinal dimension, as the Church's Magisterium strives to recall, while putting the emphasis in *Dei Verbum* on the personal-dialogical dimension based on God's self-communication in Christ.

---

[29] De Lubac, *L'Écriture dans la tradition*, 246. The author refers to Saint Bernard, *Super Missus est*, h. 4, n. 11, who has Mary say: "*Nec fiat mihi verbum scriptum et mutum, sed incarnatum et vivum*", "Let not a mute written word be done to me, but rather an incarnate, living Word" (PL 183, 86 B).

[30] *DV*, no. 10.

[31] Ibid., no. 2.

"It is clear, therefore, that sacred tradition, Sacred Scripture and the teaching authority of the Church, in accord with God's most wise design, are so linked and joined together that one cannot stand without the others, and that all together and each in its own way under the action of the one Holy Spirit contribute effectively to the salvation of souls."[32] Despite this delicate balance which has many ecumenical implications, tensions remain, and we should continue to reflect on these fundamental questions that determine the way in which to read the Scriptures, to interpret them, and to make fruitful use of them for the life and mission of the Church.

Convocatio: God calls his creatures into existence by his Word. He calls man to dialogue in his Son, and he calls the Church to share his divine life in the Spirit. I decided to conclude this part about the identity of the Word of God with a section on the Church, Spouse of the Incarnate Word. Despite the complexity of the relations between Scripture, tradition, and Magisterium, the Holy Spirit nevertheless ensures the unity of the whole, especially if we keep clearly in mind the responsorial and even nuptial dynamic of the covenantal relation. By situating the ecclesial functions of Scripture, tradition, and the Magisterium within a Marian ecclesiology, we recommend a paradigm shift in which the emphasis moves from the noetic dimension of revelation to the personal dimension. The archetypal figure of Mary allows us to highlight the dynamic dimension of the Word and the personal nature of faith as a gift of self, while inviting the Church to remain subject to the Word and available to every prompting of the Holy Spirit.

Communio: The Word of God in the Life of the Church

In this second part, I discuss the Word of God in the life of the Church, starting with the Church's dialogue with God in the Sacred Liturgy, which is the cradle of the Word, his *Sitz im Leben*.[33] Then

---

[32] Ibid., no. 10.

[33] About this expression, see Willy Rordorf, "La confession de foi et son 'Sitz im Leben' dans l'église ancienne", *Novum Testamentum* 9, no. 3 (July 1967): 225–38; Albert Vanhoye, "La réception dans l'Église de la constitution dogmatique *Dei Verbum*: Du Concile Vatican II à aujourd'hui", *Esprit et Vie* 107 (June 2004): 9.

we will discuss *lectio divina* and the ecclesial interpretation of Sacred Scripture while emphasizing the search for the spiritual sense, thus encouraging a renewed interest in patristic exegesis.

The Church's Dialogue with the God Who Speaks: The Sacred Liturgy

The Liturgy is considered to be the exercise of the priestly office of Jesus Christ, an exercise in which the integral "public worship is performed by the Mystical Body of Jesus Christ, that is, by the Head and by His members."[34] This is why the constitution *Sacrosanctum Concilium* insists on the different modalities of the presence of Christ in the Liturgy. "He is present in the sacrifice of the Mass, not only in the person of His minister, 'the same now offering, through the ministry of priests, who formerly offered himself on the cross,' but especially under the Eucharistic species."[35] Christ "is present in His word, since it is He Himself who speaks when the holy scriptures are read in the Church."[36]

It is he himself who speaks when the Sacred Scriptures are read in the Church. We cannot insist too much on the pastoral implications of this solemn conciliar statement. It reminds us that the first subject of the Sacred Liturgy is Christ himself, addressing his people and offering himself to his Father in a sacrifice of love for the world's salvation. Even though the Church seems to have the primary role in the performance of the liturgical rites, she in fact still plays a subordinate role, in the service of the Word and of the One who speaks. Ecclesiocentrism is foreign to the conciliar reform. When the Word is proclaimed, it is Christ who speaks in the name of his Father, and the Holy Spirit makes us receive his Word and share in his life. The liturgical assembly exists to the extent that it is centered on the Word and not on itself. Otherwise, it degenerates into just another social group.

By insisting in this way, the Church teaches us that the Word of God is in the first place God who speaks. Already in the first Covenant, God speaks to his people through Moses, who then brings

---

[34] *SC*, no. 7.

[35] Ibid., quoting Council of Trent, Session XXII, Doctrine on the Holy Sacrifice of the Mass, c. 2.

[36] Ibid.

back to him the people's response to Yahweh's words: "All that the LORD has spoken we will do" (Ex 19:8).[37] God speaks less to instruct us than to communicate himself and to "take [us] into fellowship [*communion*] with Himself."[38] The Holy Spirit brings about this fellowship by assembling the community around the Word and by making present the Paschal Mystery of Christ in which he hands himself over in communion. For, according to the Scriptures, the mission of the Incarnate Word culminates in the communication of the Spirit of God.[39] In this Trinitarian and pneumatological light, it appears more clearly that the Sacred Liturgy is the living dialogue between God who speaks and the community that listens and responds with praise, thanksgiving, and commitment in Christian life and mission. How can we cultivate among the faithful an awareness that the Liturgy is the exercise of the priestly office of Jesus Christ to which the Church is associated as his dearly beloved Spouse? When this original place of the Word is rediscovered, what consequences should it have on biblical hermeneutics, on the celebration of the Eucharist, and especially on the place and function of the Liturgy of the Word, including the homily?

WORD AND EUCHARIST

"The Church has always venerated the divine Scriptures just as she venerates the body of the Lord, since, especially in the sacred liturgy, she unceasingly receives and offers to the faithful the bread of life from the table both of God's word and of Christ's body."[40]

In comparing the Liturgy of the Word and the Eucharist to two "tables", *Dei Verbum* intended to emphasize with good reason the importance of the Word. This expression repeats a traditional theme that we find expressed very vigorously in the writings of Origen, for example, when he exhorts the faithful with respect to both the Word and the Body of Christ: "Now if you with good reason take

[37] We already find this responsorial dimension expressed emphatically in the description of the foundational rite of the Sinai Covenant (Ex 24:3–7), and even in the narration of the preparatory phase (Ex 19:8).

[38] *DV*, no. 2.

[39] Jn 19:30; 20:22; Acts 2:1–13; Rom 8:15–17; Gal 4:6.

[40] *DV*, no. 21.

so many precautions with regard to His Body, why would you think that negligence of the Word of God deserves a milder punishment than negligence of His Body?"[41]

If we insist on keeping the metaphor of the two tables, shouldn't we have a nuanced view about the way in which to venerate them?[42] Shouldn't we also emphasize above all their unity, because they serve the same "Bread of Life" (Jn 6:35–58) to the faithful? Whether under the form of the Word to be believed or the form of the Flesh to be eaten, the proclaimed Word and the Word pronounced over the offerings participate in one and the same sacramental event. The Liturgy of the Word bears within itself a spiritual force, which however is increased tenfold by its intrinsic connection with the actualization of the Paschal Mystery: the Word of God, who makes himself sacramental Flesh by the power of the Spirit. This sacramental mystery is accomplished by words, as the Council of Trent recalls,[43] and also by the action of the Holy Spirit, who rests upon the ordained minister and is explicitly invoked in the epiclesis.

The Spirit confers on the Word that is proclaimed in the Liturgy a power that is performative, that is, "living and active" (Heb 4:12). This means that the liturgical Word, for example, the Gospel, "is not merely a communication of things that can be known—it is one that makes things happen and is life-changing".[44] This performative power of the liturgical Word depends on the fact that the One who speaks does not intend primarily *to instruct* by his Word, but rather *to communicate himself.* The one who listens and responds does not adhere only to abstract truths; he makes a personal commitment with his whole life, thus manifesting his identity as a member of the Body of Christ. The Holy Spirit is the key to this vital communication. He is the One who fashions the sacramental and ecclesial Body of Christ, as he fashioned in Mary Christ's fleshly Body and, as Origen

---

[41] Origen, *Homilies on Exodus* XIII, 3.

[42] The redaction history of this passage from *DV* shows that a nuance was added in the final version: they used the expression *sicut et* (so too) instead of *velut* (just as) to avoid forcing the comparison along the lines of an identical veneration. See Hoping, "Theologischer Kommentar", 791.

[43] Council of Trent, Session XIII, October 11, 1551: "The Body exists under the species of bread and the Blood under the species of wine by virtue of the words" (Denzinger-Hünermann 1640).

[44] Benedict XVI, *Spe Salvi*, no. 2.

puts it, the "Body of Scripture".[45] Thus, with the Son and the Spirit, "the Father who is in heaven meets His children with great love and speaks with them."[46] How should we form disciples and ministers who are capable of highlighting the Trinitarian and responsorial dimension of the Liturgy? These pastoral incidences involve not only a reform of seminary studies but also a rehabilitation of the practice of meditating on the Scriptures.

THE HOMILY

Despite the Second Vatican Council's call for a renewal of the homily at Mass, we still experience the dissatisfaction of many of the faithful with regard to the preaching ministry. This dissatisfaction partly explains the departure of many Catholics for other religious groups. In order to remedy the gaps in preaching, we know that it is not enough to give priority to the Word of God, for it is also necessary for it to be interpreted correctly in the mystagogical context of the Liturgy. Nor is it enough to resort to exegesis or to use new pedagogical or technological methods; nor is it even enough nowadays for the minister's personal life to be in profound harmony with the Word that is proclaimed. All that is very important, but it may remain extrinsic to the fulfillment of the Paschal Mystery of Christ. What help can be given to homilists to relate life and the Word to this eschatological event that breaks into the heart of the assembly? The homily must get to the spiritual, that is, Christological depth of Sacred Scripture.[47] How can we avoid the tendency to moralism and instead cultivate the appeal to the faith decision?

The *Instrumentum Laboris* (working document) emphasized the passage Luke 4:21, which speaks about the *first homily* of Jesus in

---

[45] Origen, *Treatise on First Principles* IV, 2, 8; see Benedict XVI, Post-Synodal Apostolic Exhortation on the Eucharist *Sacramentum Caritatis* (February 22, 2007), nos. 12–13 (hereinafter *SaC*).

[46] *DV*, no. 21.

[47] See Hans Urs von Balthasar, *Light of the Word: Brief Reflections on the Sunday Readings* (San Francisco: Ignatius Press, 1993). This commentary on the Sunday readings for years A, B, and C points out the unity of the three readings from the theological perspective. This commentary, which has been published in several languages, answers a need that homilists often express. Original edition: *Licht des Wortes: Skizzen zu allen Sonntagslesungen* (Trier: Paulinus Verlag, 1987).

the synagogue in Nazareth: "And he began to say to them, 'Today this Scripture has been fulfilled in your hearing.'" The Gospel of Luke introduces this sequence solemnly, making a sort of summary of the preaching and destiny of Jesus. In a certain sense, the scene in the synagogue in Nazareth was a symbol of his life. The people are astonished by the gracious message that proceeded from his mouth, but at the end of the day, they were ready to throw him off the cliff. The beginning of his preaching was the prologue to the Paschal Mystery.

"Today this Scripture has been fulfilled in your hearing." Between the today of the Risen Lord and the today of the assembly, there is the mediation of Scripture carried by the Spirit on the lips of the homilist. All "wondered at the gracious words which proceeded out of his mouth" (Lk 4:22). Illumined by the Holy Spirit, the text, explained in a simple, familiar way, serves as a mediation for the encounter between Christ and the community. The fulfillment of Scripture thus occurs in the faith of the community, which welcomes Christ as the Word of God. The today that interests the preacher is the today of faith, the faith decision to abandon oneself to Christ and to obey him in all the moral requirements of the Gospel.

As minister of the Word, the priest makes up for what is lacking in the preaching of Jesus for his Body, which is the Church. He shares the sufferings of the preparations, the difficulties of communication, but above all, the joy of being the instrument of the Holy Spirit at the service of a very radical event: "The reception that man gives to God's offering of love which is presented to him in Christ."[48]

THE DIVINE OFFICE

God continues to speak with his people through his Son, in the Spirit, "not only by celebrating the eucharist, but also in other ways, especially by praying the divine office".[49] Christ Jesus "introduced into this earthly exile that hymn which is sung throughout all ages in the halls of heaven. He joins the entire community of mankind to

---

[48] Joseph Ratzinger, *Dogma and Preaching* (San Francisco: Ignatius Press, 2011), [approx.] 50; see also *SaC*, no. 46.

[49] *SC*, no. 83.

Himself, associating it with His own singing of this canticle of divine praise."[50] Saint Augustine writes on this subject: "It is the one Savior of His Mystical Body, our Lord Jesus Christ, the Son of God, who prays for us and in us and is Himself the object of our prayers. He prays for us as our priest, He prays in us as our Head, He is the object of our prayers as our God. Let us then recognize both our voice in His, and His voice in ours."[51]

The Divine Office is part of the exercise of the priestly office of Jesus Christ, with which the Church is intimately associated as Spouse of the Incarnate Word. The renewal of the Divine Office accomplished by the Council has produced great fruits in the Church thanks to the development of a much more widespread practice in simplified forms, which allow frequent, prayerful contact with the Word of God. This monastic and conventual practice, seasoned also with patristic readings, remains a constitutive element in the Church's tradition and consequently is an important reference point for the interpretation of Scripture in the Church. It embodies the spiritual purpose of the Sacred Scriptures and mines the unsurpassable prayer of the Psalms. As Saint Pius X explains, citing Saint Athanasius: "Though all Scripture, both old and new, is divinely inspired and has its use in teaching, as we read in Scripture itself, yet the Book of Psalms, like a garden enclosing the fruits of all the other books, produces their fruits in song."[52] The one who chants the Psalms is so to speak in front of a *mirror* in which he can find his own feelings, like Augustine, who admits that in this way "Truth filtered into my heart, and from my heart surged waves of devotion. Tears ran down, and I was happy in my tears."[53]

The Synod should recall the extent to which the fervent practice of the Divine Office, according to the proper rule of each community, remains a precious seed of community life and of joy.[54] It

---

[50] Ibid.

[51] Augustine, *Exposition on Psalm 85*, 1. English translation from *The Liturgy of the Hours according to the Roman Rite* (New York: Catholic Book Publishing, 1976), 2:367.

[52] Pius X, apostolic constitution *Divino Afflatu* (November 1, 1911), quoted in *Liturgy of the Hours*, 4:1336–37.

[53] Quoted in *Liturgy of the Hours*, 4:1337.

[54] We should mention in passing the fortunate biblical renewal of several practices and devotions that are also important occasions for meditation on Sacred Scripture: Eucharistic adoration outside of Mass, the Holy Rosary, the Stations of the Cross, etc.

embodies the *Sequela Christi*, the union of the Bride to the Bridegroom in loving intercessory prayer for the glory of God and the salvation of the world.

LECTIO DIVINA

The tradition of the Church also hands down the practice of *lectio divina* as a contemplation and savoring of Sacred Scripture, as Mary did when she meditated in her heart on all the mysteries of Jesus. "Mary sought the spiritual sense of the Scriptures and found it, associating it (*symallousa*) with the written words, the life of Jesus and the moments of discovery in her personal history.... [In this,] Mary becomes an example of faith for all of us, from the most simple soul to the most scholarly of the Doctors of the Church, who seek, consider and set forth how to bear witness to the Gospel."[55]

"I would like in particular to recall and recommend the ancient tradition of *Lectio divina*", Pope Benedict XVI writes. "The diligent reading of Sacred Scripture accompanied by prayer brings about that intimate dialogue in which the person reading hears God who is speaking, and in praying, responds to him with trusting openness of heart (cf. *Dei Verbum*, no. 25). If it is effectively promoted, this practice will bring to the Church—I am convinced of it—a new spiritual springtime."[56]

In order for us to experience the practice of *lectio divina* more fruitfully, paragraph 23 of the document *Dei Verbum* puts it in the correct light by mentioning the Church, the Spouse of the Incarnate Word, which is inspired and instructed by the Holy Spirit. This nuptial ecclesiology automatically introduces us into the atmosphere of love and reciprocity that promotes meditation on Scripture. This invaluable instruction helps us to become aware of the ecclesiological presuppositions that play a more important role than it may seem in the dialogue with God straight from the sacred text. Insofar as the Church, in her members, sees herself as a chosen, dearly beloved

---

[55] *IL*, no. 25.

[56] Benedict XVI, Address to the Participants in the International Congress Organized to Commemorate the 40th Anniversary of the Dogmatic Constitution on Divine Revelation *Dei Verbum* (September 16, 2005), *AAS* 97 (2005): 957. See also Carlo-Maria Martini, "La place centrale de la Parole de Dieu dans la vie de l'Église: L'animation biblique de toute la pastorale", *Catholic Biblical Federation* 76/77 (2005): 33.

spouse, it becomes quite natural to turn lovingly to Sacred Scripture as the everflowing source of divine love.[57]

"From this perspective, we must take into consideration, understand correctly, and retrieve the extraordinary exegesis of the Church Fathers, as well as the great medieval insight of the 'four senses of Scripture,' for they remain just as interesting today."[58] The practice of *lectio divina* will produce its fruits insofar as it is bathed in an atmosphere of confidence with regard to the Scriptures, which presupposes a textual exegesis "in the sacred spirit in which it was written".[59] In this context, we should constantly encourage "the study of the holy Fathers of both East and West and of sacred liturgies".[60]

In short, *lectio divina* can contribute much to the Church's dialogue with God, to the formation of disciples and of Christian communities, and even to bringing together the churches and ecclesial communities through their "common spiritual reading of the Word of God".[61]

It is to be hoped that the Synod will encourage the search for new, simple, and attractive strategies that are adapted to the Christian people as a whole or to particular categories of believers, to develop the taste for and practice of continuous reading, both communal and personal, of the Word of God.

The Ecclesial Interpretation of the Word of God

Problematic Elements

Ever since its apostolic origins, the interpretation of the Scriptures in the Church has given rise to conflicts and recurrent tensions. Schisms

---

[57] See Hans Urs von Balthasar, *Explorations in Theology*, vol. 2, *Spouse of the Word* (San Francisco: Ignatius Press, 1995); Hans Urs von Balthasar, *Theo-Drama*, vol. 2, *The Dramatis Personae: Man in God*, trans. Graham Harrison (San Francisco: Ignatius Press, 1990); Hugo Rahner, "Die Gott Geburt: Die Lehre der Kirchenväter von der Geburt Christi: Aus dem Herzen der Kirche und der Gläubigen", in *Symbole der Kirche* (Salzburg, Austria: O. Müller, 1964), 13–87; Luis Alonso Schökel, *Símbolos matrimoniales en la Biblia* (Estella: Verbo Divino, 1997).

[58] *IL*, no. 22 (translated by Ignatius Press).

[59] *DV*, no. 12.

[60] Ibid., no. 23.

[61] Walter Kasper, "Dei Verbum Audiens et Proclamans", *Catholic Biblical Federation* 76/77 (2005): 11. See also Groupe des Dombes, *Pour la conversion des Églises: Identité et changement dans la dynamique de communion*, ed. A. Blancy and M. Jourjon (Paris: Le Centurion, 1991).

and separations have added additional obstacles. In parallel to these unfortunate events, exegesis and theology have grown more distant not only from each other but also from the spiritual interpretation of Scripture that was current in the patristic era.[62] The contemplative model of monastic and patristic theology has given way to a speculative and often polemic model under the influence of the errors that were to be combated and of historical, philosophical, and scientific discoveries. We should add also the anthropocentric turn of modern thought, which has dismissed the metaphysics of being in favor of an immanentist epistemology. A prisoner of the enchanted confines of the *cogito [ergo sum]* (Ricoeur), man is fascinated by his own speculative prowess (Hegel), but he loses the sense of wonder with regard to the mystery of being and of revelation.[63]

In this context of separation and conflict between faith and reason, we see the unity of Scripture being called into question and interpretations of it becoming excessively fragmented. From now on, the internal relation between exegesis and faith is no longer unanimously acknowledged, and tensions increase among exegetes, pastors, and theologians.[64] Certainly, more and more often historical-critical exegesis is now being completed by other methods, some of which take up again the tradition and the history of exegesis.[65] But generally speaking, after several decades of concentrating on the human mediations of Scripture, should we not rediscover the divine depth of the inspired text without losing the valuable findings of the new methodologies?

We can never insist too much on this point, because the crisis of exegesis and of theological hermeneutics profoundly affects the spiritual life of the People of God and their confidence in the Scriptures. It also affects the ecclesial communion, because of the atmosphere of often unhealthy tension between university theology and the Church's Magisterium. Given this delicate situation, and without

[62] Hans Urs von Balthasar, *Retour au Centre* (Paris: Desclée de Brouwer, 1998), 25–57.

[63] Hans Urs von Balthasar, *Theo-Logic*, vol. 1, *Truth of the World*, trans. Adrian J. Walker (San Francisco: Ignatius Press, 2000), 23–35.

[64] On this subject see Joseph Ratzinger, "L'interprétation de la Bible en conflit: Problèmes des fondements et de l'orientation de l'exégèse contemporaine", in *L'exégèse chrétienne aujourd'hui*, ed. Ignace de la Potterie (Paris: Fayard, 2000), 65–109.

[65] Pontifical Biblical Commission, *The Interpretation of the Bible in the Church* (April 23, 1993), I, A, *Origins*, January 6, 1994.

entering into the debates between the schools of thought, the Synod must give some orientation to rectify the relations and to promote the integration of the findings of the biblical and hermeneutical sciences into the Church's interpretation of the Sacred Scripture.[66]

The dialogues along these lines that have been promoted by the Congregation for the Doctrine of the Faith should be intensified so as to study in depth, in a multidisciplinary way that respects competencies, the disputed points and thus to prepare the Church's judgment, which must carry out "the divine commission and ministry of guarding and interpreting the word of God".[67] The Pontifical Biblical Commission and the International Theological Commission play an important and highly appreciated role along these lines. The Synod could acknowledge the invaluable contribution of these organizations and encourage joint sessions[68] so as to intensify the dialogue among pastors, theologians, and exegetes. It could also suggest regional meetings of the same sort, which would help to cultivate a healthy atmosphere of communion and service to the Word of God. Furthermore, the Synod could propose taking the spiritual sense of Scripture as the axis along which to integrate this search for unity.[69]

The Spiritual Sense of Scripture

"A well-informed theologian acknowledges unambiguously", Father de Lubac writes, "that the existence of a twofold literal and spiritual sense is an inalienable fact of tradition. It is part of the Christian patrimony. Let us say it again with the Church Fathers: it [the spiritual sense] is the New Testament itself, with all its fruitfulness, revealing itself to us 'as the fulfillment and transfiguration of the Old.' "[70] According to Saint Thomas Aquinas, the spiritual sense presupposes

---

[66] See Ratzinger, "L'interpretation de la Bible en conflit"; Ignace de la Potterie, "L'exégèse biblique, science de la foi", in de la Potterie, L'exégèse chrétienne aujourd'hui, 111–60.

[67] DV, no. 12.

[68] L'interpretazione della Bibbia nella Chiesa: Atti del Simposio promosso della Congregazione per la Dottrina della Fede, Roma, settembre 1999 (Vatican City: Libreria Editrice Vaticana, 2001).

[69] See Kasper, "Dei Verbum Audiens et Proclamans", 11: "The spiritual reading of Scripture and scriptural exegesis are responses to the ecumenical and exegetical malaise."

[70] De Lubac, L'Écriture dans la tradition, 201. For a comprehensive study of the magisterial contribution made by Father de Lubac, see Rudolf Voderholzer, Die Einheit der Schrift und ihr geistiger Sinn (Fribourg: Johannes Verlag, 1998).

the literal sense and relies on it.[71] However, all symbolic or spiritual interpretation must preserve a homogeneous character with the literal sense. For "to admit the possibility of such alien meanings would be equivalent to cutting off the biblical message from its root, which is the word of God in its historical communication; it would also mean opening the door to interpretations of a wildly subjective nature."[72]

This fear of subjectivism and the lack of contemporary reflection on scriptural inspiration explain why contemporary Catholic exegesis is so slow to take a real interest in the spiritual sense of Scripture.[73] However, a significant development is taking shape along these lines: "As a general rule," the Pontifical Biblical Commission writes, "we can define the spiritual sense, as understood by Christian faith, as the meaning expressed by the biblical texts when read under the influence of the Holy Spirit, in the context of the paschal mystery of Christ and of the new life which flows from it."[74] This definition agrees nicely with the orientation of Dei Verbum, paragraph 12, which demands that biblical texts should be interpreted in the same Spirit in which they were written.

Indeed, it is the Spirit who prepared the events of the Old and New Testaments according to a progression that runs from promise to fulfillment; it is by the Spirit that these events were interpreted by prophetic words and by symbolic or sapiential rereadings, so as to lead the People of God, through purifications and a gradually deeper understanding, to the encounter with Jesus Christ, the fullness of revelation. Basically, the spiritual sense of Scripture, "the true sense remains that of the Holy Spirit."[75] "But as for me, following the counsel of the Lord, I will search for the treasures of Spirit and life hidden in the profound depths of these inspired utterances. This is my inheritance, because I am a believer in Christ. Why should I not endeavour to find the wholesome and savory food of the spirit beneath the unprofitable and unpalatable letter, as the grain amongst

---

[71] Thomas Aquinas, STh I, q. 1, art. 10 ad 1.

[72] Pontifical Biblical Commission, Interpretation of the Bible in the Church, II, B, 1.

[73] Vanhoye, "La réception dans l'Église de la constitution Dei Verbum", 3–13.

[74] Pontifical Biblical Commission, Interpretation of the Bible in the Church, II, B, 2.

[75] Hans Urs von Balthasar, "Le sens spirituel de l'Écriture", in de la Potterie, ed., L'exégèse chrétienne aujourd'hui, 184.

the chaff, the [nut]meat in the shell, or the marrow in the bone? I will have nothing to do with this letter which when tasted savours of the flesh, and when swallowed brings death. Nevertheless, that which lies concealed in it is of the Holy Ghost."[76]

The practice of the spiritual exegesis of Scripture requires here again a deeper pneumatological understanding. It is not enough just to read *under the influence of the Holy Spirit*; one must seek to perceive in the letter the Spirit who is contained in it. Thus, the Holy Spirit is not simply an extrinsic agent of the production of Sacred Scripture; he is the One who, in the Bible, expresses himself together with the Word of the Father, who is *Jesus Christ*. As this research is prolonged, it would be opportune for the Synod to inquire about the relevance of a possible encyclical on the interpretation of Scripture in the Church.

Exegesis and Theology

Exegesis and theology deal with the same subject matter, the Word of God, but from different and complementary perspectives. The exegete studies the *letter* of Scripture "with the sacred spirit in which it was written,[77] ... if the meaning of sacred texts is to be correctly worked out".[78] He is attentive to the historical genesis of the texts, to their literary genre, to their structure, but also to the relations between the different books of the Bible and between one Testament and the other. The Synod should welcome the revived interest in the canonical approach to Scripture and the efforts to propose syntheses of biblical theology as interesting steps in the progress toward an overall understanding of Scripture. The theologian, too, strives to interpret the *letter* in terms of "the unity of the whole of Scripture.... The living tradition of the whole Church must be taken into account",[79] the philosophical and other languages that mark the culture of its era,

---

[76] Saint Bernard of Clairvaux, *Sermons on the Canticle of Canticles*, translated by a priest of Mount Melleray, vol. 2 (Dublin: Browne and Nolan, 1921), Sermon 73, par. 2, p. 363.

[77] Benedict XV, encyclical *Spiritus Paraclitus* (September 15, 1920), EB 469; Jerome, *Commentary on the Epistle to the Galatians* V, 19–20 (PL 26, 417 A).

[78] *DV*, no. 12.

[79] Ibid.

and while respecting as much as possible the particular sensibilities of his own contemporaries.

Exegetes and theologians know that "the Sacred Scriptures contain the word of God and, since they are inspired, really are the word of God; and so the study of the sacred page is, as it were, the soul of sacred theology."[80] This Word of God is always and simultaneously the Word of faith, the testimony of a people and of its inspired authors. Consequently, exegetical and theological methods must reflect the interdependence of the letter and the Spirit of faith in the work of interpretation. The covenantal relation between God and his people dwells within the text itself and commands an interpretation that is not only noetic but also dynamic and dialogical. In short, exegetes and theologians either interpret the Bible rigorously in faith and listening to the Spirit, or else stick to the superficial characteristics of the text, if they limit themselves to historical, linguistic, or literary considerations.

Among the urgent tasks of scriptural research, it is important to explore theological epistemology more profoundly with the help of the Fathers of the Church and the saints. By their personal and methodical attitude of contemplative faith, they open themselves to the depth of the text, that is, to the presence of God, who speaks now through it and calls to the listener—hence their testimony to a "science of love"[81] which remains the most excellent access route to the knowledge of God. "The inspired aptness with which the least speculative saints insist on certain aspects of the Christian life can have unforeseeable effects on the living theology of the Church. Think of the Rule of Saint Benedict, the testament of Saint Francis of Assisi, the *Exercises* of Saint Ignatius [of Loyola]."[82] Even if the saints in question are not professional theologians, the particular emphases of their lives serve as "canons" and rules for interpreting revelation because "lovers are the ones who know most about God; the theologian must listen to them."[83] Saint Thérèse of the Child Jesus knew

[80] Ibid., no. 24.

[81] Saint Thérèse of Lisieux, *Manuscrits autobiographiques*, B 1 r°-v; François-Marie Lethel, "La théologie des saints comme science de l'amour", in *Connaître l'amour du Christ qui surpasse toute connaissance* (Carmel, 1989), 3–7.

[82] Hans Urs von Balthasar, "Actualité de Lisieux", conference given at Notre Dame in Paris, in *Thérèse de Lisieux, Conférence du centenaire 1873–1973*, special issue of *Nouvelles de l'Institut Catholique*, 112.

[83] Hans Urs von Balthasar, *Love Alone Is Credible*, trans. D. C. Schindler (San Francisco: Ignatius Press, 2004), 12.

that her way of spiritual childhood was an example to imitate, and Saint Paul, in the Christian Bible, holds himself up as an example.

"For a closed anthropological ethics," according to Hans Urs von Balthasar, "there will always be something scandalous about the openness with which Paul demonstrates the nature of Christian sanctity by pointing to himself (with the ultimate aim of demonstrating the dogmatic truth) and with which he undertakes, before the Church and before the whole world, an analysis of his own existence. But such openness is nothing other than the precisely and obediently reflected splendour, at the ecclesial level, of Christ's unique claim to be in himself, in his living existence, the truth of God.[84] Anton Rotzetter states, "The way in which Saint Francis understands Scripture is different in several essential points from that of his biographers. The latter are familiar with the scientific methods of that day and engage in a symbolic exegesis in which no limits are set on the imagination. It is quite different in Francis' proclamation: he has no idea of the accepted hermeneutical principles of his time. His exegesis is realist, concrete; his imagination is bound to the letter of Scripture."[85] In short, the saints contemplate with the eyes of the Spirit the depths of God that emerge from Sacred Scripture.[86] "The saints are to the Gospel what a sung score is to a printed score", writes Saint Francis de Sales.[87]

Missio: The Word of God in the Mission of the Church

We situated the Word of God in the life of the Church under the heading of Communio, because the Word received in faith introduces us into the Trinitarian communion. The experience of this communion entails an ever-deeper conversion to love and to a participation in the missionary and eschatological dynamism of the Word of

[84] Hans Urs von Balthasar, The Glory of the Lord, vol. 1, Seeing the Form, 2nd ed. (San Francisco: Ignatius Press, 2008), 194.

[85] Anton Rotzetter, "Mystique et observation littérale de l'Évangile chez François d'Assise", Concilium 169 (1981): 86.

[86] See Marc Ouellet, "Adrienne von Speyr et le samedi saint de la théologie", in Adrienne von Speyr und ihre spirituelle theologie, ed. Hans Urs von Balthasar Stiftung (Fribourg: Johannes Verlag, 2002), 31–56.

[87] François de Sales, Lettre CCXXIX [6 octobre 1604], in Oeuvres, ed. Dom Henry Benedict Mackey (Annecy, 1892–1932), 12:299–325.

God. Inspired by the Spirit of Pentecost, this Synod intends to echo this dynamism.

"The word of God grew and multiplied", the Acts of the Apostles tells us (12:24). It gained followers among the Jews and the pagans, as Peter himself testifies to the community in Jerusalem as he speaks about the outpouring of the Holy Spirit on the pagans. This is how "the word of the Lord grew and prevailed mightily" (19:20), causing the Church to grow and communicating to her the peace of the Kingdom (9:31).

Proclaiming the Gospel of the Kingdom of God

The Church, Servant of the Word

As Paul VI proclaims, "The Church ... has a vivid awareness of the fact that the Savior's words, 'I must proclaim the Good News of the kingdom of God' (Lk 4:43), apply in all truth to herself: She willingly adds with St. Paul: 'Not that I boast of preaching the gospel, since it is a duty that has been laid on me; I should be punished if I did not preach it!' (1 Cor 9:16)."[88] Evangelizing is the heart of the Church's mission. To evangelize means "to preach and teach, to be the channel of the gift of grace, to reconcile sinners with God, and to perpetuate Christ's sacrifice in the Mass, which is the memorial of His death and glorious resurrection."[89] For "evangelizing means bringing the Good News into all the strata of humanity, and through its influence transforming humanity from within and making it new: 'Now I am making the whole of creation new!' (Rev 21:5)."[90]

In carrying out her evangelizing mission, the Church receives and serves the Word of God. Through prophecy, the Liturgy, and *diakonia* (the ministry of service), she witnesses to the personal dynamism of the Incarnate Word. Bishops, priests, deacons, laypeople, and consecrated persons all live under the Word and act together with it, according to the charism they have received from the Spirit. By

[88] Paul VI, apostolic exhortation *Evangelii Nuntiandi* (December 8, 1975), no. 14 (hereinafter *EN*).

[89] Ibid., no. 14.

[90] Ibid., no. 18.

collaborating in this way with the Word of God, the Church participates in the mission of the Spirit, who gathers together "under one
Head, Christ" (see Eph 1:10) "the children of God who are scattered
abroad" (Jn 11:52).

The Historical Jesus of the Gospels

As in apostolic times, the Church announces the Kingdom of God, in
other words, Jesus, the Christ, as he is presented in the Gospels. Now
this task has been undermined by the influence of trends in exegesis
that have dug a trench between the "Jesus of history" and the "Christ
of faith". These exegetical trends have called into question the historical value of the Gospels, thus weakening the credibility of the
text. "This is a dramatic situation for faith," Benedict XVI declares,
"because its point of reference is being placed in doubt: Intimate
friendship with Jesus, on which everything depends."[91] It is true that
in the last few decades, biblical research has reestablished the historical value of the Gospels[92] and has even reaffirmed their biographical
character.[93] These findings are not yet widely known and have not
corrected the negative impact of rationalist exegesis on the spiritual
life and missionary witness of Christians.

In this context, the publication of the book *Jesus of Nazareth* by
Pope Benedict XVI is a major event that restores free access to the
authentic figure of Jesus. It shows that the divine identity of Jesus,
historically attested by the Gospels, emerges from the texts themselves and from the consistent, credible testimony of the New Testament. While appreciating the positive results of historical-critical
exegesis, the pope emphasizes its methodological limitations and
hopes for the development of "canonical exegesis" to round out the
theological interpretation of the Gospels. The liberating attitude of
Benedict XVI consists of "trust[ing] the Gospels", while presenting

---

[91] Benedict XVI, *Jesus of Nazareth*, vol. 1, *From the Baptism in the Jordan to the Transfiguration*,
trans. Adrian J. Walker (New York: Doubleday, 2007), xii.

[92] Albert Schweitzer, *Storia della ricerca sulla vita di Gesù* (Brescia: Paideia, 1986); Joachim
Jeremias, *Il problema del Gesù storico* (Brescia: Paideia, 1973).

[93] Richard Burridge, *What Are the Gospels? A Comparison with Greco-Roman Biography*
(Cambridge: Cambridge University Press, 1992).

"the Jesus of the Gospels as the real, 'historical' Jesus in the strict sense of the word."[94]

This book "is in no way an exercise of the magisterium".[95] Nonetheless, it is still a beacon that protects against reefs and shipwrecks. Its testimony brings theology and exegesis together through the harmonious union of academic competence and the personal testimony of an ecclesial authority. It goes without saying that a book like this helps to dispel the confusion sown by some media sensations,[96] and to relaunch the dialogue between the Church and contemporary culture. The Synod could acknowledge that this book is an important locus for reestablishing a contemplative culture of the Gospels.

Embodying the Witness of the God Who Is Love

The Primacy of love

When the Spirit speaks to the Church today, reminding her of the Scriptures, he calls her to a new testimony of love and unity so as to enhance the credibility of the Gospel vis-à-vis a world that is more receptive to witnesses than to teachers. "By this all men will know that you are my disciples, if you have love for one another" (Jn 13:35). This sign of mutual love prolongs God's testimony, because it embodies the same love of Jesus, who said: "Love one another; even as I have loved you" (Jn 13:34). This "as" means, love one another with the same love with which I love you. The whole priestly prayer of Jesus, a synthesis of his paschal offering, aims to associate humanity in the Trinity's testimony of unity: "The glory which you have given me I have given to them, that they may be one even as we are one. I in them and you in me, that they may become perfectly one, so that the world may know that you have sent me and have loved them even as you have loved me" (Jn 17:22–23). Gregory of Nyssa identifies glory with the Spirit,[97] who also prays with Christ that his disciples might be consecrated in the truth, in other words,

---

[94] Benedict XVI, *Jesus of Nazareth*, I:xxi–xxii.
[95] Ibid., I:xxiii.
[96] For example, Dan Brown, *The Da Vinci Code* (New York: Doubleday, 2003).
[97] Gregory of Nyssa, *Homily 15 on the Canticle of Canticles*.

consumed in [a sacrifice of] unity. This solemn prayer does show that fidelity to the commandment of love involves not only the believer's salvation, but also and above all the credibility of the Trinity in the world. "That they may all be one; even as you, Father, are in me, and I in you, that they also may be in us, so that the world may believe that you have sent me" (Jn 17:21).

The testimony of the Word of God consequently requires of missionary disciples[98] that they be authentic witnesses to the primacy of love over knowledge. Saint Paul affirms this unambiguously in the hymn to love in the First Letter to the Corinthians (13:1–13), as well as in his exhortation to the Philippians: "have the same love, be in full accord and of one mind" (see 2:2), following the example of Christ in his *kenosis*. "It is not dry [theological] manuals (full as these may be of unquestionable truths) that express with plausibility for the world the truth of Christ's Gospel; it is the existence of the saints who have been grasped by Christ's Holy Spirit. And Christ himself foresaw no other kind of apologetics (Jn 13:35)."[99]

Ecumenical Witness

Since the official entrance of the Catholic Church into the ecumenical movement, the popes have made the cause of Christian unity a priority. Moreover, ecumenical rapprochement has enabled the churches and ecclesial communities to wonder together about their own fidelity to the Word of God. Although the ecumenical meetings and dialogues have produced fruits of fraternity, reconciliation, and mutual assistance, the present situation is characterized by a certain malaise that calls for a deeper conversion to "spiritual ecumenism".[100] "This change of heart and holiness of life," according to Vatican II, "along with public and private prayer for the unity of

[98] CELAM [= Latin American Episcopal Conference], *The Aparecida Document* of the 5th General Conference of the Bishops of Latin America and the Caribbean, Aparecida, Brazil, May 13–31, 2007 (CreateSpace Independent Publishing Platform, August 5, 2013).

[99] Balthasar, *The Glory of the Lord*, 1:482.

[100] See Vatican Council II, Decree on Ecumenism *Unitatis Redintegratio* (November 21, 1964) (hereinafter *UR*); John Paul II, encyclical *Ut Unum Sint* (May 25, 1995); see also Walter Kasper, *A Handbook of Spiritual Ecumenism* (Hyde Park, NY: New City Press, 2007).

Christians, should be regarded as the soul of the whole ecumenical movement."[101]

This orientation of the Council has kept all its relevance, as the Holy Father (Benedict XVI) exhorts us "to listen to the word of God together; to practice the *lectio divina* of the Bible, that is, reading linked with prayer; letting ourselves be amazed by the newness of the Word of God that never ages and is never depleted; overcoming our deafness to those words that do not correspond with our prejudices and our opinions; to listen and also to study, in the communion of believers of all ages; all these things constitute a path to be taken in order to achieve unity in the faith as a response to listening to the Word."[102]

Among the many ecumenical witnesses of our time, we mention by way of example the Focolare movement founded by Chiara Lubich; its spirituality of unity places an emphasis on "mutual love" and obedience to the "Word of life". The pedagogy of this movement correctly prioritizes the dynamic element of love in comparison to the noetic element of the Word. This priority demands of all ecumenical partners an ever-deeper conversion to the plan of love of the Trinitarian God, which the Holy Spirit endeavors to bring to its fulfillment with "sighs too deep for words" (Rom 8:26).

It is significant that this Catholic ecumenical movement—shouldn't we just say "Catholic", that is, ecumenical?—bears the canonical name of *The Work of Mary*. We see in it a happy and harmonious blend—as it is found incidentally in other movements[103]—of the biblical movement, the ecumenical movement, and the Marian movement, thanks to a resolute practice of the Word of God, embodied and shared.[104] This witness recalls that Christian unity and its missionary impact are not in the first place "our work", but rather that of the Spirit and of Mary.[105]

---

[101] *UR*, no. 8.

[102] Benedict XVI, Homily at Vespers for the Conclusion of the Octave for Christian Unity (January 25, 2007).

[103] Particularly the Sant'Egidio community, the Taizé community, and other movements.

[104] Chiara Lubich, *Pensée et spiritualité* (Paris: Nouvelle Cité, 2003).

[105] Marc Ouellet, "Marie et l'avenir de l'oecuménisme", *Communio* 28/1 (janvier-février 2003): 113–25; Dan Ilie Ciobotea, Bernard Sesboüé, and Jacques-Noël Peres, "Marie: L'oecuménisme à l'épreuve", *L'actualité Religieuse dans le Monde* 46 (1987): 17–24.

Dialoguing with Nations and Religions

At the Service of Man

The Church's missionary activity is rooted, as we said, in the mission of Christ and of the Spirit, which reveals and spreads the Trinitarian communion in all the cultures of the world. The universal salvific import of the Paschal Mystery of Christ calls for the proclamation of the Good News to all the nations and also to all the religions. The Word of God invites every human being to a dialogue with God, who wants to save all mankind in Jesus Christ, the one Mediator (1 Tim 2:5; Heb 8:6; 9:15; 12:24). The missionary activity of the Church testifies to her love for the whole Christ that includes every culture. In her efforts to evangelize cultures, this activity aims at the unity of humanity in Jesus Christ, but while respecting and integrating all human values.[106] As Saint Paul exhorts us, "Finally, brethren, whatever is true, whatever is honorable, whatever is just, whatever is pure, whatever is lovely, whatever is gracious, if there is any excellence, if there is anything worthy of praise, think about these things" (Phil 4:8).

In her liturgical dialogue with God, the Church intercedes for all, especially for the poor. Her passion for the Word of God draws her in the footsteps of the poor, chaste, and obedient Jesus, so as to bring hope, reconciliation, and peace to all situations of injustice, oppression, and war. As in the case of the "Good Samaritan", this care about the human being, whoever he may be, expresses the Church's compassion for all human suffering and her willingness to help the poor and the afflicted. Conscious of the presence of Jesus at her side, as on the road to Emmaus, she interprets Scripture as he does, "beginning with Moses and all the prophets" (Lk 24:27), and explaining to every human being the mystery of Jesus the Savior: "Was it not necessary that the Christ should suffer these things and enter into his glory?" (Lk 24:26).

This exegesis of Jesus, repeated incessantly by the Church, authenticates the Christological interpretation of the Old Testament, which

---

[106] Vatican Council II, Decree on the Missionary Activity of the Church *Ad Gentes* (December 7, 1965), no. 11 (hereinafter *AG*); *EN*, no. 20; John Paul II, Encyclical on the Permanent Validity of the Church's Missionary Mandate *Redemptoris Missio* (December 7, 1990), no. 3.

the Church Fathers, after Origen and Irenaeus, developed broadly. Nowadays, considering the tragic history of the relations between Israel and the Church, we are invited not only to make reparation for the injustice committed against the Jews, but also to have "a new respect for the Jewish interpretation of the Old Testament".[107] Moreover, a respectful and constructive dialogue with Judaism can serve to deepen both parties' interpretation of Sacred Scripture.[108]

Interreligious Dialogue

Among the partners of the Church's various dialogues with the nations, the Jewish people occupy a unique place as heir of the first Covenant, with whom we share their Sacred Scriptures. This common heritage invites us to hope, "for the gifts and the call of God are irrevocable" (Rom 11:29). As we read in Saint Paul's impassioned testimony in the Letter to the Romans: "I am speaking the truth in Christ, I am not lying; my conscience bears me witness in the Holy Spirit, that I have great sorrow and unceasing anguish in my heart. For I could wish that I myself were accursed and cut off from Christ for the sake of my brethren, my kinsmen according to the flesh. They are Israelites, and to them belong the sonship, the glory, the covenants, the giving of the law, the worship, and the promises; to them belong the patriarchs, and of their race, according to the flesh, is the Christ, who is God over all, blessed for ever. Amen" (9:1–5). And "lest you be wise in your own conceits, I want you to understand this mystery, brethren: a hardening has come upon part of Israel, until the full number of the Gentiles come in, and so all Israel will be saved; as it is written" (11:25–26).

Next come believers in the Muslim faith; they, too, are rooted in the biblical tradition, professing the one God. In confronting secularization and liberalism, they are allies in defending human life and in affirming the social importance of religion. Dialogue with them is more important than ever in the current circumstances in order "to promote together for the benefit of all mankind social justice and

---

[107] Pontifical Biblical Commission, *The Jewish People and Their Sacred Scriptures in the Christian Bible* (February 12, 2002), preface by Joseph Cardinal Ratzinger (Rome, Solemnity of the Ascension, 2001).

[108] Ibid., nos. 9, 11, 21–22, 85–86.

moral welfare, as well as peace and freedom".[109] The witness of the Martyrs of Tibhirine in Algeria in 1996 lifts this dialogue to a level that perhaps has never been reached before in history, with regard to service to mankind and to the reconciliation of peoples. The bold initiatives of Pope Benedict XVI plead for perseverance in the pursuit of dialogue with Islam.

Last but not least are the human beings "from every tribe and tongue and people and nation" (Rev 5:9) who are under the heavens, for the Lamb who was immolated shed his blood for them all. The Word of God is especially destined for those who have never heard it because, in God's heart and in the Church's missionary awareness, the last have the grace of being the first.[110]

In a world that is on the path to globalization, with the new means of communication, the mission field is open to new initiatives for evangelization in a spirit of authentic inculturation. We are in the internet era, and the possibilities of access to Sacred Scripture have proliferated.[111] The Synod must listen, discern, and encourage the projects for transmitting and culturally transposing the Sacred Scriptures into all these new "languages" which are waiting to serve the Word of God.

The First Letter of John asks, "Who is it that overcomes the world but he who believes that Jesus is the Son of God? ... And the Spirit is the witness, because the Spirit is the truth. There are three witnesses, the Spirit, the water, and the blood; and these three agree. If we receive the testimony of men, the testimony of God is greater" (5:5, 7–9).

Jesus still comes, in the Church, "to bear witness to the truth" (Jn 18:37) and to communicate to those who believe in his name the knowledge of the Father that he possesses in its fullness. This message of John explains the primary purpose and the primary concern of the Synod: to listen anew to God who speaks and to receive

---

[109] Vatican Council II, Declaration on the Relation of the Church to Non-Christian Religions *Nostra Aetate* (October 28, 1965), no. 3.

[110] *AG*, no. 10.

[111] For example, the *Biblia Clerus* of the Congregation for the Clergy provides very valuable resources; the volume draws on several works, among them the *Bible chrétienne* written by Dom Claude-Jean Nesmy and Mother Élisabeth de Solms, Benedictines of La Pierre qui Vire and Solesmes, published by Éditions Anne Sigier.

him, and to ask for the grace of a renewed faith in his Incarnate Word. Conscious of the ecclesiological renewal connected with the dynamic, dialogical concept of revelation, we suggested ways of studying in greater depth the Word of God, starting from Mary's faith as it is prolonged in the life of the Church, the Liturgy, preaching, *lectio divina*, exegesis, and theology.

The application of this Marian paradigm presupposes a pneumatological deepening of the ecclesial tradition and of scriptural exegesis, one that realizes the performative power of the Word of God, while distinguishing it carefully from the Eucharistic presence. More than a library for the erudite, the Bible is a temple where the Bride of the Song of Songs listens to the admissions of her Beloved and celebrates his kisses (1:1–2). "The one who is instructed by the Holy Spirit understands everything", Saint Silouan writes. "His soul feels as though it were in Heaven, for the Holy Spirit Himself is in Heaven and on earth, in Sacred Scripture and in the souls of all who love God."[112]

This perspective, which is more dynamic than noetic, calls for a more contemplative theology rooted in the Liturgy, the Church Fathers, and the lives of the saints, an exegesis practiced in faith in keeping with its object, and also a philosophy of being and of love.

It opens the way to a more fruitful spiritual reading of the Bible, to an ecclesial interpretation of Scripture, and to a revitalization of the Church's missionary dialogue in all its forms. More diligent and regular attention to the Scriptures will revive the missionary consciousness of the Church and her love for man, the image of God longing for the divine resemblance.

Saint Caesarius of Arles frequently exhorted his diocesan priests never to neglect what he described as "the food of [the] soul forever": "I beseech you, beloved brethren, be eager to engage in divine reading whatever hours you can."[113] Often, at the end of the day, he liked to ask his priests, concerning their meditation on the Word of God, "What did you eat today?" May we have that same availability, that same taste for the Word of God, and ask ourselves in turn the same question: "What have we eaten today?"

---

[112] Saint Silouan of Mount Athos, *Écrits spirituels*, Spiritualité orientale 5 (Abbaye de Belle-fontaine, 1976/1994), 30.

[113] Caesarius of Arles, Sermon VIII, in *Sermons*, 49.

Chapter 2

The Word of the Lord Abides Forever

" 'The Word of the Lord abides forever' (1 Pet 1:25).... This word, which abides for ever, entered into time. God spoke his eternal Word humanly; his Word 'became flesh' (Jn 1:14). This is the good news."[1] The post-synodal apostolic exhortation *Verbum Domini* begins with this statement of the mystery of the Word of God, which causes joy in the Church. Dear friends, I am very honored to be invited to share this joy with you, and I greet very cordially all the members of this prestigious university community of the Sacred Heart. I thank you for giving me the opportunity to echo the October 2008 Synod of Bishops on *the Word of God in the life and mission of the Church.*

Allow me to invoke Saint Ambrose in your midst, by recalling what the Church teaches through him in the breviary these days: "Open your mouth to the word of God", he writes. "Open your mouth; it is He who speaks. David also said: 'I will hear what the Lord God will speak in me,' and the Son of God Himself said: 'Open your mouth wide, and I will fill it.' "[2]

Supported by this great saint from Milan, who was delighted and requisitioned by the Word of God, I pray the Holy Spirit to perfect in you what he crowns eternally in God himself: the communion of love of the Father and the Son. This communion of love is our eternal destiny, but it is also our present, illuminated by faith in the

---

This essay is based on a conference delivered at the Università Cattolica del Sacro Cuore in Milan, March 2, 2011.

[1] Benedict XVI, Post-Synodal Apostolic Exhortation on the Word of God *Verbum Domini* (September 30, 2010), no. 1 (hereinafter *VD*).

[2] Ambrose of Milan, *Homily on Psalm 36*, 65–66, CSEL 64:123–25 (citing Ps 85:8 and Ps 81:10).

Word-made-flesh. May we live it fully and bear witness to it, because this grace is intended for everyone.

Since you are members of a university community, I will approach the theme of the Word of God from the angle of rationality, which is dear to our Holy Father Benedict XVI. This approach will help us to grasp better our own responsibility to give an account of our Christian hope when faced with the dominant culture of our time. Therefore, to start with, I will discuss the crisis of Christianity at the beginning of the third millennium in order to put in perspective the essential message of the post-synodal apostolic exhortation *Verbum Domini*. There is a reason why we speak more and more about a new evangelization, and a new Roman dicastery has just been created to promote the work of carrying it out. Isn't it time to deepen the foundations of our civilization through a serene dialogue between faith and reason?

The Crisis of Christianity in Our Time

To get to the heart of the contemporary problem, I will echo two speeches by Benedict XVI, one as cardinal when he was Prefect of the Congregation for the Doctrine of the Faith, during an official conference at the Sorbonne in Paris, at the close of the second millennium, on November 27, 1999,[3] the other as the pope at the opening of the Synod on the Word of God, on October 6, 2008. Two very different, but complementary speeches: one very academic, discussing the crisis of Christianity at the end of two thousand years of European civilization, the other introducing the work of the Synod by a meditation on Psalm 119:89: "For ever, O LORD, your word is firmly fixed in the heavens."

The Truth of Christianity?

The speech at the Sorbonne begins in this way: "At the close of the second Christian millennium, it is in the very area of its first great expansion, in Europe, that Christianity finds itself deep in crisis,

---

[3] Joseph Cardinal Ratzinger, *Truth and Tolerance: Christian Belief and World Religions*, trans. Henry Taylor (San Francisco: Ignatius Press, 2004), 162–81.

arising from the crisis concerning its claim to truth."[4] Referring to a
Buddhist parable, Cardinal Ratzinger then describes the skepticism
that rules contemporary thought, and that calls into question the
Christian vision: "The theory of creation seems to have been made
obsolete by [the theory] of evolution; the teaching on original sin
by our knowledge of man's origins; critical exegesis relativizes the
figure of Jesus and puts a question mark against His consciousness of
being the Son; it seems doubtful whether the Church really originates from Jesus, and so forth."[5]

Then, widening the perspective on the relations between faith
and reason, he continues in these words: "The philosophical basis of
Christianity has become problematic through the 'end of metaphysics'; as a result of modern historical methods its historical foundations
are left in twilight. So from that viewpoint it seems an obvious step
to reduce the content of Christianity to symbolism, to ascribe to it
no more significance than one would to any myths from the history
of religions—to regard it as one form of religious experience, which
should humbly take its place alongside the others."[6]

In this sense we can continue to remain Christian but without
claiming to adhere to a definitive and restricting truth, but rather as a
cultural expression of the general religious sensibility that is expressed
in this way in Europe and in another elsewhere. Having thus described
the phenomenon of relativism, which he will denounce later as a
true "dictatorship", the author then demonstrates that "the apparent
equanimity of the farewell to truth about God and about the essential
nature of our selves, the seeming content[ment] at no longer having
to bother about this, is deceptive." Also, "man cannot come to terms
with being born blind and remaining blind, where essential things are
concerned. The farewell to truth can never be final."[7]

I cannot set forth here the Ratzingerian vision of the emergence of
Christianity from the perspective of the history of religions. He maintains that its success does not depend on the assertion of the political
hegemony of this religion over the others, but rather of its rational
superiority compared with the mythical explanations of other religions.

---

[4] Ibid., 162.
[5] Ibid., 163.
[6] Ibid.
[7] Ibid., 164–65.

Nowadays, the author keenly observes, the situation appears to be reversed. In the name of a rational superiority—scientific positivism— the Christian religion is downgraded to the rank of an outdated vision that can no longer be naively embraced as the truth. But this scientific positivism which is expressed in a general theory of evolution does not succeed, basically, in giving a reasonable account of reality and its foundation. It stops at a description of phenomena by means of chance and variations that, in the living world, is designated as natural selection, that is to say, by the method of reproduction plus variation.

Having noted the rational defect of the general theory of evolution, Ratzinger then raises the debate to another level: "The question is whether reality originated on the basis of chance and necessity (or, as Popper says, in agreement with Butler, on the basis of luck and cunning) and, thus, from what is irrational; that is, whether reason, being a chance by-product of irrationality and, floating in an ocean of irrationality, is ultimately just as meaningless; or whether the principle that represents the fundamental conviction of Christian faith and of its philosophy remains true: 'In principio erat Verbum' ['In the beginning was the Word']."[8] Also, "now as then, Christian faith represents the choice in favor of the priority of reason and of rationality."[9]

Furthermore, this priority of the rational is not only a requirement of theoretical reason in its quest for meaning and truth; it is also a requirement of practical reason, an ethical requirement. Indeed, where the ethos of evolution fails as a first philosophy, Christianity offers an alternative as a rational and practical religion. Because "this evolutionary ethic that inevitably takes as its key concept the model of selectivity, that is, the struggle for survival, the victory of the fittest, successful adaptation, has little comfort to offer.... It ultimately remains a bloodthirsty ethic."[10] "All this is of very little use for an ethic of universal peace, of practical love of one's neighbor, and of the necessary overcoming of oneself, which is what we need."[11]

[8] Ibid., 181.
[9] Ibid.
[10] Ibid., 182.
[11] Ibid., 182–83.

In conclusion, Ratzinger maintains that the attempt to restore to Christianity, in this crisis of humanity, its full meaning as *religio vera* [the true religion] must rely on both orthodoxy and orthopraxis, on metaphysics and ethics. "At the most profound level its content will necessarily consist—in the final analysis, just as it did then—in love and reason coming together as the two pillars of reality: the true reason is love, and love is the true reason. They are in their unity the true basis and the goal of all reality."[12]

Realism of the Word

In the wake of this fundamental speech on the rationality of Christianity and the profound nature of the Logos, we can easily see the importance that the Synod on the Word of God had for Benedict XVI, and his expectations with regard to the theological and pastoral perspectives of this assembly. Before tackling the text of the post-synodal exhortation *Verbum Domini*, I would like to quote again his meditation at the opening of that same Synod, which expresses a fundamental truth in very simple language: "Furthermore, the Word of God is the foundation of everything, it is the true reality. And to be realistic, we must rely upon this reality. We must change our idea that matter, solid things, things we can touch, are the more solid, the more certain reality." Note that this speech does not disqualify the sciences, which study the laws of material reality and exploit its technological possibilities for the well-being of the human race; it refers to the reality underlying all these realities. The pope continues his meditation:

> At the end of the Sermon on the Mount the Lord speaks to us about the two possible foundations for building the house of one's life: sand and rock. The one who builds on sand builds only on visible and tangible things, on success, on career, on money. Apparently these are the true realities. But all this one day will pass away. We can see this now with the fall of large banks: this money disappears, it is nothing. And thus all things, which seem to be the true realities we can count on, are

---

[12] Ibid., 183.

only realities of a secondary order. The one who builds his life on these realities, on matter, on success, on appearances, builds upon sand.[13]

The Holy Father then concludes by reaffirming:

Only the Word of God is the foundation of all reality, it is as stable as the heavens and more than the heavens, it is reality. Therefore, we must change our concept of realism. The realist is the one who recognizes the Word of God, in this apparently weak reality, as the foundation of all things. Realist is the one who builds his life on this foundation, which is permanent.[14]

Verbum Domini: To Renew the Faith of the Church in the Word of God

Revelation as Encounter

The post-synodal apostolic exhortation *Verbum Domini* marks an important step in the search for a new evangelization that responds to the challenges of our secularized societies, characterized by the scientific culture. *Verbum Domini* provides a doctrinal, pastoral, and missionary response to the current problems of transmitting the faith to the people of our time, in particular to the young generations who have fully accepted the new languages of the internet and of the new world that constitutes the "digital continent". The Synod of Bishops on *the Word of God in the life and mission of the Church* paved the way for a response to these challenges. In order to appreciate them properly, it is important to recall the notion of revelation developed at the Second Vatican Council in the Dogmatic Constitution on Divine Revelation *Dei Verbum*.

This constitution marks a turning point in the way divine revelation is understood. Before the Council, divine revelation was presented in a more abstract and static way by speaking of a collection

---

[13] Address of Pope Benedict XVI at the Opening of the 12th Ordinary General Assembly of the Synod of Bishops (October 6, 2008).

[14] Ibid.

of truths to believe. *Dei Verbum* presents divine revelation in a more dynamic way, centered on the personal encounter with Christ, "who is both the mediator and the fullness of all revelation", and "through this revelation, therefore, the invisible God out of the abundance of His love speaks to men as friends and lives among them, so that He may invite and take them into fellowship with Himself."[15]

This dynamic and personal vision of revelation presupposes a living exchange where God speaks and his people listen, a dialogue in which the Word of God elicits a personal and communal response, made up of praise, thanksgiving, and obedience to the divine will. This vision inspired the liturgical reform, the major documents of the Council on the Church and the different decrees on the priesthood, consecrated life, the apostolate of the laity, and the missionary activity of the Church, obviously without forgetting ecumenism.

Forty years later, the post-Synodal Exhortation *Verbum Domini* takes up for its part the task of promoting at all levels this dynamic conception of revelation as an encounter with Christ. This is why it insists on listening to the Word of God, on personal and community prayer with the Word, particularly in the context of the Divine Office, the celebration of the sacraments, and especially the Holy Eucharist, where the nuptial encounter par excellence between God and his people takes place.

The Partners of the Encounter

Pope Benedict states, "God makes himself known to us as a mystery of infinite love in which the Father eternally utters his Word in the Holy Spirit. Consequently, the Word, who from the beginning is with God and is God, reveals God himself in the dialogue of love between the divine persons, and invites us to share in that love."[16]

God is love not only in his relationship with us but in himself, as the Trinity of love. This is what the Holy Father Benedict XVI masterfully told us again in his first encyclical. He is in himself, dialogue, exchange, encounter. His mystery of communion is infinite

---

[15] *DV*, no. 2.
[16] *VD*, no. 6.

and transcendent, but he is also a space open to the participation of his creatures. The Incarnation of the Word is the unfolding of it in the economy of salvation, inaugurating this participation himself by his own existence in the flesh and by the gift of faith to those who receive it.

"Consequently," the document adds, "created in the image and likeness of the God who is love, we can thus understand ourselves only in accepting the Word and in docility to the work of the Holy Spirit. In the light of the revelation made by God's Word, the enigma of the human condition is definitively clarified."[17]

The entire Second Vatican Council is evoked in these few sentences, in particular the Pastoral Constitution on the Church in the Modern World *Gaudium et Spes*. We cannot overemphasize the correspondence between these two great documents: on the one hand, the opening up to man of the Divine Persons' dialogue of love, and on the other hand, the definitive enlightenment that brings to man the revelation of his being created in the image and likeness of God, who is Love.

The fact that these two fundamental dimensions of Christianity have been forgotten partly explains its eclipse in modern and contemporary culture. Because for centuries, in theology and even in preaching, the Trinitarian mystery was relegated to the rank of an abstract speculation without meaning concretely for the Christian life; at the same time, theological anthropology drifted toward an individualist conception of the person, for lack of a Trinitarian vision of man as *Imago Dei*. Consequently, an individualistic conception of salvation predominated, obscuring the social relevance of Christianity. The questions of justice and peace, the questions of life and love, for example, were approached from the moral perspective without the underlying anthropology being solidly articulated on the basis of Christology, that is to say, on the basis of participation in the Trinitarian life.

John Paul II and Benedict XVI helped to correct these omissions thanks to magisterial developments that we find, among others, in the post-synodal exhortation *Familiaris Consortio*, the apostolic letter *Mulieris Dignitatem*, and the encyclical *Deus Caritas Est*. To my way of thinking, the new evangelization will be fruitful and lasting in the

[17] Ibid.

measure in which it will enlighten, in depth, the identity of man as a being of communion and his relation to the Trinitarian communion in Christ.

The Marian Paradigm

Once it has recalled these doctrinal foundations of the encounter between God and his people, *Verbum Domini* insistently invites to listen anew to the Word of God, in the Spirit, as the Virgin Mary did, this young woman "who by her assent decisively cooperated with the entrance of the eternal into time".[18] *Verbum Domini* issues here an appeal for a more profound contemplation and theology of the Word in the light of Mariology: "Devout and loving attention to the figure of Mary as the model and archetype of the Church's faith is of capital importance for bringing about in our day a concrete paradigm shift in the Church's relation with the word, both in prayerful listening and in generous commitment to mission and proclamation."[19]

There we have an invaluable instruction for renewing the faith of the Church in the Word of God. It is enough, for example, to meditate on the scene of the Annunciation in order to enter into the dialogue of Mary with the Holy Trinity. This dialogue would not cease to grow as the event of the Incarnation of the Word led Mary on the road to her cousin Elizabeth, to Cana and Capernaum, and finally to the Cross and the Cenacle of Pentecost. What could be more fascinating, indeed, than the very intimate communion of Mary with the Word-made-flesh!

What could be more fascinating than our faith-filled participation in this dialogue!

As we contemplate in the Mother of God a life totally shaped by the word, we realize that we too are called to enter into the mystery of faith, whereby Christ comes to dwell in our lives. Every Christian believer, Saint Ambrose reminds us, in some way interiorly conceives and gives birth to the word of God: even though there is only one

---

[18] *VD*, no. 27.
[19] *Propositio* 55, quoted in *VD*, no. 28.

Mother of Christ in the flesh, in the faith Christ is the progeny of us all. Thus, what took place for Mary can daily take place in each of us, in the hearing of the word and in the celebration of the sacraments.[20]

The Church's faith in the Word of God is unceasingly renewed, starting from the contemplation of the Mother of God, in her union with Christ and with the Spirit. For Mary is the perfect icon of the Virgin Church, Spouse and Mother of the Lamb of God.

Verbum Domini: Renewing the Interpretation of Sacred Scripture

Between Mary and the Church, there is a parallel that inspires the renewal of faith in the Word of God. The same parallel can also inspire the renewal of the interpretation of Sacred Scripture in the Church. For the Church gave birth to the Scriptures as Mary gave birth to the Word Incarnate, by the grace of the Holy Spirit. The Church possesses an intimate knowledge of the Scriptures that establishes its authority in order to interpret them. "I would not believe the Gospel, had not the authority of the Catholic Church led me to do so.", writes Saint Augustine.[21] This is why *Verbum Domini* forcefully and clearly reaffirms as a first principle that "the Bible is the Church's book, and its essential place in the Church's life gives rise to its genuine interpretation."[22]

Interpreting in the Spirit of the Church

"Sacred Scripture must be interpreted in the light of the same Spirit through whom it was written."[23] From this fundamental assertion, *Verbum Domini* asks for a deeper reception of the hermeneutical principles of *Dei Verbum*, number 12.[24] Hence, the three basic criteria "for an appreciation of the divine dimension of the Bible are

---

[20] *VD*, no. 28.

[21] Augustine, *Contra epistulam Manichaei quam vocant fundamenti* V, 6 (PL 42, 176), quoted in *VD*, no. 29.

[22] *VD*, no. 29.

[23] *DV*, no. 12 (translated by Ignatius Press).

[24] See *VD*, no. 34.

(1) interpreting the text while taking into account *"the unity of the whole of Scripture"*—we speak today about "canonical exegesis"; (2) then taking into account *the living Tradition of the whole Church"*; and finally (3) respecting *"the analogy of faith"*.[25]

It is important to explain these criteria briefly in order to understand their significance and importance.

THE UNITY OF SCRIPTURE

The first criterion is the unity of Scripture. What causes the unity of Scripture as a whole? Clearly, the Bible is a library of several books, and contemporary historical-critical exegesis has taught us a lot about the human composition of the text. But the Bible is also the Book of a Divine Author. The unity of Scripture as a whole depends on this Divine Author, who inspired the biblical authors.

> The same Spirit who acts in the incarnation of the Word in the womb of the Virgin Mary is the Spirit who guides Jesus throughout his mission and is promised to the disciples. The same Spirit who spoke through the prophets sustains and inspires the Church in her task of proclaiming the word of God and in the preaching of the Apostles; finally, it is this Spirit who inspires the authors of sacred Scripture.[26]

"All divine Scripture is one book," writes Hugh of Saint Victor, "and this one book is Christ, speaks of Christ, and finds its fulfilment in Christ."[27] The divine Spirit, who speaks in and through the biblical texts, first guided the events and their interpretation in order to lead the People of God to the green pastures of divine life in Christ.

TRADITION

The second criterion is to take into account the whole of tradition. Indeed, historical-critical exegesis has shown notable progress as to philological and literary analysis, but it has done little to develop the spiritual sense of Scripture. This is the heritage of patristic exegesis,

---

[25] Ibid.
[26] Ibid., no. 15.
[27] Hugh of Saint Victor, *De Arca Noe* 2, 8 (PL 176, 642C-D), quoted in *VD*, no. 39.

which is centered on the Christological interpretation of the Old Testament and its fulfillment in the New Testament.

Saint Gregory the Great summarizes it in this way: what "the Old Testament promised, the New Testament has shown; what the former announced in a hidden way, the latter openly proclaims as present. This is why the Old Testament is the prophecy of the New Testament; and the best commentary on the Old Testament is the New Testament."[28]

Verbum Domini reminds us that this exegesis of the Fathers still retains its value. It assumes the definition that the Pontifical Biblical Commission gives of the spiritual sense of Scripture:

> The meaning expressed by the biblical texts when they are read under the influence of the Holy Spirit in the context of the Paschal Mystery of Christ and of the new life which results from it. This context, in fact, exists. The New Testament recognizes in them the fulfillment of the Scriptures. Therefore, it is normal to reread the Scriptures in the light of this new context, which is that of life in the Spirit.[29]

THE ANALOGY OF FAITH

The third criterion for the interpretation of Scripture is, according to *Dei Verbum*, the analogy of faith that can be linked to the analogy of the Word of God of which *Verbum Domini* speaks. The expression "Word of God" actually covers a diversity of meanings as divine word, creative word, historical and literary word; this diversity of meanings is nevertheless unified by the convergence of the meanings on Christ, the fullness of revelation.[30]

According to the *Catechism of the Catholic Church*, the analogy of faith discussed in *Dei Verbum* is commonly understood in the theological tradition as "the coherence of the truths of faith among themselves and within the whole plan of Revelation".[31] As stated at the 12th Ordinary General Assembly of the Synod of Bishops, "It may

---

[28] Gregory the Great, *Homily on Ezechiel* I, VI, 15 (PL 76, 836 B).

[29] Pontifical Biblical Commission, *The Interpretation of the Bible in the Church* (April 15, 1993), II, A, 2.

[30] See *DV*, no. 2.

[31] *Catechism of the Catholic Church*, no. 114.

be useful to recall in this regard an analogy developed by the Fathers of the Church between the Word of God who becomes 'flesh' and the Word which becomes 'Book.' "[32] As Saint Ambrose said, "The teachings of the Scriptures are His Body (that of the Son)."[33]

When we interpret Scripture, we must take into account this analogy between the Incarnate Word and Sacred Scripture, between the truth in person and all the particular truths concerning salvation. All these divine and human dimensions of the truth are closely interconnected. The discernment of the meaning of Scripture by the Church and her authentic Magisterium is consequently worked out based on the criteria of the unity of Sacred Scripture, the unity of tradition, and the unity of faith.

Exegesis and Theology

In this light we understand the insistence of *Verbum Domini* on a renewal of the ecclesial interpretation of Sacred Scripture. Because a certain kind of modern exegesis would like to interpret Scripture scientifically by abstracting from the faith. *Verbum Domini* denounces this reading, which remains on the surface of the text and reduces the Bible to a document of the past. The erroneous position of this exegesis rests on the presupposition that faith and reason are opposed.[34]

This secularized exegesis, which feeds into the positivist mentality, has harmful methodological consequences. It excludes divine intervention in history and consequently reduces the divine dimension of Sacred Scripture. Benedict XVI wants a "theological" development of exegesis up to the "highest academic levels", so that the danger of a dualism between exegesis and theology can be overcome and the two levels of exegesis, historical and theological, can be adequately developed. "In a word," notes the Pope, "where exegesis is not theology ..., and conversely, where theology is not essentially the interpretation of the Church's Scripture, such a theology no longer has

[32] Final message of the 12th Ordinary General Assembly of the Synod of Bishops (October 5–26, 2008), no. 5.

[33] Ambrose, *Treatise on the Gospel of St. Luke* 6, 33.

[34] See *VD*, no. 36.

a foundation."[35] Furthermore, he himself gives the example of such theological exegesis in his book on Jesus of Nazareth.

The development of a theological exegesis is of capital importance for the renewal of the spiritual life of the people of God. Because where dualism rages between exegesis and theology, harm and damage ensue for the spiritual life, because the truth of the Scriptures is no longer perceived as a foundation and fulcrum.[36] An exegesis conducted in faith, and therefore truly theological in its content and method, makes it possible to restore the unity of interpretation, and therefore the confidence of the faithful in Sacred Scripture.

To Deepen the Life in the Spirit

Interpreting Scripture according to the Church's criteria has consequences for the formation of the faithful: "A notion of scholarly research that would consider itself neutral with regard to Scripture should not be encouraged. As well as learning the original languages in which the Bible was written and suitable methods of interpretation, students need to have a deep spiritual life, in order to appreciate that the Scripture can only be understood if it is lived."[37]

Understanding Sacred Scripture presupposes, indeed, an act of faith, and even of conversion. Before his conversion, Saint Augustine had learned from Saint Ambrose the typological interpretation of Scripture, which shows the convergence of the Old Testament on Jesus Christ, but he remained interiorly incapable of taking the step of faith. That was when the grace of conversion was given to him by the Holy Spirit as he was reading a passage from Saint Paul: "Put on the Lord Jesus Christ, and make no provision for the flesh, to gratify its desires" (Rom 13:14). His spiritual life, finally free from rational prejudices and carnal attachments, became the key to his astonishing penetration into the mysteries of faith contained in Sacred Scripture.

Saint Anthony the Abbot, the founder of Eastern monasticism, had a similar experience and a very fruitful encounter with Christ in

---

[35] Ibid., no. 35.
[36] See ibid., no. 35.
[37] Ibid., no. 47.

Scripture, just as Saint Thérèse of the Child Jesus did, who enthusiastically testifies about her vocation to love, which she discovered in reading chapters 12 and 13 of the First Letter to the Corinthians. The apostolic exhortation evokes at length this rich experience of the saints, which helps us to understand that Sacred Scripture contains more than ideas or maxims; it is full of the Spirit, who is encountered by anyone who believes. He it is—and he alone—who leads to the entire truth, that is, to the Trinitarian communion to which Sacred Scripture testifies.

The men and women who have a living experience of faith experience the truth of Sacred Scripture, its coherence and its unity, despite the diversity of the writings; they feel a joy and peace that urges them to seek the meaning of their life more and more in Scripture, like Saint Augustine, who found in it "at last the answer to his deep inner restlessness and his thirst for truth".[38]

> By applying yourself in this way to *lectio divina*, search diligently and with unshakable trust in God for the meaning of the divine Scriptures, which is hidden in great fullness within. You ought not, however, to be satisfied merely with knocking and seeking: to understand the things of God, what is absolutely necessary is *oratio*. For this reason, the Saviour told us not only: "Seek and you will find," and "Knock and it shall be opened to you," but also added, "Ask and you shall receive."[39]

The Word of the Lord abides forever. The post-synodal apostolic exhortation *Verbum Domini* reaffirms the faith of the Church in the Word of God and thus responds to the challenge of relativism, which calls into question the truth of Christianity. The fullness of meaning that emanates from this Word makes us exult in joy with Mary. Reason and faith are in harmony there, because Benedict XVI reminds us that "the true reason is love, and love is the true reason."[40] The beauty and the specificity of faith is to give eternal life, this eternal life that is to "know you the only true God, and Jesus Christ whom you have sent" (Jn 17:3).

[38] *VD*, no. 38.
[39] *VD*, no. 86, citing Origen, *Epistola ad Gregorium* 3.
[40] Ratzinger, *Truth and Tolerance*, 183.

Dear members of the university community, "His word engages us not only as hearers of divine revelation, but also as its heralds."[41] In the midst of a world in search of meaning, we are living witnesses of a Word and above all of a Presence. Eucharistic communion with him who sends us makes us witnesses, not by external constraint but by interior necessity. To this end, let us take responsibility for the mission in the same spirit that Saint Bernard strove to communicate to his disciples: "The man who is wise, therefore, will see his life as more like a reservoir than a canal. The canal simultaneously pours out what it receives; the reservoir retains the water till it is filled, then discharges the overflow without loss to itself."[42] We will be credible witnesses of the living God if we allow the Spirit of God to fill our hearts with his Word.

"Indeed," says *Verbum Domini*, "sharing in the life of God, a Trinity of love, is complete joy (cf. 1 Jn 1:4). And it is the Church's gift and unescapable duty to communicate that joy, born of an encounter with the person of Christ, the Word of God in our midst.... There is no greater priority than this: to enable the people of our time once more to encounter God, the God who speaks to us and shares his love so that we might have life in abundance (cf. Jn 10:10)."[43]

---

[41] *VD*, no. 91.

[42] Bernard of Clairvaux, *On the Song of Songs I*, trans. Kilian Walsh (Kalamazoo: Cistercian Publications, 1981), sermon XVIII, no. 3.

[43] *VD*, no. 2.

Chapter 3

A Synodal Church

In his historic speech given on October 17, 2015, on the occasion of the fiftieth anniversary of the institution of the Synod of Bishops, Pope Francis, exercising his discernment as the supreme pastor of the Church, declared significantly that "it is precisely this path of *synodality* which God expects of the Church of the third millennium."[1] Since the beginnings of his pontificate, he has been inviting this very same Church to think of herself as essentially "going forth",[2] in other words, missionary.

Therefore, we must understand the notion of *synodality* within the logic of faith in God's calling for his people. To the world's way of thinking, we speak about democracy and participation, more or less on the basis of the self-affirmation of individuals and peoples, but in the Church, we speak about synodality, in other words, about communion in faith and mission with reference to him whose Church is a sacrament for humanity. With this concept, the Holy Father concretely specifies and makes more effective the missionary essence of the Church, which was reaffirmed during the Second Ecumenical Council of the Vatican.

This statement by the current pontiff, though solemn and engaging, is not altogether new; rather, it is a more incisive renewal of the conciliar approach, which confirms and broadens the synodal practice

---

This essay is based on a talk given at the 37th General Assembly of the Episcopal Conference of Latin America (CELAM), Tegucigalpa, May 15, 2019.

[1] Francis, Address at the Ceremony Commemorating the 50th Anniversary of the Institution of the Synod of Bishops (October 17, 2015).

[2] Francis, apostolic exhortation *Evangelii Gaudium* (November 24, 2013), no. 25 (hereinafter *EG*).

of his predecessors. John Paul II, for example, expressed his preference for a synodal method in ecclesial responsibility and desired to be recognized as the *pope of the Synods*. He wrote:

> Part of the preparation for the approach of the Year 2000 is the *series of Synods* begun after the Second Vatican Council: general Synods together with continental, regional, national, and diocesan Synods.... These Synods themselves are part of the new evangelization: they were born of the Second Vatican Council's vision of the Church. They open up broad areas for the participation of the laity, whose specific responsibilities in the Church they define. They are an expression of the strength which Christ has given to the entire People of God, making it a sharer in his own Messianic mission as Prophet, Priest and King.[3]

With Pope Francis, we find ourselves facing a choice not only of style but of substance: he proposes to the whole Church a *missionary conversion*, starting from the base and involving all the faithful in their witness to the Gospel. The bishops obviously remain central to the *synodal Church* with the renewed role of the *Synod of Bishops*, but they are strongly urged to make an effort to change their thinking; this involves them in a restoration of pastoral activity, interpreted in a synodal key:

> Synodality is not an external habit. It has a mysteric significance, which is contained in this little prefix: *syn-*, "together," the fruit and condition of the coming of the Holy Spirit who loves unity and concord. Synodality is the external form assumed by the mystery of communion in the life of the Church: Christians are synodal, in other words, "traveling companions," bearers of God, bearers of the temple, bearers of Christ and of the Spirit, as Saint Ignatius of Antioch puts it.[4]

Synodality therefore does not primarily mean organization, but interior communion with God, which is expressed in external witness:

> Synodality is therefore a style that springs from this life of grace which conforms us to the Lord Jesus. Synodality arises from below. It starts by

---

[3] John Paul II, apostolic letter *Tertio Millenio Adveniente* (November 10, 1994), no. 21.

[4] Gualtiero Bassetti, *Discorso per l'apertura del Consiglio episcopale permanente della CEI*, April 1, 2019.

listening, in which everyone has something to learn from the other, in willingness to be in tune, to welcome one another. It shows in one's language and conduct, in our relations, in the choices made in everyday life. It gives rise to synodality, approaches reality with a willingness to learn and to become involved.... As a process, experienced in the tension between going forward and keeping together, synodality is also tiring. It requires an evangelical spirituality and ecclesial belonging, continual formation, willingness to accompany, and creativity.[5]

Therefore, we must understand the notion of *synodality* within the logic of faith in God's calling for his people. It is a matter not only of working toward a more adequate consultation with the people of God, but also of acknowledging that the presence of the Spirit dwells within this people at the root of their faith, thus configuring their ontological-sacramental membership. The operative dimension of synodality is significant to the extent that one walks by faith, following the Gospel, going out to meet the various cultures with an evangelizing dynamism, without letting oneself be contaminated by worldly mentalities and ideologies.

The Theological Foundations of Synodality

In order to reflect calmly and theologically on the significance of *synodality*, as the mature fruit of a journey that has been made since Vatican Council II, it is helpful to refer either to the abovementioned speech on the occasion of the Commemoration of the 50th Anniversary of the Institution of the Synod of Bishops, or to the recent document by the International Theological Commission entitled *Synodality in the Life and Mission of the Church*,[6] or to the apostolic constitution that followed it, *Episcopalis Communio*,[7] by which the Holy Father reformed the Synod of Bishops that had been instituted by Saint Paul VI in 1965. These three documents, which I recommend reading in unabridged form, can be considered as an

[5] Ibid.
[6] See International Theological Commission (ITC), *Synodality in the Life and Mission of the Church* (March 2, 2018).
[7] Francis, Apostolic Constitution on the Synod of Bishops *Episcopalis Communio* (September 15, 2018).

authoritative clarification of what is meant by and included in this *walking together* implied in the notion of synodality. Here I intend to reflect on several features that help us to describe the theological-pastoral dimension of it.

In order to have a correct theology of synodality, we first have to affirm its Trinitarian root, which qualifies the ecclesial *communion* as a people gathered by the Holy Trinity, called through the action of the Holy Spirit "to live communion, which comes about through sincere self-giving, union with God, and unity with our brothers and sisters in Christ".[8] This source in the *very bond of love (nexus amoris)* in the Trinitarian life, in which the community of believers is called to participate sacramentally,[9] makes synodality "not simply a working procedure, but the particular form in which the Church lives and operates".[10] It takes shape first as *infallibility* of the People of God as a whole "in the act of believing", and therefore as a *participation* of all the baptized in the eschatological mission of the Church, each one through the gift-charism or ministry that he has received (1 Cor 12:11), according to this logic of the *hierarchical communion* taught by Vatican Council II.[11] The context in which such a joint membership is fully realized, where the synodal path of the Church is therefore found in its permanent form, is the Eucharistic *synaxis*, which brings about this *communion of saints* (1 Cor 11:17), or the union with the Triune God and the unity of the human persons, which comes about through the mediation of the Holy Spirit in Jesus Christ, making the believers participants in the multiform divine grace. Consistently, then, the document by the Theological Commission explains that "the Trinitarian, anthropological, Christological, pneumatological, and Eucharistic dimensions of God's plan of salvation, which is at work in the mystery of the Church, are the theological horizon which has been the context for the development of synodality across the centuries."[12]

In other words, the idea of a *synodal Church* means first a qualitative leap in our awareness that we all participate together in the Trinitarian communion, through the gift of the Holy Spirit poured

[8] ITC, *Synodality*, no. 43.
[9] Ibid., no. 46.
[10] Ibid., no. 42.
[11] See *LG*, no. 12.
[12] ITC, *Synodality*, no. 48.

out in our hearts, which is renewed permanently through the paschal Eucharistic gift of the Lord. The Holy Spirit is the principle and the soul of the ecclesial communion; without him, no one can profess that Jesus is Lord. All of us equally are introduced into the Trinitarian relations through the baptismal grace of divine adoption, accomplished by him, who bestows on us furthermore a personal charism with which to serve the community, the Body of Christ.

At the root of the Church's missionary character and synodality, therefore, is the presence and action of the Holy Spirit, who brings about the communion in faith that stirs up the witness and the activities of the Church. Such a faith saves not only through adherence to the mystery of Christ, but through testifying to him: "If you confess with your lips that Jesus is Lord and believe in your heart that God raised him from the dead, you will be saved. For man believes with his heart and so is justified, and he confesses with his lips and so is saved" (Rom 10:9–10).

It is not enough to "believe in your heart" in order to be justified; it is necessary to "confess with your lips" in order to be saved; this means giving witness to others, which implies community. The faith lives and grows if it is communicated; otherwise, it weakens and dies. Pope Francis sums up this intrinsic dynamic of the faith with the paired terms *disciple-missionary*, a binomial that comprises the whole structure of the Church's missionary conversion and of the transformation of her ordinary pastoral care in a missionary key. The moving forward together that constitutes synodality is a path in faith manifesting the joy of salvation in the testimony of the mission.

In his address to the Synod, Pope Francis emphasized that a common path like this is first of all a dynamism of listening, conducted at all levels of the Church's life, in order to perceive the voice of the Spirit in *the faith of the whole Church*, according to the ancient maxim that was dear to the Christendom of the first millennium: "What concerns everyone must be negotiated by all." If, as the pope often recalls, "the *sensus fidei* prevents a rigid separation between an *Ecclesia docens* [teaching Church] and an *Ecclesia discens* [learning Church], since the flock likewise has an instinctive ability to discern the new ways that the Lord is revealing to the Church",[13] then "the renewal

---

[13] Francis, Address during 50th Anniversary of Institution of Synod of Bishops.

of the Church's synodal life demands that we initiate processes for consulting the entire People of God",[14] because a "synodal Church is a Church of participation and co-responsibility".[15] With that, we define the path of ecclesial self-consciousness, which already became particularly acute during the nineteenth century, through prophetic voices like those of Johann Adam Möhler (1796–1838), Antonio Rosmini (1797–1855), and John Henry Newman (1801–1890); by identifying with the normative sources of Scripture and tradition, and by hoping for the biblical, liturgical, and patristic renewal that followed, they emphasized that "the whole Church, by the action of the Holy Spirit, is the subject or 'organ' of Tradition; and that lay people have an active role in the transmission of the apostolic faith."[16]

The pope, seeking to practice the ecclesiology of communion of Vatican II, invites the Church to realize, precisely along the difficult path of listening, how synodality "offers us the most appropriate interpretive framework for understanding the hierarchical ministry itself".[17] In order to understand the structure of the mystery of communion—of the Church and in the Church—there must in fact be an acknowledgment of the profound connection between the concept of synodality and that of collegiality. The latter is "the specific form in which ecclesial synodality is manifested and made real through the ministry of Bishops on the level of communion of the local Churches in a region, and on the level of communion of all the Churches in the universal Church. An authentic manifestation of synodality naturally entails the exercise of the collegial ministry of the Bishops."[18] In fact, concretely, the first level of the exercise of synodality is actualized in the particular Church, where all the various components of the ecclesial body are called to collaborate with the bishop for the good of the community itself: over the course of history, the synodal exercise of the bishop's ministry, founded sacramentally on Holy Orders, has been the principal way in which the synodal path of the People of God, guided by the Holy Spirit, has been and

---

[14] ITC, *Synodality*, no. 65.

[15] Ibid., no. 67.

[16] ITC, *Sensus Fidei in the Life of the Church* (June 10, 2014), no. 41, quoted in ITC, *Synodality*, no. 39.

[17] Francis, Address during 50th Anniversary of Institution of Synod of Bishops.

[18] ITC, *Synodality*, no. 7.

continues to be accomplished, at various levels—provinces, ecclesi-astical regions, particular councils—up to the level of the Universal Church, thanks to the proper charism of the Successor of Peter.[19] Incidentally, in keeping with a communional logic of mutual service, the same pontiff suggested understanding the Church as an inverted pyramid, with the top located beneath the base; that is where the "ministries" are found, because "it is in serving the people of God that each bishop becomes, for that portion of the flock entrusted to him, *vicarius Christi*, the vicar of that Jesus who at the Last Supper bent down to wash the feet of the Apostles (cf. Jn 13:1–15). And in a similar perspective," the pope concludes, "the Successor of Peter is nothing else if not the *servus servorum Dei*."[20] He, in fact, being "not ... above the Church; but within it as one of the baptized, and within the College of Bishops as a Bishop among Bishops, called at the same time—as Successor of Peter—to lead the Church of Rome which presides in charity over all the Churches."[21]

At the juridical level, it is necessary however to specify that the collegiality of the acts of the episcopal body is bound up with the fact that the "universal Church cannot be conceived as the sum of the particular Churches, or as a federation of particular Churches."[22] According to the Congregation for the Doctrine of the Faith, "It is not the result of the communion of the Churches, but, in its essential mystery, it is a reality *ontologically and temporally* prior to every *individual* particular Church."[23]

Similarly, the episcopal college should not be understood as the sum total of the bishops set over the particular churches, nor as the result of their communion, but rather, as an essential element of the Universal Church, it is a reality prior to the office of headship over a particular Church.[24] This theological-juridical clarification may seem subtle and

---

[19] See ibid., no. 29.

[20] Francis, Address during 50th Anniversary of Institution of Synod of Bishops.

[21] Ibid.

[22] John Paul II, Address to the Bishops of the United States of America (September 16, 1987), no. 3.

[23] Congregation for the Doctrine of the Faith, Letter to the Bishops of the Catholic Church on Some Aspects of the Church Understood as Communion *Communionis Notio* (May 28, 1992), no. 9, *AAS* 85 (1993): 843.

[24] Among other reasons, as is obvious to everyone, there are many bishops who, while performing their properly episcopal duties, do not head a particular Church.

superfluous, but it recalls the logic of faith that is founded on the gift of God and not on human consent.

The Principles on Which Synodality Is Founded

Although it does not use the term *synodality*, the conciliar constitution *Lumen Gentium* states in paragraph 32 the equal dignity of all Christians as its fundamental principle: they share "a common dignity as members from their regeneration in Christ, having the same filial grace and the same vocation to perfection; possessing in common one salvation, one hope and one undivided charity." The holy pastors, the ordained ministers, and the lay faithful, despite the hierarchical diversity of the offices and responsibilities, have one and the same dignity (*dignitas*), that of the "children of God", and are all equally engaged (*actio*), each according to his own state in life and particular tasks, in spreading the Kingdom of God and building up the Body of Christ. This equality is what prompted Saint Augustine to say, in a homily addressed to the faithful of Hippo on the anniversary of his episcopal ordination: "For you I am a bishop, with you, after all, I am a Christian. The first is the name of an office undertaken, the second a name of grace; that one means danger, this one salvation."[25] He also said, "I hope the fact that I have been bought together with you gives me more pleasure than my having been placed at your head."[26]

For several centuries, because of complex contingencies of various kinds, the principle of the substantial equality between those who make up the People of God was overshadowed by the hierarchical principle, which of course is also essential to the Church's constitution. This evolutionary process, which started in the fourth century, gained ground in the medieval era and was definitively affirmed in the sixteenth century, in opposition to the anti-hierarchical principles of the Protestant Reformation. Thus, a verticalist ecclesiology prevailed, founded on authority, in which the Church came to be presented chiefly as an *unequal society*, divided dualistically into superiors and subjects, clerics and laypersons: *coetus ducens et coetus ductus* [the leading

---

[25] Augustine, *The Works of Saint Augustine*, pt. 3, vol. 9, *Sermons on the Saints*, trans. Edmund Hill, O.P. (Hyde Park, N.Y.: New City Press, 1994), sermon 340, 1 (PL 38, 1483).
[26] Ibid.

group and the group that is led], resulting in the radicalization of the famous passage attributed to Saint Jerome and quoted by Gratian (in the twelfth century): "*Duo sunt genera christianorum*, there are two kinds of Christians, clerics and lay people."[27]

The ecclesiology of Vatican II, which is based essentially on communion (it is not only a juridical society),[28] goes beyond such a unilateral conception and regards the Church as a sacrament of salvation, "sign and instrument of communion with God and of unity among all men",[29] while explicitly confirming the hierarchical principle, which is divinely instituted and therefore cannot be reformed; the conciliar view places at the basis of the Church's constitutional structure the principle of radical "equality with regard to dignity and ... activity",[30] thus eliminating the artificial dualism between clergy and laity, and calling them all to an effective participation in and shared responsibility for ecclesial life and activity. From this perspective, the structure of the Church appears theologically and juridically in a profound unity and harmony. The hierarchical principle is tempered by the principle of equality, and, in turn, the principle of equality is integrated and activated by the principle of organicity and functional diversity. There is a co-responsibility and a cooperation on everyone's part in building up the Body of Christ, for the growth and development of the People of God. Through canon 208, the principle of equality "of dignity and action", expressed theologically in the dogmatic constitution *Lumen Gentium*, has become a basic principle of canonical order.[31]

Consequently, according to canon 209, the Christian's first and fundamental duty, which summarizes and qualifies all the others, is to maintain always, in every manifestation of his individual and social life, a vital communion with the Church, along the lines indicated by canon 205. The condition and foundation for this communion, which is at the same time a right, is intimate communion with God, and it is expressed concretely through union with the brethren in the

---

[27] *Decretum Gratiani*, c. 7, c. XII, q. 1. See Luigi Chiappetta, *Il Codice di Diritto canonico: Commento giuridico-pastorale* (Bologna: EDB, 2011), 280.

[28] *Code of Canon Law: Latin-English Edition* (Washington, D.C.: Canon Law Society of America, 1983), can. 204, §2 (hereinafter CIC).

[29] See *LG*, nos. 1, 9.

[30] CIC, can. 208.

[31] Chiappetta, *Il Codice di Diritto canonico*, 281.

faith, and above all with the lawful pastors. It involves furthermore some precise duties both toward the Universal Church and toward the particular Church (§2) to which one belongs according to law. Canon 529, §2, also recalls that there is moreover a parochial communion to preserve and promote.

Similarly, according to canon 210, the vocation to holiness is not the privilege of specific persons or categories in the Church: the vocation to holiness is universal.[32] "Everyone," the Council says, "whether belonging to the hierarchy, or being cared for by it, is called to holiness.... All the faithful of Christ, of whatever rank or status, are called to the fullness of the Christian life and to the perfection of charity."[33]

Toward a Synodal Church in Latin America

On the basis of the theological and canonical foundations that serve as principles for the concept of *synodality*, and the exercise of it in the Church, we can boldly go ahead to adapt the *walking together* of a synodal Church to all ecclesial contexts. The actualization of synodality in the sense presented above demands a *pastoral conversion* that implies in the Latin American context (and not only there) going beyond certain paradigms that are still present in the ecclesiastical culture, among them "the concentration of responsibility for mission in the ministry of Pastors; insufficient appreciation of the consecrated life and charismatic gifts; rarely making use of the specific and qualified contribution of the lay faithful, including women, in their areas of expertise."[34]

In this sense, in other words, by overcoming self-referentiality and verticalist authoritarianism,

> synodality takes shape in the fact of experiencing that the Church is a living body in which everything holds together; a body characterized by this fraternal communion in which the members, who are distinct

---

[32] LG, no. 11.

[33] The pertinent paragraphs from *Lumen Gentium* are no. 39 (holiness of the Church); no. 40 (the universal vocation to holiness); no. 41 (the multiple forms); no. 42 (the path and the means of holiness).

[34] ITC, *Synodality*, no. 105.

but not distant, share the gifts, the charisms, the ministries.... Synodality must help us precisely to live in *greater fraternity*: alone, we can do nothing; our strength depends on the unity of our being and of our action. We must practice synodality as a method of life and of government in our diocesan communities, starting with the involvement of the laity, men and women, and also with methods with which we advance shared responsibility and decision-making processes. Besides, we ask ourselves: where can our people express this *flair* that the Holy Father has many times recognized as theirs? In what forms and in what spaces? Maybe it would not be a bad idea to start again from a commitment to revitalize the diocesan Councils, both priestly and pastoral, and parish Councils themselves: if these participatory organizations function, then communion and co-responsibility become effective.[35]

At the continental level, several priorities for Latin America have been discussed in recent years that remain at the top of the agenda for a synodal Church. For example, a more determined and significant involvement of the laity in public life and, for this purpose, dialogue between pastors and politicians, are prospects that should be furthered resolutely, by means of meetings and dialogues at various levels. On the other hand, although staunch Christians who are involved in public life have converging objectives, they cannot dispense with an adequate formation, which these meetings can develop and motivate. Similarly, it is good to welcome the initiative to form Catholic leaders, which is spreading enthusiastically on the continent, after a very stimulating Roman encounter with extensive participation by qualified men and women. To me it seems fair to emphasize that Latin America needs a feminine kind of synodality, in other words, a radical revision of women's situations and status on the continent, by a qualitative leap that changes the *macho* mentality and fights against the violence that women put up with, the exploitation of them personally, and the poverty that is endured by many abandoned and exploited women. This priority is all the more necessary because today, in part because of better education compared with the past, women are pillars of parish communities but often suffer from the clerical mentality of their pastors. Their progressive access to higher education is an enormously important cultural fact, and there is no

---

[35] Bassetti, *Discorso per l'apertura del Consiglio episcopale.*

longer any justification for relegating them to marginal roles and not integrating them into decision-making processes. The vitality of a synodal Church in Latin America will depend on *cultural conversion*,[36] which presupposes the authentic and urgent promotion of women on the continent.

Finally, after the impulse of the continental mission that implanted everywhere the spirit of missionary discipleship, and after the apostolic exhortation *Evangelii Gaudium*, which made the missionary commitment of the Aparecida Conference universal, Latin America faces the challenge of demonstrating that the measures that have been taken lead, with the vigorous prompting of Pope Francis, to a decisive commitment to a synodal Church. This commitment does not ignore the fact that the great majority of the faithful do not participate directly in the structures and synodal organizations of our dioceses. Consultations among the People of God rarely reach a significant percentage of our faithful. This should not discourage us, because the first objective of synodality is not the measurable visibility of walking together, but the growth of the faith of the People of God who walk in history with the Risen Christ.

Indeed, the Church's experience throughout history since her origins is that of a people whose members are poor, who walk with few resources but with Spirit and life, supported by the myriads of saints who have revitalized the Church permanently, starting with their love for the poor. For his part, Pope Francis invented the expression *a poor Church for the poor*, so that in the strength of charity and of the evangelical counsels, the synodal Church may go ahead as a people made up of the poor, listening to the Spirit, and at the service of the brethren in the humility of faith. Today as always, the Church's path in response to God's call remains the evangelization of the poor, an awareness that Latin America restored to the Universal Church.

This is why the final word on synodality must return to the mystery of faith that constitutes the People of God as an assembly gathered in the unity of the Father, of the Son, and of the Holy Spirit,[37]

---

[36] See Marc Ouellet, "La mujer a la luz de la Trinidad y de María-Iglesia", in Pontificia Comisión para América Latina, *La Mujer, pilar en la edificación de la Iglesia y de la sociedad en América Latina*, Actas de la Reunión Plenaria 6–9 de marzo de 2018 (Rome: Libreria Editrice Vaticana, 2018), 93–94.

[37] See *LG*, no. 4.

so as to insist on the absolute priority of evangelization and education in the faith. Otherwise, the pilgrim people lose the sense of belonging to God and allow themselves to be attracted to deceitful paths that end up ruining families, confusing young people, and destroying man and woman in their search for happiness.

In this sense, popular piety has always been, and is more than ever today, an antidote to the consumerism and ideological colonialism that invade markets, schools, parliaments, and households. Marian devotion in particular, in the many shrines that venerate the Mother of God on this continent, serves as a permanent guide to the crowds that walk together, with the sense of tenderness and mercy, which helps them to follow Jesus and to remain hopeful despite adverse conditions, injustices, the degradation of our common home [i.e., the environment], corruption, and forced migrations that sow insecurity and death along the roads of the continent.

God's path for the Church in the third millennium takes the form and style of *synodality*. This perspective, which is a challenge to our faith, is not only the pedagogical method of a pope who is calling us to a missionary conversion; it is the activation of the breath of the Holy Spirit, who urges each and every one of us to believe in the Risen Lord and to act in communion, in keeping with the dignity and responsibility of the members of the Body of Christ, which has been sent into the world.

Many people understand synodality as a higher, organic concept, according to the democratic sensibility of our era; this perspective is not wrong but remains superficial: the qualitative leap is first of all the awareness of the One Spirit who animates and moves each and every one by grace and according to his own charism. In other words, synodality in a synodal Church presupposes that mission is first of all *witness* together with the first and principal Missionary who is the Holy Spirit.

Part II

Sacrament

Chapter 4

The Holy Spirit
and the Church's Sacramentality

It was from the side of Christ as He slept the sleep of death upon the
cross that there came forth "the wondrous sacrament of the whole
Church".

— *Sacrosanctum Concilium*, no. 5

One of the major decisions by the Ecumenical Vatican Council II, if
not the most important, was to articulate the ecclesiological renewal
starting with the idea of sacrament that opens the Dogmatic Constitution on the Church *Lumen Gentium*: "The Church, in Christ, is
in the nature of sacrament—a sign and instrument, that is, of communion with God and of unity among all men."[1] In order to spell
out this view of the "nature and universal mission" of the Church,
the conciliar constitution immediately introduces three paragraphs
specifying the role of the Divine Persons in the Trinitarian plan of
salvation, which leads to a remarkable quotation from Saint Cyprian:
"Thus, the Church has been seen as 'a people made one with the
unity of the Father, the Son, and the Holy Spirit.'"[2] From the outset, then, we are oriented to a Trinitarian ecclesiology of a sacramental nature, formulated at the conclusion of the paragraph on the
Person and the mission of the Holy Spirit. We have here an entire
program, which the reception of the Council has implemented only

This essay is based on a talk given in Einsiedeln, Switzerland, for the Freundeskreis Hans
Urs von Balthasar, December 2, 2023.
[1] *LG*, no. 1.
[2] Ibid., no. 4, quoting Saint Cyprian, *De Orat. Dom.* 23 (PL 4, 553).

partially, as Joseph Cardinal Ratzinger regretted at the turn of the year 2000.[3]

The elaboration of "an ecclesiology that was theo-logical in the proper sense", as Ratzinger puts it, remains a work in progress, despite the abundant postconciliar ecclesiological literature, which has concentrated preferably on the notion of communion, without developing in parallel and equally energetically the sacramental dimension of the Church, leaving obscure, for example, the analogy between the Incarnate Word and the Church that concludes the chapter on the mystery of the Church: "As the assumed nature, inseparably united to Him, serves the divine Word as a living organ of salvation, so, in a somewhat similar way, does the social structure of the Church serve the Spirit of Christ, who vivifies it, in the building up of the body (cf. Eph 4:16)."[4]

The following essay endeavors to fill a certain gap in Catholic theology and pastoral practice by showing how the Holy Spirit and the Church's sacraments prolong the corporeality of the Risen Christ. The Holy Spirit's perspective is rarely taken into account, and consequently this makes theology less flavorful (cf. Mt 5:13) and pastoral

---

[3] Joseph Ratzinger, "The Ecclesiology of the Constitution *Lumen Gentium*", in *Pilgrim Fellowship of Faith: The Church as Communion*, trans. Henry Taylor (San Francisco: Ignatius Press, 2005), 123–52, esp. p. 125: "The Second Vatican Council certainly did intend to subordinate what it said about the Church to what it said about God and to set it in that context; it intended to propound an ecclesiology that was theo-logical in the proper sense. The way in which the Council's teaching has been received, however, has hitherto overlooked this determinative prefix to all the various individual ecclesiological statements; people have pounced upon individual phrases and slogans and have thus fallen short of the great overall perspectives of the Council Fathers."

[4] *LG*, no. 8. Of the abundant ecclesiological bibliography, I remember in particular Heribert Mühlen, *Una mystica persona: La Chiesa come il mistero dello Spirito Santo in Cristo e nei cristiani: una persona in molte persone* (Rome: Città Nuova, 1967); Otto Semmelroth, "Die Kirche als Sakrament des Heils", in *Mysterium Salutis, IV.1* (Einsiedeln: Johannes Verlag, 1972); Jean-Guy Pagé, *Qui est l'Église?* (Montréal: Bellarmin, 1977–1979); Hans Urs von Balthasar, *Explorations in Theology*, vol. 2, *Spouse of the Word* (San Francisco: Ignatius Press, 1995); Hans Urs von Balthasar, *Theo-Drama*, vol. 3, *The Dramatis Personae: The Person in Christ*, trans. Graham Harrison (San Francisco: Ignatius Press, 1990); Angelo Scola, *Chi è la Chiesa? Una chiave antropologica e sacramentale per l'ecclesiologia* (Brescia: Queriniana, 2005); J. Rigal, *L'Église, obstacle et chemin vers Dieu* (Paris: Cerf, 1983); Rémi Cheno, *L'Esprit-Saint et l'Église: Institutionnalité et pneumatologie, vers un dépassement des antagonismes ecclésiologiques*, Cogitatio Fidei (Paris: Cerf, 2010); Alain Nisus, *L'Église comme communion et comme institution: Une lecture de l'ecclésiologie du cardinal Congar à partir de la tradition des Églises de professants*, Cogitatio Fidei (Paris: Cerf, 2012); Roland Varin, *L'Église sacrement universel du salut: Chemin et but du dessein de Dieu*, Bibliothèque de la Revue thomiste (Paris: Parole et Silence, 2021).

practice less creative. I do not claim to have overcome the difficulty of communicating academic research in simple language, but I pray to the Holy Spirit to make my systematic reflection accessible for you and for those men and women who will discover its spiritual and pastoral import.

The Spirit and the Church from a Sacramental Perspective

Let us begin our essay with several considerations about the Holy Spirit as Trinitarian love incarnate in the Church.[5] This will help us to understand the very close collaboration between the Divine Persons of the Word and the Spirit in salvation history. As a result, this will also facilitate an understanding of the analogy between the Body of Christ, instrument of the Divine Word, and the Church, instrument of the Divine Spirit in the sacramental order.

Sacred Scripture mentions the Spirit, already in the Book of Genesis, as the creative Breath, then in the prophets as the Inspirer of their mission; elsewhere he is associated with Wisdom and the Word. In the fullness of time, he accompanies the mission of the Incarnate Word from his conception to his confirmation as Son of God by his Resurrection from the dead (Rom 1:4). He is designated in the writings of Saint John as "the Spirit of truth, who proceeds from the Father" (Jn 15:26), whose function in the economy of salvation is to interpret Christ, as Christ is the interpreter of the Father.[6]

---

[5] See Mühlen, *Una mystica persona*; Hans Urs von Balthasar, *Explorations in Theology*, vol. 3, *Creator Spirit*, trans. Brian McNeil (San Francisco: Ignatius Press, 1993); Balthasar, *Explorations in Theology*, vol. 2, *Spouse of the Word*; Hans Urs von Balthasar, *Explorations in Theology*, vol. 4, *Spirit and Institution*, trans. Edward T. Oakes, S.J. (San Francisco: Ignatius Press, 1974); François Bourassa, "L'Esprit Saint, 'communion' du Père et du Fils", *Science et Esprit* 29/3 (1977): 251–81; Yves Congar, *Je crois en l'Esprit Saint* (Paris: Cerf, 1979–1980); Paul Evdokimov, *Lo Spirito Santo nella tradizione ortodossa* (Rome: San Paolo edizioni, 1971); Luis Francisco Ladaria, *Jesus y el Espiritu: la uncion* (Burgos: Monte Carmelo, 2013); Jean Zizioulas, *L'être ecclésial* (Geneva: Labor et Fides, 1981); for a critical analysis of a certain pneumatological deficiency in the Latin tradition, see Alberta Maria Putti, *Il difficile recupero dello Spirito: Percorsi e luoghi teologici della Pneumatologia nella tradizione latina del secondo millennio* (Rome: PUG, 2016).

[6] Hans Urs von Balthasar, *Theo-Logic*, vol. 3, *The Spirit of Truth*, trans. Graham Harrison (San Francisco: Ignatius Press, 2005), 17: "The Spirit's entire role is to guide us into the truth and to declare it; all the other, manifold utterances concerning the Spirit that we find in John and in the Scriptures of the Old and New Covenants come back to this fundamental

In the life of the Trinity, the Holy Spirit appears as the third gift, the *Donum doni*, which proceeds from the Father but results also from the response of the Son (*Filioque*) in the Trinitarian love. His ineffable personality is beyond our grasp and cannot be enclosed within a category; this is why Scripture speaks about him by means of symbols such as wind, fire, water, and dove. Theologians strive to understand his personal property in the divinity by means of various analogies, none of which is completely satisfactory. In the love which God is, he is seen as the "we" of the Father and of the Son, even though this "we" does not express him totally, since he, too, is an "Other" of the same nature in relation to them. Hans Urs von Balthasar says, "He is the love between Father and Son by being simultaneously their fruit and hence their witness."[7] Balthasar then adds more precisely: "The Spirit is both the expression of what is most 'subjective' in the divine love and, at the same time, the 'objective' witness of this 'subjective' love between Father and Son."[8]

One way to explore in greater depth the concrete bond between the Spirit and the Church is to analyze the relations between the Holy Spirit and the multiform expressions of "the Body of Christ" that are applied to Jesus, to the Eucharist, and to the Church. The Gospels testify that the Incarnate Word was conceived by the Holy Spirit and that he was accompanied by him throughout his life in the flesh until his death on the Cross and his Resurrection. Theology has understood, moreover, that Christ's corporeality was not dissolved by his Resurrection; rather, it was transfigured and consolidated in such a way as to be capable of prolongation in a Eucharistic and even an ecclesial form. These nuanced meanings of "Body of Christ" express the unity of the mystery of the Covenant that is guaranteed by the presence and the action of the Holy Spirit. Yves Congar writes: "One and the same Spirit is at work in the three realities that bear the same name of body of Christ and are dynamically linked—by His dynamism: [1] Jesus, born of Mary, who suffered, died, was raised again to life and glorified; [2] the bread and wine that have been made

---

role. As we have seen, the Son, [having] become Incarnate, was the adequate declaration of the Father, but this declaration remained closed to men so long as the Spirit 'had not been given' (Jn 7:39)."

[7] Ibid., 18.

[8] Ibid., 141.

Eucharist, and [3] the communional [i.e., Mystical] Body of which we are the members."[9]

The sequence of the three bodies (Jesus, the Eucharist, the Church), distinct but unified by the Holy Spirit together with the glorified Christ, are the fundamental sacramental framework of the mystery of the total incarnation of the Trinitarian love; the Church unceasingly meditates and studies this mystery in greater depth so as to understand her own nature and universal mission. For this purpose she can rely on the medieval tradition explored by Father de Lubac: "Over and above the institutional unity that was clear to any observer, since the time of Saint Paul faith recognized within it an internal unity. It assigned to it a mysterious source of life: the very Spirit of Christ. Such was the teaching behind the *lex orandi*, repeated over and over again by theologians."[10]

Latin theology is heir to the Alexandrian tradition that accentuates the vision of the *logos-sarx* as foundation of the Eucharist, under-scoring the causality of the Divine Logos united to the flesh of the Incarnate Word. The Antiochian tradition takes into account more the role of the Holy Spirit with regard to the reality of Christ's Body, both in what concerns the process of the Incarnation and in its sacra-mental transformation. Saint Thomas synthesizes the two perspectives while favoring the Alexandrian approach. The key to a satisfactory synthesis is to articulate the relation between the Word and the Spirit according to their respective complementary missions, which depend on the order of their procession in the immanent Trinity.

I already began to study the mystery of the Church from the per-spective of the Holy Spirit in the theology of the priesthood;[11] now

---

[9] Yves Congar, *Je crois en l'Esprit Saint. III. Le fleuve de Vie coule en Orient et en Occident* (Paris: Cerf, 1980), 340–41.

[10] Henri Cardinal de Lubac, S.J., *Corpus Mysticum* (Notre Dame, Ind.: University of Notre Dame Press, 2006), 88: "*Ecclesia sancta corpus est Christi, uno Spiritu vivificata.... Ecclesia sancta, id est, universitas fidelium, corpus Christi vocatur propter Spiritum Christi quem accepit.*" "The Holy Church is the body of Christ, made alive by the one Spirit.... The Holy Church, that is, the totality of the faithful, is called the body of Christ because of the Spirit of Christ, which she receives." The "theologians" de Lubac has in mind are Hugh of Saint Victor (PL 176, 416) and Isaac of Stella (PL 194, 1801). See also Fulgentius, *Ad Monimum* (PL 65, 189 C); Cardinal Humbert (*Libelli de lite*, t. 1, p. 235).

[11] Marc Ouellet, "L'Esprit Saint et le sacerdoce du Christ dans l'Église", in *Pour une théologie fondamentale du Sacerdoce*, Actes du Symposium du Centre de Recherche et d'anthropologie des vocations, Rome, 17–19 février 2022 (Paris: Cerf, 2023), 115–33.

we must bring this reflection to the point that is crucial for a sacramental ecclesiology: the celebration of the Eucharist as a mystery of the Covenant, which joins the Triune God and his created image, the Church, through the mediation of the Incarnate Word. The latter gives his Body as a real symbol of his Person to the Church, which receives it in faith and allows herself to be made fruitful by his Spirit, becoming as a result one Body with him in an unparalleled nuptial mystery. This sacramental mystery invites us to reflect more deeply on how the Holy Spirit works in the sacraments, more especially in the Eucharist. Is he not situated on both sides of the sacramental event, in other words, on the side of the objective presence of Christ's Body and on the side of the Church's faith in receiving it and allowing herself to be made fruitful by God's gift?

Furthermore, the current anthropological situation requires a sacramental theology that is more open to the symbolic dimension, and broader than the Scholastic notion of sign. The development of the nuptial symbol, for example, is an important resource for theology, but it is also an invaluable aid in evangelization. I have devoted a lot of effort to this research in my earlier works, convinced that in our time this biblical and patristic symbol can advantageously take on the role that hylomorphism has played since the Middle Ages. Encouraged by Saint John Paul II, I became convinced that the nuptial symbol, notwithstanding all the cultural pressures and confusions, can serve as a catalyst to overcome the current disaffection with regard to the sacraments and to propose a more attractive face of the Church for the purpose of evangelization. I do not intend to provide a new monograph in this regard, besides the one that I already published on the theology of marriage and of the sacraments,[12] but I would like to bring my own reflections to a higher level of synthesis and unity. Pastoral experience and research in this regard have led me to a Trinitarian, paschal, and nuptial vision; I would like to provide a summary of it here. This involves a somewhat technical argument, but it is worth

---

[12] Marc Ouellet, *Divine ressemblance: Le mariage et la famille dans la mission de l'Église* (Québec: Anne Sigier, 2006); Marc Ouellet, *Divina somiglianza: Antropologia trinitaria della famiglia* (Rome: Lateran University Press, 2004); Marc Ouellet, *Mystère et sacrement de l'amour* (Paris: Cerf, 2014), esp. part 3: "Trinité et nuptialité: Pour une théodramatique eucharistique du mystère nuptial", 225–352.

the effort because it results in an overall view that is fruitful for the spiritual life and pastoral care.

Systematic Perspective

I introduce the systematic part of my presentation with a quotation from *Lumen Gentium*, paragraph 48, which establishes the essential theme of my talk:

> Christ, having been lifted up from the earth has drawn all to Himself (see Jn 12:32). Rising from the dead (see Rom 6:9) He sent His life-giving Spirit upon His disciples and through Him has established His Body which is the Church as the universal sacrament of salvation. Sitting at the right hand of the Father, He is continually active in the world that He might lead men to the Church and through it join them to Himself and that He might make them partakers of His glorious life by nourishing them with His own Body and Blood.

The Trinitarian and sacramental identity of the Church comes from the Spirit, who proceeds from the Father (Jn 15:26), and it is rooted in the historical and eschatological gift of Jesus Christ; the latter became incarnate, as the Word of God, in an ordinary human existence, which concluded with his prophetic witness and his sacrificial offering "once for all", *pro nobis* [for us], on the Cross; an offering of love that was accepted by the Father and glorified by the power of the Holy Spirit, who raised him from the dead. As a result, the Trinitarian face of God was manifested, appearing on the worldly scene through the exaltation of this Man to the right hand of the Father and the sending of the Holy Spirit as Advocate, Consoler, the Paraclete charged with bringing to its eschatological conclusion the fruitfulness of Christ's Cross for the salvation of the world.

From the Resurrection onward, the Holy Spirit appears on the scene according to his hypostasis, and his earlier relation with Christ is now inverted, for now he is the one who takes over so as to guide believers "into all the truth" (Jn 16:13). Until that point, the Spirit discreetly and actively accompanied the Incarnate Word, serving as mediation for him so that he could live out his loving obedience to the Father in all truth, both human and divine.[13] Now he takes in hand the continuation of the Incarnation of the Word according to a new, sacramental modality, which will be the proper, ecclesial mode of the Holy Spirit in the economy of salvation. The Church, as a sacramental reality, is born of this mission of the Holy Spirit, who presides at the constitution of its sacramentality. As an inseparable partner of the Incarnate Word, the Spirit indeed presides at the accomplishment of the Baptism-Confirmation that constitutes the ecclesial Body of Christ; moreover, he "fluidifies" the body and blood of Christ, who died and rose again in order to make it food that can be assimilated by the faithful and thus to configure the growth of the ecclesial Body.

In doing this, the Holy Spirit obviously does not display himself as an autonomous protagonist; instead, in keeping with his personal property, the fact that he is "a Person from Persons",[14] he takes what is from Christ and from the Father so as to put the finishing touches on it, to make it visible and operational in the Church, whose identity and sacramental mission must reflect and embody Trinitarian love until the eschatological end of the economy of salvation.

The turning point that marks his personal entrance on the scene according to his own mode is Christ's Resurrection, in which he comes as proceeding from the Father to confirm in his name and with his power this Son of man who cannot remain a prisoner of death and hell, because he conquered sin and death by his loving obedience

[13] See Balthasar, *Theo-Drama*, 3:201: "It is the identity of character and mission that really makes the world drama into a theo-drama. For this identity is only possible if the Person has been given a mission, not accidentally, but as a modality of his eternal personal being; if, as Thomas says, the Son's *missio* is the economic form of his eternal *processio* from the Father. This mission of the Son draws the mission of the Spirit in its wake, in a twofold form: first, the Spirit is sent from the Father upon the incarnate Son, and then the Spirit is sent from the Father and the exalted Son upon the Church and the world." This becomes clear also in light of the author's controversial expression concerning the Trinitarian inversion. See ibid., 3:191: "What we have termed 'inversion' is ultimately only the projection of the immanent Trinity onto the 'economic' plane, whereby the Son's 'correspondence' to the Father is articulated as 'obedience'."

[14] See Heribert Mühlen, who draws from the encyclical *Mystici Corporis* the basis for his thesis about the Holy Spirit as "a person (a Spirit) in several persons (in Christ and in us)". According to him, "the most important teaching in the Encyclical, which is expressed most forcefully, is that the uncreated Spirit of Christ is the unitary principle in the plurality of the persons who are members of the Church" (*Una mystica persona*, 93).

unto death. He must be confirmed Son of God with power through the Spirit of holiness (Rom 1:4). He works therefore quite according to the Trinitarian logic, by raising Christ from the dead and by exalting him at the right hand of the Father in heaven—hence the fundamental axiom that, to my way of thinking, governs pneumatology: the moment of Christ's Resurrection in the economy of salvation is the economical manifestation of the moment of the procession of the Holy Spirit in the immanent Trinity. The sequence of events starting from the Incarnation of the Word leads, indeed, to the Paschal Mystery of Christ, the fruit of which is the outpouring of the Holy Spirit, *Spirit of Truth*, the intra-Trinitarian end of the genealogy of the Divine Persons and the crowning of the incarnation of Trinitarian love in the economy of salvation.

The Spirit of the Risen Lord places the final seal of the Trinity on the plan of the Covenant. He manifests its fruitfulness by allowing himself to be poured out as *Donum Dei et Donum doni* [Gift of God and Gift of the gift] upon his created partner, lifting him up from among the dead and exalting him at the Father's right. The Trinity as an event of eternal love thus establishes its final stage of donation and manifestation in the economy of salvation. This is the properly nuptial stage which inaugurates the nuptials of the Risen Lord as the eschatological Bridegroom with his Bride, the Church, thanks to the Holy Spirit, who has been poured out; as a result, the latter takes charge of the ecclesial proclamation of the Gospel of God, and he goes into action for the consummation of the wedding of the Church sacrament, which existentially tends toward the eschatological fullness of the Kingdom.

The Holy Spirit appears here simultaneously and paradoxically as the One who brings about Christ's Resurrection and the fruit of the Paschal Mystery. He was given to Jesus all along his path of incarnation as the Spirit of the Son, imbuing him with grace and strength and dwelling in the innermost depths of his human nature so that he might faithfully carry out his mission to the end. Now the Spirit is given to him in fullness (Jn 7:39); he comes upon him powerfully as the Spirit of the Father, who raises him from the dead and confirms who he is, thus making him attain not only his divine glory in his flesh but also a fullness of humanity that now transcends the limits of time, space, and capabilities as we know them.

From this moment on, the *Eschaton* is present in history as the in-breaking of the Kingdom that transcends the chronology of creation by assigning to it the glorious end toward which the whole economy of salvation tends. The mission of the Holy Spirit is to make this Kingdom come in all the elect, together with the glorified Christ, through the gift of his own Person, which crowns the work of the Incarnate Son. Hence, the sacramental order of the Church, which prolongs the Incarnation of the Word in a pneumatological modality with the seven sacraments, tasks it to articulate the Body of Christ that is the Church in its covenantal mode, so that the nuptial encounter between the Trinity and humanity might be accomplished in the Eucharistic celebration as the inaugural coming of the Kingdom. In this activity, which is sacramental in the strict sense and is the basis of the wider sacramentality of the ecclesial community, the Spirit's mission is always to glorify the Father and the Son in their own work, by perfecting it and by devoting himself to it as their ultimate fruit and their supreme gift.

The Holy Spirit consequently takes elements from creation—water, bread, wine, oil—and by means of sacramental words, he bestows on them his presence and power, so that these elements then produce effects that come no longer from their own nature but rather from the Spirit dwelling in them. It should be noted, however, that before the sacramental use of these material elements, the Spirit provided for the reception of the ultimate gift that he is, by raising exponentially the faith of the Church-Bride, starting with the participation of the Virgin Mary in the Redeemer's Passion. He had already guaranteed her *fiat* to the mystery of the Incarnation at the Annunciation. He had anticipated her participation in the sacramental economy by her maternal role at Cana. He prolonged her unconditional *fiat* at the foot of the Cross by making it fruitful once again through the death of the Word, her Son, thus expanding her spiritual maternity to include all humanity. As the New Eve, Mary precedes in a way the sacramental economy, since she is its Mother by her perfect availability to the Holy Spirit, which associated her to all the suffering love of the Redeemer. These bloody nuptials were sealed by the last breath of the Crucified, the prelude to the gift of the Spirit, which the Risen Christ would then breathe upon the Apostles for the remission of sins and the configuration of the whole sacramental economy, from the seven sacraments to the Church-sacrament that radiates the Trinitarian communion into the human community until the fullness of the Kingdom.

The sacramental economy thus, from the Marian-nuptial perspective, becomes part of the prolongation of the Incarnation of the Word and of his glorification. Christ the Lord exercises his Lordship over the universe from his heavenly throne, which never leaves his earthly Cross in the past, because nothing of what Christ lived and suffered has been lost; all is glorified, that is, preserved, made eternal, elevated in the glory of the eschatological Kingdom. This is why the memory of the Spirit can take from his goods, which are indeed still available, and distribute them to the Church, in a different form that is no less real and substantial. The Eucharist is the clearest demonstration of this.

In commemorating the Paschal Mystery, the Holy Spirit takes the Master's words and gestures during his last paschal meal and bestows on them his own power, which confirms Christ's own authority; indeed, by making it universal, he completes the efficacy that he intended for his divine words, which were pronounced once and for all. For the purpose of these gestures and words of the institution of the Eucharist is precisely communion with Christ in the Spirit, which results when the faithful eat of his crucified and risen Body. The sacramental action of the Holy Spirit, moreover, allows these gestures and words, pronounced once and for all, to preserve their unique value through the identification that he can make between what is eschatological, the Paschal Mystery, and what belongs to a specific time, the Eucharistic rite in all its cultural and cultic modalities on all the altars of the world from the Last Supper until the parousia.

The Spirit certainly does perform an objective action suited to commemorate Christ's gift in a sacramental form, but his first contribution is situated on the side of the recipient's faith, without which the sacramental reality, like the Word, would fall into nothingness. The Spirit is doubly receptive in the immanent Trinity; he eternally embraces the Word of love that he receives from the Father. His first mission in the economy of salvation is to prolong this reception and this embrace in the consciousness of believers, thus introducing them into the mystery of the Covenant. At Baptism, he fashions consequently the believer's adherence to the Word of the Lord and to his death and Resurrection, which implies self-renunciation and a commitment to live for the Lord. Through the Eucharist, he refines the configuration of the believer's whole life to Christ crucified, through the gift of active charity that builds up the community.

Furthermore, he gives special charisms to the members of the Body of Christ, each according to his vocation and mission at the service of the community. This subjective way of enlivening communion in the Church through faith and charity corresponds to his personal mode of loving in the Trinity, which is that of a fruitful, radiant receptivity that he shares now with all, perfectly attuned to the objective gift of Christ the Lord. This outpouring explains how the Trinitarian communion brings about the unity of the People of God; this is not a vague model of communion that we construct under pressure from a democratic culture, but rather an authentic divine-human communion shared in souls and even in ecclesial structures and relations.

This is why we must say that the whole sacramental structure of the Church, starting from Baptism to the Last Rites, aims to configure the Trinitarian identity of the Church, of each one of her members, and of their ultimate nuptial and missionary communion. Given that the whole sacramental order is the celebration of the Eucharist, which is not one sacrament among others but in a way the summit of all the sacraments, so, too, we must specify its very particular contribution to the constitution of the Church. Although it is true that Baptism precedes the Eucharist and lays the foundation of faith as membership in the ecclesial Body, this membership remains incomplete as long as the baptized person does not exercise the priesthood for which he is qualified, as long as he does not participate personally and spiritually in the true adoration, in the sacrificial offering of Christ to his Father, for the new and eternal Covenant of all humanity.

This Eucharistic participation associates the thirst of suffering humanity to the offering of Christ to God and obtains in return the outpouring of the communion of the Father and the Son in the Spirit. Thus, the celebration of the Eucharist not only has a purpose of communion and ecclesial unity, but also reveals the universal nature of this communion and consequently makes the Church's universal mission more dynamic. Isn't it the first and final purpose of this universal mission to obtain the outpouring of the Holy Spirit on all humanity by the power of the Eucharistic offering of the Paschal Mystery?

Consequently, the Eucharist contains all the dimensions of the Church's identity: the remission of sins, the sanctification of the members of the ecclesial Body, the intensification of charity and therefore of unity, but also this outreach to the rest of humanity that still awaits the Gospel. In short, it is the summit of evangelization. All these effects of the celebration of the Paschal Mystery in its Eucharistic form are based, however, on the outpouring of the Person of the Holy Spirit, uncreated grace, who communicates his own identity of Person-communion to the Church-communion.

Who Is the Church?

The passage from the Trinitarian communion to the ecclesial communion through Eucharistic communion prompts us now to ask a further question, which will bring out the Trinitarian quality of the Church's unity. It is the question about the Church as a person. Who is the Church? Balthasar formulated the question and discussed it in depth, offering an answer that seems obscure to many, particularly because of the Marian dimension of his ecclesiology. The theologian from Basel maintains that on the side of uncreated grace, the Holy Spirit makes sure that the ecclesial community participates in some way in the Trinitarian unity, according to the beautiful remarks by Saint Ignatius of Antioch that are repeated in *Lumen Gentium*, paragraph 4. But if we inquire about the created dimension of the person of the Church, he sees in the Virgin Mary, to whom I alluded earlier, the "inchoate subjectivity"[15] of the Church, which includes her relation to the totality of the members because of her role as Bride of the immolated Lamb and as Mother of the Church. Even the Eucharistic Body results from her maternity in the order of grace, because those who through their ministry help bring about the sacrament do so by virtue of the faith that they receive from the Holy Spirit and from Mary, the Mediatrix of all grace, who is associated with the Redeemer's fullness. That being said, the unity of the Church that proceeds from the Eucharist is dynamic, unitive,

---

[15] Hans Urs von Balthasar, "Who Is the Church?", in *Explorations in Theology*, 2:143–92. See also Balthasar, *Theo-Drama*, vol. 3.

and missionary, because the Holy Spirit, poured out in each celebration, assures the permanent vitality of the ecclesial body, harmony between the pastors and the faithful, the regeneration of Church structures, the flourishing of charisms, the missionary passion, the eschatological tendency toward a fulfillment that is already contained in the mystery being celebrated but is progressively appropriated by the ecclesial body until the final parousia.

Who is the Church? As a people, she is a collective unified by the Trinity; as Body of Christ, she is one with her divine-human Head; as Bride of the Lamb, she is distinguished by a nuptial love that is all the more unifying because he was obtained at the price of her total compassion with the sacrifice of the Bridegroom-Redeemer; as living Temple of the Holy Spirit, she is raptured above herself in an outburst of adoration of the Father through Christ and in the Spirit. In short, no real symbol of the Church adequately expresses her personality; she cannot be hypostatized as though she were the hypostasis of the Holy Spirit, in parallel and in reciprocity with the Incarnate Word. With regard to her, we must express ourselves in personal terms, but while acknowledging that her name is Mystery, because the Spirit, who weds, inhabits, and inspires her, bears with him the Father and the Son in a circumincession that makes her a supra-personal we, a personality that is indefinable yet pregnant with the mystery of love.[16] The particular role of the Holy Spirit with regard to her consists in what he perfects[17] and glorifies, guaranteeing as a result the share of the Father and of the Son within his own causality. Balthasar writes: "The Son gives the Spirit to the world both as 'His' Spirit (the Spirit of obedience out of love for the Church, crying 'Abba, Father,' as the Spirit of the *Son*) and as the *trinitarian* gift that, henceforth, will be inseparably the Spirit of Father and Son and, hence, can become the Church's unifying power."[18]

In the words of Saint Irenaeus, the Father's two hands, the Word and the Spirit, have a mission to work together in a perfect harmony so as to bring about the sacrament par excellence, which alone

[16] See Balthasar, "Who Is the Church?"; Scola, *Chi è la Chiesa?*, 54–55, 133–34.

[17] See Jean-Paul Lieggi, "Lo Spirito 'causa perfezionante': Su alcuni tratti della pneumatologia dei Cappadoci", in Associazione Teologica Italiana, *Tempo dello Spirito: Questioni di pneumatologia* (Milan: Glossa, 2020), 107–31.

[18] Balthasar, *Theo-Logic*, 3:294.

can transform the People of God into a sacramental people—priest, prophet, and king—the bearer of salvation. Similarly, the fact that the Spirit has a role to play in the hypostatic union does not obscure the fact that the concrete human nature of Jesus belongs immediately to the Word; on the contrary, it guarantees the respectful and adequate adaptation of this nature to its altogether singular Christic belonging.[19] Likewise, the fact that the Holy Spirit is the Architect of the sacramental order in no way detracts from the Incarnate Word's own causality; it contributes to its actualization (memorial) and to its perfecting, in tune with the Risen Christ's mode of existence. The latter from now on acts according to his divine identity, which is fully united to his glorified human nature, which has the Holy Spirit at its disposal as an indispensable Trinitarian partner for an extended and properly sacramental activity. For, within the framework of the Trinitarian plan, he, the ultimate Agent and the Fruit, is the One who has the mission to unite what is distinct, to universalize what is unique, to gather what is scattered. Christ handed himself over to this Partner totally, to the point of allowing him to make use of him [Christ], in a Eucharistic way, for the building up of his ecclesial Body.

Finally, this pneumatological perspective reconciles divergent positions in such a way as to account more fully for the truths of the faith in the sacramental domain. The sacrificial aspect of the Eucharist, for example, which gave rise to many unsatisfactory theories of the Mass as sacrifice, receives a simple explanation that resolves the paradox by integrating the Holy Spirit's action with the impact of the Resurrection. For Christ's Resurrection is brought about by the power of the Holy Spirit (Rom 1:4), who as a result safeguards his corporeal substance by raising it to a higher degree, according to an increased mode of substantiality that we must call "pneumatic". This substantial mode of the risen Body is the basis for the possibility of sacramental transubstantiation, to which the Holy Spirit contributes by recalling Christ's words, which are pronounced by the minister. This objective memorial of the Paschal Mystery includes the sacrifice of the Cross, for Christ's Resurrection does not merely concern

---

[19] Walter Kasper, *Jésus le Christ* (Paris: Cerf, 1977), 380: "The sanctification of Jesus' humanity by the Spirit and by His gifts is not just an accidental consequence of the sanctification by the Logos by virtue of the hypostatic union; on the contrary, it is the condition for it."

his passage from the state of a cadaver to the state of one risen from the dead; it recapitulates his whole human story by glorifying his Body in all that it lived through, which culminates in his paschal and nuptial sacrifice.

The involvement of the Father and of the Holy Spirit in Christ's Resurrection authorizes us to understand it not as a mere accidental modification of Christ's natural body—little more than a return to life, in a way—but rather as a qualitative leap, an increase of substantiality due to the fullness of the Spirit, who is then communicated to it (Jn 7:37). In receiving the fullness of his anointing, the Christ then passes, so to speak, into the sphere of the Spirit. In this passage he brings with him his whole life and very especially his sacrifice of the Cross, which is raised to a new coefficient of reality by the fact of his glorification. So that nothing of Christ's life or of his story was lost, all is raised high, consolidated, eternalized, by his glorification. Otherwise, devotion to the Heart of Jesus would make no sense, and devotion to the Child Jesus would be pointless—so would devotion to the Passion, which is so full of spirituality in the ecclesial tradition.

Otherwise, the Church's sacramental life would have no foundation; the Mass would be a figurative, ritual reproduction of a sacrifice sunk deep in the past and guaranteed only by a transcendent divine causality that is applied arbitrarily. Whereas the Eucharistic sacrifice is in fact the Holy Spirit making available the unique event of the Cross, which is definitively glorified in the Risen Lord at the right hand of the Father, it is made available so as to assimilate the faithful and to be assimilated by them through the memorial of the sacramental rites.

The importance of these pneumatological considerations for the spirituality of the faithful, popular devotion, and the pastoral ministry of the sacraments, of the Eucharist in particular, is plain for all to see. The Holy Spirit is the Artisan and the Artist of our union with Jesus Christ, of our adoration of his Eucharistic Body, of our membership in his ecclesial Body, and of our commitment to witnessing to the Trinitarian communion on earth among men. Without him, faith, theology, and the Church's pastoral care lack the creative and apostolic breath with which to give life and hope to the world. Thanks to him, the community of the baptized makes up the Body with Christ their Head, the ministers go into action to serve to the community the Word and the sources of life which are the sacraments, and all Christian men and women are graced and made aware of and responsible for a personal charism for the building up of a synodal Church and for her mission.

The perspective that we have just sketched sheds light on the sacramental nature of the Church starting from the Trinitarian communion that prolongs the mystery of the Incarnation according to the Holy Spirit's own nuptial modality. From it results a harmonious, integrated vision of the mysteric and social dimensions of the Church, hinging on the Eucharist and pointing everywhere to the Risen Christ. The task remains of articulating this structure in detail by showing the relations of complementarity and community between the priesthood of the baptized and the priesthood of the ordained ministers, always in a pneumatological perspective, at the service of the Church's universal mission. My hope is that where disaffection for the faith and the sacraments is endemic, as is largely the case in our secularized societies, the Holy Spirit will liberate a new kerygmatic breath [i.e., of proclamation] in the hearts of pastors, prophets, theologians, and catechists, inspired by the Eucharistic nuptials of the Trinity and humanity at the heart of the Church, the sacrament of salvation.

Chapter 5

The Distinction and Communion between the Priesthood of the Baptized and the Ministerial Priesthood

It is difficult to exaggerate the importance and significance of the Second Vatican Ecumenical Council for the missionary transformation of the Church in our time, which counts among its centerpieces a renewed theology of the priesthood.[1] First, the question of the sacramentality of the episcopate was settled, including episcopal collegiality, which makes it possible now to frame and resituate the Catholic vision of the priesthood; then the ecumenical opening and the experience of numerous dialogues allowed for mutual enrichments

---

This essay is based on a talk given in Switzerland for the Freundeskreis Hans Urs von Balthasar, December 2, 2023.

[1] Voir Juan Esquerda Bifet, *Teologia de la espiritualidad sacerdotal* (Madrid: BAC, 1976), with an extensive international annotated bibliography, chap. 19, pp. 314–68; Report of the International Théological Commission, *The Priestly Ministry* (1970); Gustave Martelet, *Théologie du sacerdoce. Deux mille ans d'Église en question* (Paris: Éditions du Cerf, 1984–1990); Gisbert Greshake, *Priester sein* (Freiburg im Breisgau: Herder Verlag, 1991); Joseph Ratzinger, *Kunder des Wortes und Diener eurer Freude*, Gesammelte Schriften 12 (Freiburg im Breisgau: Herder Verlag, 2010); Miguel Nicolau, "El Episcopado en la constitucion 'Lumen Gentium'", *Salmanticensis* 12 (1965): 451–507; Giuseppe Rambaldi, "Natura e missione del Presbiterato nel decreto 'Presbiterorum Ordinis'", *Gregorianum* 50 (1969): 239–61; Joseph Coppens, ed., *Sacerdocio y Celibato* (Madrid: Biblioteca Autores Cristianos, 1971); Gerhard Ludwig Müller, *Priesthood and Diaconate*, trans. Michael J. Miller (San Francisco: Ignatius Press, 2002); Marc Cardinal Ouellet, *Friends of the Bridegroom: For a Renewed Vision of Priestly Celibacy*, trans. Benjamin Crockett (Irondale, Ala.: EWTN Press, 2019); Martin Troupeau, *L'unité du sacrement de l'ordre dans la réforme des ordinations de 1968*, LQF (Münster: Aschendorff Verlag, 2022); Romano Penna, *Un solo corpo: Laicità e sacerdozio nel cristianesimo delle origini* (Frecce Roma: Carocci editore, 2020).

thanks to the complementary perspectives. Certain agreements clearly demonstrate this and hold out hope for new progress.[2]

For example, the renewal of the common priesthood of the baptized[3] offers a way of coming together with our Protestant brothers, while a rather remarkable pneumatological and Trinitarian advance at the Council builds bridges toward the Eastern, Orthodox, and other traditions. It is necessary to respond to this ecumenical commitment of the Council through the patient search for a reconciliation of differences, in order to respond to the Lord's prayer for the unity of his disciples, and to the current missionary challenges of Christianity given the phenomena of secularization and scientific reprogramming of the *homo technicus*.

My contribution to this search explores the relation between the Holy Spirit and the exercise of the priesthood in the Church. Concretely and precisely, I am interested in the conciliar affirmation concerning the distinct participation of the baptized and of the ordained ministers in the one priesthood of Christ. This affirmation needs to be viewed in a pneumatological light in order to justify the difference in nature, and not only in degree, between these two participations. Hence, I structure my talk in two main points: (1) some preliminaries on the Holy Spirit and Christ's priesthood; (2) the pneumatological and Trinitarian integration of the two participations in Christ's priesthood in the Church.

This more in-depth understanding challenges us not to justify a confessional position but rather to open an ecclesiological perspective that allows us precisely to go beyond the differences between the confessions. Besides this ecumenical intention, it is necessary to help overcome the conflicts and negative tensions that sometimes appear in the practice of the ministers in the pastoral field; our essay offers an ecclesiological vision that aims to avoid sterile polarizations and

[2] See Walter Kasper, *Harvesting the Fruits: Basic Aspects of Christian Faith in Ecumenical Dialogue* (New York: Continuum, 2009); Nicholas Lossky et al., *Dictionary of the Ecumenical Movement* (Geneva: World Council of Churches, 2002); Jeffrey Gros, Harding Meyer, William G. Rusch, eds., *Growth in Agreement II: Reports and Agreed Statements of Ecumenical Conversations on a World Level 1982–1998* (Eerdmans, 2000); Carlo Lorenzo Rossetti, *Uniti nel Nome del Padre: Una Chiave per la Comunione tra Cattolici e Ortodossi sullo Spirito Santo e il Primato del Papa* (Siena: Edizioni Cantagalli, 2021).

[3] *LG*, no. 10.

to integrate positively the various complementary charisms that are given by the Holy Spirit with a view to a more synodal Church.

The Holy Spirit and the Priesthood of Christ

Let us begin by referring to the Trinitarian structure of the priesthood, which will be explained further on, and which is identifiable in the figure of Christ, the High Priest of the New Covenant; it can be traced back to three fundamental aspects: offering, mediation, communion. The Holy Spirit appears very explicitly in the communion aspect, in keeping with his hypostasis in the Trinity and his own mission in the economy of salvation in company with the Incarnate Word. Indeed, we should not forget that the Spirit participates in Christ's priesthood from the first moment of his Incarnation; since the Son of God was conceived by the Holy Spirit, he took flesh from the Virgin Mary under his action, which then lasted for the whole time of his earthly mission.

The Spirit thus configured Christ's priesthood by imprinting on his human existence the traits of the Son of God, by making his humanity filial, not only as an example for the men and women who would believe in him, but with the power of communicating to them a participation in his own filial condition. This would be initiated later by the public life and preaching of Jesus, but it would be accomplished at the end by the gift of his Spirit, the Spirit of the Son, as the fruit of his death and Resurrection. A gift that will be decisive for the disciples' participation in his priesthood as it appears from the solemn proclamation of Jesus in the Temple: "If any one thirst, let him come to me and drink. He who believes in me, as the Scripture has said, 'Out of his heart shall flow rivers of living water'" (Jn 7:37–38). John explains that Jesus was pointing out the Spirit, whom those who were to believe in him had to receive, because "the Spirit had not been given, because Jesus was not yet glorified" (7:39).

The priesthood of Christ is therefore constituted and configured by the Holy Spirit, who participates intimately in his incarnation of the Trinitarian love in history. This participation concerns, first of all, the hypostatic union in which the Holy Spirit unites the divine and human natures, without confusion or separation, in the Person of the Incarnate

Word;[4] it continues through the historical and existential development of this union (anointing, per Irenaeus) in the Redeemer's mission, which unfolds under the sign of loving obedience even unto death;[5] it culminates in the paschal event in which the Father, acknowledging the work of his Divine Son, raises him from among the dead by the power of his Spirit (Rom 1:4). The Body of Christ is then engulfed by the fullness of the Spirit of the Father, becoming radiant with the Holy Spirit, indeed with the life-giving Spirit, as the High Priest who can bring reconciled humanity into the Trinitarian communion.

For our purposes, we must remember here that Christ's priesthood as mediation inseparably includes the participation of the Spirit not only as its fruit, but also as its prerequisite. For the Redeemer's loving obedience is made possible by the grace of the Holy Spirit, who mediates the will of the Father for him. This soteriological obedience expresses in the economy of salvation his eternal procession as Son from the Father; and the glorification of Christ by the Holy Spirit confirms the divinity of the Incarnate Son and the perfect unity of the Father and the Son in the common work of reconciling the world with God. In short, the Paschal Mystery of Christ manifests the Trinitarian economy of salvation in which the Holy Spirit confirms the fruitfulness of the New Covenant by his own outpouring, which makes humanity's participation in the Trinitarian community effective. The Church will be the concrete manifestation of this under her sociological form as the People of God, a form that acquires a sacramental meaning by the work of the Holy Spirit specifically, yet always carried out in concert with the Risen Christ, the sole Mediator of the New Covenant.[6]

---

[4] This same aspect can be expressed by the theme of *the anointing* so eloquently developed by Irenaeus: "In the name of 'Christ' is implied the One who anointed, the One who was anointed, and the very Anointing with which He was anointed: the One who anointed is the Father, the One who was anointed is the Son, and He was anointed in the Spirit, who is the Anointing." *Adversus Haereses* III, 18, 3.

[5] Thomas Aquinas, *Super Epistolam B. Pauli ad Hebraeos lectura*, cap. IX, 1, 3: "The reason why Christ shed His blood was the Holy Spirit, by whose impulse and motion He did this, that is to say, by the love of God and of neighbor", quoted in Antoine Gugenheim, *Jésus-Christ, Grand Prêtre de l'Ancienne et de la Nouvelle Alliance: Étude du commentaire de Saint-Thomas d'Aquin sur l'Épitre aux Hébreux* (Paris: Parole et Silence, 2004), 297–99.

[6] Hans Urs von Balthasar builds the third part of his pneumatology in the *Theo-Logic*, vol. 3, *The Spirit of Truth*, trans. Graham Harrison (San Francisco: Ignatius Press, 2005), drawing inspiration from the vision of Irenaeus of Lyon of the relationship between the Son and the Spirit,

To speak of the priesthood of Christ, therefore, essentially involves three fundamental aspects that emanate from his incarnate figure: offering, mediation, and communion. Jesus Christ is the One sent by the Father to mankind, in order to embody his love and to offer in return the sacrifice of expiation for sins, which restores the communion of mankind with God through the paschal gift of the Holy Spirit. The three aspects articulate the Trinitarian structure of the priesthood: the offering is, first of all, that of the Father, who gives his Son to the world (Jn 3:16), then that of the Son, whose mediation is to take on our sinful flesh in order to offer it to the Father, redeemed, in response to his love. The Incarnate Son thus obtains from the Father the outpouring of the Holy Spirit, who raises him from the dead, absolves the sin of the world, and gives believers access to the eternal life of the Father and of the Son in the communion of the Spirit.

This Trinitarian structure of the priesthood is brought about through the mystery of the Incarnation and of the Church, in which the Holy Spirit plays his own role, which we still need to clarify and highlight—because it is necessary to explain the very close relationship between the Holy Spirit and the Church in a way that simultaneously brings out the continuity with the economy of the Incarnation and the difference that results from the Spirit's own personality as a mystery of communion.

The fundamental relationship of the Spirit to the Church is described eloquently in *Lumen Gentium*, paragraph 4: "The Spirit dwells in the Church and in the hearts of the faithful, as in a temple" (cf. 1 Cor 3:16; 6:19). "In them He prays on their behalf and bears witness to the fact that they are adopted sons" (cf. Gal 4:6; Rom 8:15–16, 26). This is the fundamental perspective that in its dignity and importance takes precedence over all other manifestations of the Spirit; it is a question of his witness to filial adoption that is at the foundation of the Church's mission; the Spirit enlivens, sanctifies, renews, equips, and directs this Church "with hierarchical and charismatic gifts and adorns [it] with His fruits", beautifying it and leading it "to perfect union with its Spouse". This remarkable paragraph concludes by quoting Saint Cyprian, who said that the Universal Church appears as "a people made one with the

---

"the Father's two hands" (see pp. 165–218); this vision nicely articulates the common work of the Son and the Spirit, each according to his hypostasis: "Furthermore, 'the Father's two hands' are those with whose assistance He carries out the entire world project—from creation, via the redemption, to its final consummation in God" (p. 167).

unity of the Father, the Son and the Holy Spirit".[7] Based on this fundamental pneumatological synthesis, which emphasizes filial adoption, the Trinitarian unity of the People of God, and the nuptial dimension of the Church, we are equipped to highlight the shared responsibilities of the common priesthood of the baptized and of the hierarchical priesthood of the ministers in a way that builds communion and stimulates collaboration among everyone for the mission.

Let us return briefly, however, to the data of Sacred Scripture on Christ's priesthood as mediation. Although the New Testament is rather quiet about the priesthood, the Letter to the Hebrews takes up the priestly theme vigorously by exalting the one priesthood of Christ and by noting how it is different compared with the external, ritual priesthood of the Old Covenant. The priesthood of Christ, High Priest of the New Covenant, opens access to God by virtue of his own sacrificial offering to the Father in the Spirit (9:14).[8] The contrast with the ancient worship is unfathomable, but all the same must not be rigidified with regard to the figure of the priest. Saint Thomas Aquinas writes: "Christ is the source of all priesthood: the priest of the old law was a figure of Christ, and the priest of the new law acts in the person of Christ."[9] Moreover, the First Letter of Peter applies the priestly idea to the people of the New Covenant,[10] and Saint Paul takes up the idea of the priesthood of the faithful in the Letter to the Romans,[11] as well as in the Letter to the Ephesians.[12] These are important, but relatively exceptional, passages in the New Testament writings.

---

[7] Saint Cyprian, *De Orat. Dom.* 23 (PL 4, 553).

[8] We must not make the contrast too rigid, because the institutions of the Old Covenant, prophecy, priesthood, kingship, are positive realities, figures awaiting their fulfillment in Christ. The figure of the High Priest, in particular, transcends the Levitical institution and constitutes a prefiguration of the High Priest of the New Covenant. See Antoine Guggenheim, *Jésus-Christ, Grand Prêtre de l'Ancienne et de la Nouvelle Alliance* (Paris: Parole et Silence, 2004), chap. 5.

[9] Thomas Aquinas, *STh* III, q. 22, art. 4c, quoted in *Catechism of the Catholic Church (CCC)*, 2nd ed. (Vatican City: Libreria Editrice Vaticana, 2019), 1548.

[10] "Like living stones be yourselves built into a spiritual house, to be a holy priesthood, to offer spiritual sacrifices acceptable to God through Jesus Christ" (1 Pet 2:5); "You are a chosen race, a royal priesthood, a holy nation, God's own people, that you may declare the wonderful deeds of him who called you out of darkness into his marvelous light. Once you were no people but now you are God's people; once you had not received mercy but now you have received mercy" (1 Pet 2:9–10).

[11] "I appeal to you therefore, brethren, by the mercies of God, to present your bodies as a living sacrifice, holy and acceptable to God, which is your spiritual worship" (Rom 12:1).

[12] "Be renewed in the spirit of your minds, and put on the new man, created after the likeness of God in true righteousness and holiness" (Eph 4:23–24).

Although our framework does not allow for a presentation of the biblical sources of Christ's priesthood, nevertheless, we will mention some classic places to which I refer: chapter 12 of the Letter to the Romans, chapter 4 of the Letter to the Ephesians, and especially the Letter to the Hebrews, which is the fundamental New Testament document on the subject.

Let us clarify, however, that these texts show us how Christ's priesthood is the major articulation of the loving plan of the Most Holy Trinity. For the Lord's mediation includes the creation of the universe; the Incarnation of the Word; the Paschal Mystery of Christ; the outpouring of the Holy Spirit; the birth of the Church and her growth through its sacramental mysteries; the pilgrimage of the priestly People of God toward the eschatological fulfillment of all things "that God may be all in all".

The hymn of Christ, Head of the universe, from the Letter to the Colossians, best summarizes this priestly perspective (1:15–16, 18–20): "He is the image of the invisible God, the first-born of all creation; for in him all things were created.... All things were created through him and for him.... He is the head of the body, the Church.... For in him all the fulness of God was pleased to dwell, and through him to reconcile to himself all things, whether on earth or in heaven, making peace by the blood of his cross." Here, the Apostle Paul draws the immediate consequences of this mystery for the faith of the Christian believers by testifying to his own participation in this mystery (1:24), and by demanding that their way of life be conformed to the image of the Son of God, while in the Letter to the Ephesians, at the end of his solemn evocation of the divine plan, Saint Paul explains the pneumatological dimension of Christ's priesthood: "In him you also ... have believed in him, were sealed with the promised Holy Spirit, who is the guarantee of our inheritance until we acquire possession of it, to the praise of his glory" (1:13–14). The whole priesthood of Christ culminates in this communication of the Holy Spirit which brings to fulfillment the Trinitarian plan of salvation. Mankind attains the end for which it was created by participating in this priesthood of Christ, up to and including the full possession of the Holy Spirit, the Spirit of glory, who consummates the fruitful communion of the New Covenant.

This is the horizon that frames our reflection on the relationship between the common priesthood of the baptized and the hierarchical priesthood of the Church's ministers. We start with Baptism for the sake of the foundation and to avoid the usual way of discussing the question starting with the ministerial priesthood, often at the expense of the priestly dimension of Baptism. The latter is not limited to the aspect of offering according to the expression in Romans 12:1; it also includes the aspect of mediation, although some renowned authors, including Albert Vanhoye, reserve the mediatory aspect to the ministerial priesthood, too exclusively in my opinion.[13] Indeed, Baptism consecrates the person as a member of the Body of Christ, effecting an ontological and ecclesial identification that associates him with Christ's entire priesthood, inasmuch as his Body is the instrument of his filial offering and redeeming sacrifice.

By becoming sons and daughters of God through Baptism, Christians are associated with the filial priesthood of Christ with their whole being, as members of his Body, becoming, as a result, temples of the Holy Spirit and "cooperators" in the gift of the Holy Spirit to the world. For the Incarnate Son of God participates, by his obedience, in the outpouring of the Holy Spirit in the economy of salvation, as he participates by his divine filiation in the joint spiration of the Holy Spirit in the immanent Trinity. Analogically, the priesthood of the baptized not only has an ascending filial dimension as an agreeable offering to the Father or as intercession on behalf of mankind; it also has a concrete descending dimension, a vital communication of the Holy Spirit, who descends from the Father through Christ and passes through the corporeality of the servants and handmaids of God, whose active charity penetrates mankind, aids it, serves it, and sanctifies it. The conciliar texts on the mission of the laity speak of the Holy Spirit, who gives them life and sanctifies them for participation in worship,[14] for the prophetic office,[15] and for the royal office,[16] spreading in the world abundant spiritual fruits in the Spirit of the Beatitudes proclaimed in the Gospel.

What concrete shape, then, does this prophetic, royal, and cultic form of the priesthood of the baptized take? First of all, the shape of

---

[13] See Albert Vanhoye, *Il sacerdozio della nuova alleanza* (Bologna: EDB, 1992), 49–50. It is possible to safeguard the distinction in nature between the two participations in the one priesthood of Christ without cutting off one essential part of it, as we will see further on.

[14] *LG*, no. 34.

[15] Ibid., no. 35.

[16] Ibid., no. 36.

the community of faith, hope, and love, because the Holy Spirit is the source of communion and solidarity in the mission. The Holy Spirit, who enlivens the baptized, becomes incarnate, in a way, in this people belonging to God, a people unified and structured in living and missionary communities, where the Divine Persons, in circumincession, give themselves to human persons in communion and participation. In this sense, the universal priesthood of the Church, founded on the presence of Christ and the indwelling of the Holy Spirit, involves an exchange of gifts, which implies the interaction of the Divine Persons with human persons for an expanded communication with the world that is to be evangelized. For intercessory prayer, the gift of self, sacrifices, works of mercy, charisms, holiness, etc., build a fruitful relationship between God and the world.

The world is then invited and, above all, attracted and drawn in by the Spirit to put its faith in Christ and in the Trinity; communion with them offers to it a foretaste of the joy of salvation in the experience of ecclesial communion. In this way, the priesthood in the Church is not only one charism among others, one particular office of many within her bosom, but a life of communion that involves her whole being, all her activities, all her relationships *ad intra* and *ad extra*, having as their substance and supreme goal holiness in love, through the action of the Holy Spirit poured out and possessed as a down payment before being tasted in fullness. For at the bottom of the multiple exchanges of gifts that take place in the Church, there is the reflection and even a participation in the Trinitarian life, an exchange of intra-Trinitarian love that is mediated *ad extra* through the Incarnation of the Son in Jesus Christ and, analogically, through the incarnation of the Spirit in the Church; these two concrete and complementary manifestations of the gift of God to the world are unfolded in each other and with each other, in historical and eschatological continuity in what we recognize as the sacramental nature of the Church.

In everyday human life, this far-reaching priesthood means serving the glory of God through the humble and persevering practice of the virtues of faith, hope, and, above all, charity. Indeed, every act of love of God and neighbor, even if it is hidden and inconspicuous, is theophoric: it bears God. It is supported by God as a created reality, but it is also the bearer of God in his act of total gift to his creatures in the Holy Spirit. For in the fullness of time, the Holy Spirit, being poured out, not only adds some aesthetic details to the work of the Father and the Son; he universalizes the sacramentality of the paschal Christ through his Body, which is the Church, extending the incarnation of Trinitarian love according to the modality of his own hypostasis *communion*, progressively effecting the *connubium* [marriage] of the Trinity and mankind in a symphony of exchanged gifts and reciprocal glorifications. This symphony already anticipates here on earth the glory of the Kingdom in the humble face of Mary-Church,[17] the Bride without spot or wrinkle, consecrated to serve today and throughout the centuries the glory of God all in all. Who will deny that the service of this eminent member of the Church, Spouse and Mother, is a fruitful mediation of the priestly fullness of Christ?

Because of its purpose and its fruit, which is the gift of the Holy Spirit, the one priesthood of Christ consequently confers on all its beneficiaries a participation in its pneumatic fruitfulness, precisely in terms of participation in his mediation. The uniqueness of the Christ's priesthood does not exclude but includes the mediation of the Church-sacrament as a believing community, thanks to the two specific forms in its bosom; the Holy Spirit ensures that it is dependent on Christ's mediation and that it unfolds properly through his Person-communion. To speak about the Church's participation in Christ's priesthood, consequently, does not mean to affirm a mediation that is autonomous with respect to the unique mediation of Christ, but rather to affirm a fructification of the latter through the Holy Spirit, who is its fruit and who communicates its virtue and richness by his own Person united to the Church.

The Pneumatological and Trinitarian Integration of the Differentiated Participation in Christ's Priesthood in the Church

All the foregoing developments lead us to derive the participation in Christ's priesthood in the Church from a pneumatology that establishes a Trinitarian and nuptial ecclesiology, setting the stage for the

---

[17] See Gisbert Greshake, *Maria è la Chiesa. Un tema antico, una sfida per il presente* (Brescia: Queriniana, 2020); *Maria-Ecclesia: Perspektiven einer marianisch grundierten Theologie und Kirchenpraxis* (Regensburg: Friedrich Pustet, 2014); Hans Urs von Balthasar and Joseph Cardinal Ratzinger, *Mary: The Church at the Source*, trans. Adrian Walker (San Francisco: Ignatius Press, 2005).

articulated communion of the Divine Persons and human persons within the historical and eschatological horizon of the Church. God willed to incarnate his love and his grace in the sacramental structure of the Church, because the Incarnation of the Word in Christ is his definitive and irreversible choice, a choice that must continue in history in a more universal way through the mission of the Holy Spirit. It is up to the Holy Spirit to continue the mission of Christ by accepting it and expanding it to mankind as a whole through the sacramental mediation of the Church. This entails a real participation in the Trinitarian communion stemming from the paschal sacrifice of the Incarnate Word, by virtue of Baptism and the other sacraments. The Holy Spirit accomplishes this sacramental universalization of Christ's mission by allowing himself to be poured out by the Father and the Son, and by giving himself to the Church in an indescribable and unparalleled manner. The nuptial analogy, for example, is fitting for the relationship of Christ with the Church, but not for the relationship of the Holy Spirit with the Church, because the Spirit is not so much the partner of the Church as her nuptial bond with Christ, *he* is the "we" by whom the subjectivity of the Church is rooted in the Trinitarian communion.

This ineffable presence of the Holy Spirit is the foundation of the Church's participation in the Trinitarian communion, and the principal agent of the differentiation of the sacramental gifts and of the numerous interactions between the Divine Persons and human persons. The sacramental structure of the Church, which aims at the divine-human communion of the New Covenant and brings it about, presupposes the representation of the Divine Persons by human persons, so that the communion of the invisible God with his Covenant partners may be made sacramentally visible and effective.

In the case of Baptism, it is not a question of representation but rather of the identification of each baptized person, and of the community of the baptized, with the Son, and through him, with the Father in the Spirit. For it is the Spirit who always brings about communion, without confusion or separation, between the Divine Persons and the ecclesial community, who configures the grace of divine filiation in the soul of the baptized, in an indelible manner that the concept of sacramental character expresses. This character (*sfragis*) imprints the seal of filiation as an irreversible gift signifying the irrevocability of God's gifts, even when the human creature betrays and denies the gift received. Just like the Pasch of Christ necessarily leads to the gift of the Holy Spirit, so, too, the Baptism that prolongs it marks the subject with an irrefutable "pneumatic" seal—hence the permanent possibility for the baptized, in any state of grace or sin, to offer themselves to the Father with Christ, in the power of the Spirit, who is always available to make the filial priesthood of the baptized bear fruit.

In the case of the Sacrament of Holy Orders, it is not a matter of a pure and simple identification of the priest with Christ, which is already accomplished by Baptism, but rather of a sacramental representation of the paternal dimension of Christ's mission. For in the economy of the Incarnation, Christ manifested himself as the Son, who is obedient to the Father and subject to his parents, but he also revealed himself as the Apostle of the Father, the minister of the Father: "He who has seen me has seen the Father" (Jn 14:9). This is, in my humble opinion, what is at the basis of the distinction between the two participations of the Church in the one priesthood of Christ.[18]

It is important to grasp correctly this crucial aspect that places us at the heart of the mystery of the Incarnation and of its sacramental continuity in the Church. If the Word of God was conceived by the Holy Spirit and was accompanied by him throughout his Incarnation, it was so that he might live out fully his human condition and his mission as Son of the Father assisted by his filial Spirit, in order to carry out to the end his redemptive mission, which included bearing the sin of the world in his offering of love on the Cross and obtaining the Father's absolution in response to his sacrifice. Now, this absolution of the Father is signified and given to him in the very act of his Resurrection from the dead by the power of the Holy

---

[18] We can also express this distinction by speaking about the subjective filial priesthood of Christ and about his objective priesthood of representing the Father. This second aspect is secondary, because it is tied to the temporal economy of the Incarnation and does not persist in eternal life. This is true of Christ and of his ministers who represent him by virtue of an objective gift entrusted to them for the time of the economy of the Church. In heaven the offices disappear and the filial priesthood remains, the shared enjoyment of the full reality of the Divine Persons and the human persons. See Marie of the Trinity, *Filiation et sacerdoce des chrétiens* (Paris: Lethielleux, 1986).

Spirit. That is when the fullness of the Holy Spirit is communicated to him as the Spirit of the Father, the sovereign Spirit who absolves sins, raises the dead, *pneumatizes* the humanity of Christ to make it a life-giving Spirit, capable of continuing in history under a new *sacramental*, corporal modality in the Church, Body and Bride of the Risen Christ.

The essential distinction between the two participations in the one priesthood of Christ is founded, therefore, on the pneumatology that distinguishes the Spirit from the Son, at the source of the filial priesthood, and the Spirit from the Father, at the source of the paternal priesthood of ordained ministers. In this light it is obvious that the two are ordered to each other, the more fundamental being the eternal filial priesthood, in the service of which the sacramental hierarchical priesthood unfolds for the time of the economy of salvation.[19]

The Sacrament of Holy Orders is clearly instituted by God in this pair of sayings by Christ at the Last Supper and on the evening of the Resurrection: "Do this in remembrance of me" (Lk 22:19), and "Receive the Holy Spirit. If you forgive the sins of any, they are forgiven; if you retain the sins of any, they are retained" (Jn 20:22–23). The *exousia* (*potestas*) proper to the ordained ministry proceeds from the Spirit of the Father raising Christ from the dead and conferring on him henceforth a power that radiates from his transfigured humanity. He is capable of communicating this power by his physical breath, which the Church would express later on by the imposition of hands, so as to authorize his ministers to proclaim the Word with authority and to celebrate the sacraments for the building up of the Church. Thus, the ecclesial Body of Christ is expressed as a "pneumatic" Body truly configured and made personal by the Spirit, to the point where it assumes the social configuration of a people, but also the mystical figure of the Bride of Christ—hence, the nuptial meaning of the Sacrament of Holy Orders to assure the representation of the Bridegroom and the power to actualize permanently his

[19]Dario Vitali, "Nuovi cammini per la ministerialità ecclesiale", *PATH* 20, no. 1 (2022): 48: "The 'Copernican revolution' of the Council finds here its structural principle: indeed, the pyramidal structure of the Church, which lasted for centuries, comes to be destroyed at the moment when it is affirmed that the two distinct modalities of participating in Christ's priesthood are ordered to each other". Dario Vitali, "Sacerdozio comune e sacerdozio ministeriale o gerarchico: rilettura di una questione controversa", *Rassegna di Teologia* 52 (2011): 39–60.

Eucharistic nuptials *in Persona Christi Capitis* (in the Person of Christ the Head).

It follows that this sacrament also contains a stable "pneumatic" character which configures the subject and makes him capable of representing Christ the Head precisely as an Apostle of the Father, sacramentally signifying the sovereign initiative of the Father throughout the divine plan, and guaranteeing at the same time the apostolicity of the Church's mission. Thus, the Church lives daily from the Eucharist, a mystery of the New Covenant, a nuptial mystery, a theandric mystery configured by the Trinitarian bond of the Spirit—the Spirit of the Father and of the Son—communicated in full by the Risen One!

The profound meaning of the Sacrament of Holy Orders would then certainly be to signify to the community that it does not own the unique mediation of Christ independently as its property, but must always receive it as a gift. Beyond this fundamental meaning, however, we could see in it another meaning: a reminder to the whole Church that the one priesthood of Christ refers radically to the Father from whom she permanently receives her participation in it, both for the fundamental grace of divine filiation and for the hierarchical and charismatic gifts that proceed from the generosity of the Father, through the Son, in the Spirit.

In this way, the perspective of the priesthood is expanded in the Trinitarian sense of a participation in the Spirit of the Father and of the Son, the same Spirit of communion that manifests its filial aspect in the common priesthood of the baptized, and its paternal aspect in the ordained ministry of the ministers. The two sacramental manifestations thus converge in building up the ecclesial communion in which the peaceful and joyful complementarity between the faithful and the ministers is founded and nourished at the source of the communion of the Divine Persons. This participation in the loving relations between the Father and the Son sanctifies human relations, purifies relations that sometimes involve conflict, puts into perspective the questions of power and authority, and, above all, opens up a space of freedom for the Holy Spirit's own creativity.

The relationship between the authority and the community is no longer centered on the very human dimension that is often in conflict and is centered instead on grace, that is, the communion of the Divine Persons given in participation in the filial identity of the baptized and the paternal identity of the ordained ministers, both being inhabited and sanctified by the Spirit of the Father and of the Son. Such a grace is not a dream, an ideal, a mere symbol; it is the ontology of the Divine Persons and of human persons who are exercising communion in the Spirit. He gives access to his paternal and filial "we" by allowing himself to be infused into souls and into ecclesial relations founded on Baptism and the Sacrament of Holy Orders. But his personal gift is not limited to these two services that he renders to the Father and to the Son by radiating their presence in the relations between the baptized and the hierarchical ministers. He also expresses himself in an "overflowing" that corresponds to his own identity in the Trinitarian life.

Indeed, although the fruitfulness of this Trinitarian perspective first appears in the communion between pastors and the faithful, it truly flourishes and blossoms in the development of a richly charismatic ecclesial community. For ecclesial communion, strengthened by harmonious participation in the relations of filiation and paternity, liberates the sphere proper to the Spirit, who then expresses himself by an abundance of charisms and a flowering of vocations of all kinds, secular, marital, religious, and priestly, at the service of the Church's sacramental mission. The presence of the consecrated life in particular, in all its forms as the *sequela Christi*, is a testimony to the freedom and gratuitousness of the Holy Spirit, who builds unity in love starting from respect for diversity, complementarity, and reciprocity. Just as in the Trinity, the love that is the Spirit flows back on the love of the Father and of the Son, giving them an ineffable "plus", so, too, in the economy of the Church, the witness of consecrated life flows back on the spirituality of the ministers and of the faithful, stimulating them to selflessness and the perfection of charity, for a more fruitful witness to communion and the ecclesial mission.

The ordained "sacramental" ministry refers to the Father, whom Christ represents, and his ministers after him, by virtue of a specific gift of the Spirit of the Father, but without rigidifying the identification in a "sacral" or "idolatrous" sense. Any excess of sacralization in this area leads to abuses of power and the phenomena of rejection. The key to understanding the "sacramental" nature of this "ministerial" identification is the mediation proper to the Holy Spirit, whose personal characteristic is to unite by distinguishing, to unite without confusing. Therefore, it is he who unites the minister to the One whom he represents in a real way in this *sacramental-pneumatic* order in which the distinction remains in the union, with this allowance that respects the subject's freedom and his possible or real failure, but nevertheless guaranteeing to the ministerial mediation an efficacy that is partially independent of the moral value of the minister. This is the *ex opere operato* dimension of the ordained ministry, which applies to strictly sacramental acts, but not in the same way to the whole life of the priest.

It appears from this pneumatological consideration that the ordained ministry must be understood as an ontological reality that permanently configures the person, and not as a simple social function without a permanent character. This configuration is not on the order of the subject's personal sanctification, but on the order of his objective charism for the service of the ecclesial community.[20] In fact, the whole sacramental order is ontological, because it is "pneumatological"! The Holy Spirit fills the Church with the presence of the Divine Persons; he enriches human persons by joining them together and making them socialize from within the Trinitarian relationships. Indeed, by his grace the Spirit molds the personal and ecclesial relationships, making them substantial and influential. His own action along the lines of communion relates the baptized and the ministers reciprocally on the basis of the sacramental gifts that bring into play the ontology of the Trinitarian relationships and the sociology of human relationships.

In short, everything is carried out by the Person of the Holy Spirit, who is, so to speak, the Trinitarian hypostasis of the Church.[21] He joins the Trinity and mankind in a nuptial mystery for which there is no analogy, uniting them by distinguishing them in love, safeguarding the

---

[20] The very well-articulated study of the liturgical sources of the renewed theology of the priesthood by Martin Troupeau provides, in conclusion, an overall confirmation of the pneumatological considerations that I have tried to broaden from a dogmatic perspective; see Troupeau, *L'unité du sacrement*, 407: "In addition to this service to the community which is common to the three degrees, we propose thinking about the unity of the sacrament from the angle of pneumatology: the Spirit is poured out on the ministers of the different orders so that they may build up the Church as a holy people, by guiding it, sanctifying it, and teaching it."

[21] Balthasar, "Who Is the Church?": "This inchoate subject, the Church, is fulfilled only in the mystery of the Holy Spirit, who is embedded in her as her inmost ground, and who can therefore constitute it in its perfected state because he is a Divine Person precisely as testifying to the eternal opposition of the Persons" (p. 191).

Creator-creature difference, while filling the chasm between the thrice
Holy God and the mass of sinners, not by a penal exclusion, but by
the *kenotic* sacrificial inclusion of Trinitarian love manifested in Christ,
crucified and risen "to the praise of his glorious grace" (Eph 1:6).

This Trinitarian and nuptial approach provides a profound ecclesiological basis for the current research into a synodal Church: communion, participation, and mission. For we discover that the personal
and institutional relations in the ecclesial communities are animated
interiorly by dynamic, articulated participation in the Trinitarian
relations. These are understood in their distinctions and unity, which
thoroughly imbue the complex and diversified, albeit sometimes
difficult interplay of human and ecclesial relationships, bringing a
grace of healing, sanctification, and fruitfulness. From this emanates
a "spirituality of communion" for everyone in the Church, which
changes the situation at a pastoral level and goes beyond slogans; from
this also results a "missionary mysticism" beyond voluntarism, for it
springs from the most profound universality of love, embodied in the
Church and entrusted to her care to evangelize the whole world until
the fullness of the reign of God, who is all in all.

The formula that can summarize the comprehensive vision which
has been proposed here is the pneumatological formula of the *Ecclesia, Sacramentum Trinitatis*. The Church is constituted, in fact, by
the divine missions of the Word and of the Spirit, who establish
and structure its participation in the Trinitarian communion upon
its faith in the priesthood of Christ, the one mediator of salvation;
this faith enables it through Baptism to be his Body and his Bride
in the Spirit, the People of God on a pilgrimage to the Kingdom,
a people of priests, a royal priesthood, a holy nation. This priestly
people, sign and instrument of the Trinitarian communion in the
service of the unity of the human race, is constituted as such in two
specific participations, according to the Spirit of the Father and the
Spirit of the Son, with a view to a total gift of the Trinitarian life to
its Covenant partner in history and through it to all humanity that is
awaiting salvation. The mutual reference of the two participations,
far from enclosing them within this communion, projects them outward together under the apostolic impulse of the ministers for the
evangelization of the world.

The Church is the dawn of the Kingdom insofar as it already "sacramentally" incarnates the eschatological communion promised to all mankind; her ecclesial relations of communion and mission, founded among others on the sacraments of Baptism, the Eucharist, and Holy Orders, express the involvement of the Divine Persons in the communion of human persons in whom the Holy Spirit dwells with all the richness of his Trinitarian identity: the Spirit of the Father in the gift of the hierarchical ministry, the Spirit of the Son in the personal and existential offering of the community of the baptized, the Spirit of communion and freedom in the abundance and flourishing of the charisms in the service of communion and mission.

This Trinitarian perspective of ecclesiology and this pneumatological integration of the Church's twofold participation in the one priesthood of Christ make it possible not only to frame the missionary pastoral work of the Church better, but also to resolve the age-old conundrums and recurring conflicts. Such a priestly perspective, radically focused on participation in the Trinitarian communion, could have a notable impact on all vocations by sowing enthusiasm for a true ecclesial communion that is missionary because it is attractive, welcoming, and in solidarity with the coming of the Kingdom of God starting in the present life.

Chapter 6

The Missionary Future of a Synodal Church

Pope Francis has published two messages during the Synod on Synodality; the preliminary phase of its work has just been concluded. The first is an ascetical kind of message, cautioning against spiritual worldliness: *Holy, Not Worldly.*[1] The Holy Father takes this theme from a prophetic warning by Father Henri de Lubac in his *Meditation on the Church*, which is one of the leitmotivs of his pontificate. The second, more mystical, message applies the teaching of Thérèse of the Child Jesus and the Holy Face about the little way of holiness to this hour of synodal and missionary research. It is worthwhile listening to two significant passages that will introduce our topic:

> I feel concern that God is loudly calling the entire Church to remain vigilant and to fight with the strength of prayer against every concession to spiritual worldliness. This battle has a name: it is called holiness. Holiness is not a state of beatitude which one has reached once and for all. It is instead the incessant, tireless desire to remain attached to the cross of Jesus, letting ourselves be shaped by the logic that comes from the gift of self and from resisting the enemy who flatters us by convincing us that we are self-sufficient. It would do us well to remember what Jesus said: "Without me you can do nothing" (Jn 15:5). Holiness is therefore remaining open to the "more" that God asks of us and that is manifested in our adherence to our daily lives.[2]

This essay is based on a talk given in Switzerland for the Freundeskreis Hans Urs von Balthasar, December 3, 2023.
[1] Francis, *Santi, non mondani: La grazia di Dio ci salva dalla corruzione interiore* (Rome: LEV, 2023).
[2] Ibid., 9–10. See Henri de Lubac, *Méditations sur l'Église* (Paris: Aubier-Montaigne, 1953), 321. The theme of spiritual worldliness is discussed in *EG*, nos. 93–97.

This first message exhorts us to a dynamic holiness, following Jesus on the path of self-giving, vigilance, and openness to grace, which always leads us further onward in the newness of God. The second passage summarizes in a few lines the significance of Thérèse of the Child Jesus for a synodal, missionary Church. "In the heart of Thérèse, the grace of baptism became this impetuous torrent flowing into the ocean of Christ's love and dragging in its wake a multitude of brothers and sisters. This is what happened, especially after her death. It was her promised 'shower of roses'."[3]

The pope makes this comment after quoting a prayer by Thérèse that illustrates the missionary charism by attraction with which the Holy Spirit graced her:

> That is my prayer. I ask Jesus to draw me to the flames of his love, to unite me so closely to him that he live and act in me. I feel that the more the fire of love burns within my heart, the more I shall say *"Draw me"*: the more also the souls who will approach me (poor little piece of iron, useless if I withdraw from the divine furnace), the more these souls *will run swiftly in the odour of the ointments of their Beloved*, for a soul that is burning with love cannot remain inactive.[4]

Dear friends, when little Thérèse made her way into the Synod Hall, it was for many participants a breath of fresh air and encouragement on the rather laborious road that initiates us into a more synodal Church. I welcomed this initiative of the Holy Father with all the more emotion and gratitude because Thérèse played an important role at the start of my own vocation. Indeed, reading *The Story of a Soul* at the age of seventeen set me on fire and confirmed my priestly and missionary vocation. The main reason for my gratitude, however, is more objective: it is the spiritual and missionary depth of her contemplative witness that came to call all of us, bishops and non-bishops, traveling companions, both men and women, to a surge of spiritual fervor in the assembly. May it please God that this rose

---

[3] Francis, Apostolic Exhortation on Confidence in the Merciful Love of God *C'est la confiance* (October 15, 2023), no. 13, quoting Thérèse of Lisieux, *Her Last Conversations* (Washington, D.C.: Institute of Carmelite Studies, 1977), 62.

[4] Thérèse of Lisieux, Ms C, 36r, in *Story of a Soul* (Washington, D.C.: Institute of Carmelite Studies, 1996), 257, quoted in Francis, *C'est la confiance*, no. 12.

which fell from heaven may inspire the continuation of the work and bear mature fruits at the next session of the Synod and beyond.

A Modality of the Synod of Bishops That Is Open to the Signs of the Times

The phase that has just ended in fact raised many questions and confirmed a process of discernment with a view of a synodal conversion that is still to be clarified and distinguished from some ideological interests that try to adapt the Church to the democracies of this world. *Santi, ma non mondani!* [Holy, but not worldly!], the Holy Father repeats endlessly, especially for ordained ministers, but his exhortation is valid for all Christians and for all the discernments that the Church makes. The synodal experience that we have just had was not centered on resolving a doctrinal or moral question. It was above all an exercise of "conversation in the Holy Spirit" so as to learn better to listen to one another in order to hear better the Spirit of God together. The exercise consisted of lengthy exchanges, in groups of around ten persons, in which everyone spoke out about the theme for reflection, then, going around the table a second time, commented on what he remembered from the other interventions, so as to conclude together with a common reflection to be shared at the plenary session. This method of "conversation in the Spirit" really contributed to developing a more prayerful and fraternal climate among everyone, and to keep the assembly from drifting toward a parliamentary style of discussion.

The Synod unfolded, therefore, under the banner of listening and freedom of expression, to follow up the vast consultation. Although at the start it was affected too much by a functional mentality oriented to structural changes, as it went along it became more interior and centered on an in-depth examination of Christian identity, giving priority to Christian initiation and the formation of missionary disciples, keeping an interest in participatory structures but organizing more activities for the conversion of persons. The synodal assembly asked, furthermore, that specialized studies be made on new questions of a scientific, anthropological, or ethical sort, which could require discernment in the future. The floor is now open to the theologians who must examine these questions in greater depth, limit the topics to be discussed, and root the functional and organizational aspects in the mysteric dimension of the Church. In all likelihood, the conclusion of the synodal process in October 2024 should lead to a deeper understanding of synodality that can make a turning point in the missionary vocation of the People of God as a whole.

This is precisely the theological and vocational reason that motivated the organization of the symposium toward a fundamental theology of the priesthood at the Vatican in February 2022.[5] This academic initiative developed the theological and spiritual dimension of the synodal research by drawing attention to God's call to all baptized persons. The missionary future of the Church vitally depends on this broad vocational promotion, because otherwise the synodal process would run the risk of slipping into a parliamentary style that is more susceptible to worldly ideologies, in which the discussion of ideas prevails over the vocation and involvement of the persons. This would only increase the confusion and division that already reign in some circles in which people seek either to impose views that are foreign to the logic of the faith or else to discredit the pope and the Synod wholesale.

The synodal assembly, for its part, revealed that there is an ongoing, ever-deeper realization of the dignity of all baptized persons. This is reflected in its method of working, which promoted the development of a real fraternity, nourished by the complementarity of vocations between the bishops, the men and women religious, and the laypersons. We hoped that this experience would continue and extend to the whole Church so as to create a new atmosphere of communion and participation in mission, in which the contribution of each man and each woman would be more welcome and appreciated. At the point we have reached, it is clear that the Holy Spirit is animating this synodal and missionary research of the Church, with the positive yet not exclusive method of "conversation in the Spirit", which was experienced at various levels of the research, even in the phase of the

---

[5] See Marc Cardinal Ouellet, ed., *A Fundamental Theology of the Priesthood*, vol. 1, *Proceedings of the Symposium Sponsored by the Center for Research and Anthropology of Vocations*, Rome, February 17–19, 2022 (Mahwah, N.J.: Paulist Press, 2023). For additional information, see the website of the Center for Research and Anthropology of Vocations (CRAV) at https://crav -vocation.org/en/contents/.

Synod of Bishops. It is important for current theological reflection on synodality to be up to this "change of era" in order to discern the "signs of the times"[6] and to promote an intercultural and missionary dialogue that involves the People of God.

Pope Paul VI already invited the Church to such a dialogue during the ecumenical Vatican Council II with his encyclical *Ecclesiam Suam*: "The Church must enter into dialogue with the world in which it lives. It has something to say, a message to give, a communication to make."[7] The saintly pontiff, and with the Council with him, wanted a new atmosphere of dialogue with the world so as to proclaim the Gospel but also to listen to and welcome whatever is beautiful and good in the experience of our contemporaries.[8] This attitude of fraternal dialogue inaugurated a new style of mission, one that is more aware of cultural mediations and is interested particularly nowadays in the major problems that affect humanity as a whole: peace, poverty, the future of the planet, migrations. This does not mean making the explicit proclamation of the Gospel secondary, but rather proclaiming it with respect for cultures, seeking the way that is in keeping with the dignity of every human person and with religious traditions, counting more on the force of charity and on the attractive witness of local vibrant missionary communities.

After these reflections on the synodal event, which tested a method that is open but in need of further definition for the future,[9] I will develop now a theological perspective on the future of the Church's mission to contribute to this necessary, in-depth examination with the help of some elements that emerged from the discussions, in particular proclamation of the kerygma, the spirituality of communion, discernment of the signs of the times, the complementarity and reciprocity of vocations, intercultural and religious ecumenical dialogue. The itinerary will be divided into two parts: (1) toward a Church that

---

[6] See Francis, Apostolic Letter in the Form of a Motu Proprio *Ad Theologiam Promovendam* (November 1, 2023), nos. 1, 8, by which the new statutes of the Pontifical Academy of Theology were approved, November 1, 2023.

[7] Paul VI, encyclical *Ecclesiam Suam* (August 6, 1964), no. 65.

[8] See *GS*, nos. 53–54.

[9] A good 25 percent of the participants in this Synod of Bishops were nonbishops: men and women religious, priests, and laypeople with a right to vote equal to that of the bishops; although this format *ad experimentum* was a positive experience, it would be regrettable if this formula was imposed unilaterally as the "Synod of Bishops".

is entirely priestly and missionary; (2) the communion of vocations: a challenge for our times.

Toward a Church That Is Entirely Priestly and Missionary

During the celebration of the fiftieth anniversary of the institution of the Synod of Bishops, in October 2015, the Holy Father Francis made a solemn and programmatic appeal for a synodal Church: "We must continue along this path. The world in which we live, and which we are called to love and serve, even with its contradictions, demands that the Church strengthen cooperation in all areas of her mission. It is precisely this path of *synodality* which God expects of the Church of the third millennium."[10] This appeal is based on the vocation of the People of God to witness to the faith that they received in Baptism: "After stating that the people of God is comprised of all the baptized who are called to 'be a spiritual house and a holy priesthood,' the Second Vatican Council went on to say that 'the whole body of the faithful, who have an anointing which comes from the holy one (cf. 1 Jn 2:20, 27), cannot err in matters of belief.'"[11]

"To love the world in which we live", "to strengthen cooperation in all areas", "to be a spiritual house and a holy priesthood": these are the Holy Father's fundamental guidelines for the whole Church. Above all, this means counting on the baptismal dignity of all the members of the People of God and inviting each one to live out his vocation, according to his own charism, in communion with the ecclesial community as a whole. The Church is indeed altogether priestly and missionary through the grace of Baptism, which makes her participate in the priesthood of Christ and in the anointing of the Holy Spirit, by which she is infallible *in credendo* [in believing].

Vatican Council II recalled that there are two forms of participating in Christ's priesthood, which are complementary and centered on each other so as to render to God the worship that is due to him, and also to communicate to the world the gift of the Holy Spirit. These

---

[10] Francis, Address at the Ceremony Commemorating the 50th Anniversary of Institution of Synod of Bishops (October 17, 2015).

[11] Ibid., quoting *LG*, nos. 10, 12.

two forms, baptismal and ministerial, about which we have already spoken, embody the twofold movement, ascending and descending, of Christ's priesthood. The ascending movement, which is of a cultic nature, leads by the covenantal logic of their union to the descending movement, which is of a missionary nature and broadens the gift of the Holy Spirit to the world. Thus, the Trinitarian communion that constitutes the People of God and confers its unity upon it[12] is communicated to the world through the faith of the members of the Body of Christ, through the baptismal and hierarchical structure of the Church. The communion of the Divine Persons, which proceeds from the Father through the Son in the Spirit, is prolonged and embodied then in the ecclesial community thanks to the mediation of the priesthood of Jesus Christ, a gushing source of the Spirit and of all vocations.

This priestly kind of approach to mission has the advantage of highlighting the mysteric nature of the Church, which a "ministerial" approach does not manage to integrate to the same degree. Some, in fact, would have wanted to plan the synodal discussion around the formula "Toward a Church that is entirely ministerial", but this was disputed because of its ambiguity and its limitations in expressing the Christian apostolic identity. Wanting an entirely ministerial Church would run the risk of prolonging a "clerical" model and a mentality of the same order, by describing all sorts of apostolate as "ministry". The most serious danger would be "clericalizing" laypeople by an ambiguous highlighting of roles within the ecclesial organization, whereas the mission of the laity consists above all in witnessing to Christ in the world and imbuing their family life and their temporal tasks with the Spirit of the Gospel. In the Church, all are "missionary disciples", but all are not "ministers". Ministries are the job of some, according to specific charisms, institutional or otherwise.

Let us acknowledge at the outset that our Catholic tradition is marked by a clerical mentality, at least in the West. Everything gravitates around the ordained minister. Moreover, we suffer from the consequences of this, which the serious crisis of sexual abuse has revealed and exacerbated. In this regard, it is high time for sincere self-criticism and for openness to synodal forms of collaboration. Our

[12] *LG*, no. 4.

Catholic tradition generally does not give a shining example of recognizing the dignity and the competence of baptized persons in their mission in the midst of the world. For example, laypeople should be consulted systematically on the complex questions that emerge from scientific and technological developments concerning life, ethics, the economy, politics, the digital culture, art, etc. There is also a lack of appreciation for and promotion of charisms in the Christian communities, for lack of sensitivity to the presence of the Holy Spirit and to his sometimes surprising or even unsettling action. Every reform presupposes initiatives and changes that alter the equilibrium and open up new missionary opportunities. Think of the development of Catholic action before the Council, or the experience of the worker priests, the emergence of the ecclesial movements, etc. Vatican Council II unfroze this situation, but the dominant mentality is still slow to integrate the talents and gifts that the Holy Spirit pours out on the priestly people for the building up of the local churches.

These limitations and this slowness, however, do not justify the position of some theologians, even at the Synod, who tend too much to pit the Kingdom of God against the Church. They accentuate the difference and the discontinuity between the Church and the Kingdom in a way that devalues the institutional Church in favor of a self-proclaimed prophetic ministry that does not always have true worth. They forget then that the Kingdom of God is Jesus Christ living in his ecclesial Body according to a modality of Incarnation over which the Holy Spirit presides; a Kingdom of God that is therefore already here and not just relegated to some future fullness, notwithstanding all the historical limitations of the Church.[13] The charismatic prophetic ministry is therefore called to assist humbly the prophetic ministry of the institutional Church; otherwise, it runs the risk of serving a spirit that has more affinity with the *Zeitgeist* than with the Spirit of communion of the Father and of the Son. In this same vein, some isolated opinions have mentioned ideologies that level the anthropological and charismatic differences, perhaps in the hope of establishing democratic decision-making processes, but explicit protests in the assembly revealed a healthy resistance to these cultural pressures.

---

[13] This tendency comes to a great extent from Latin America, where one can still perceive an ideological influence that is probably unconscious and fortunately outmoded: a certain Marxist-oriented theology of liberation.

Through Baptism, each person is constituted a member of the Body of Christ and, by that title, receives a mission to fulfill as such with the personal charism that the Holy Spirit assigns to each man and each woman, in this way to one and in that way to another (1 Cor 7:7) for the service of the community. All things considered, the deputation of all the members to witness to divine charity is what determines the substance of all personal mission within the ecclesial communion (see 1 Cor 13). The particular ministries certainly play an important part in this, but it is a subordinate part, derived from the fundamental dignity bestowed by the grace of divine adoption. This distinguished grace includes the requirement of personal testimony, which is of a different order compared to the testimony that is required by the exercise of a ministry, however important it may be. For the filial grace of a baptized person qualified him first of all to be a member of the Body of Christ and involved the whole person, whereas the charism of the ordained or instituted minister concerns the exercise of a particular function, even though the subject who performs it involves his baptismal identity in the service that is to be rendered.

This primacy of personal testimony over functional service is based on baptismal dignity but also on the Eucharistic compost in which all vocations grow. Indeed, the Trinitarian identity of the Church and of each member of the People of God proceeds fundamentally and permanently from the joint missions of the Incarnate Word and of the Holy Spirit, who prolong their active and fruitful presence in the community through the proclamation of the Word of God and the gift of the sacraments. These divine missions constitute the deepest identity of the People of God and enlighten their prayer, their witness, and their awareness of mission, at the place where the mystery of the Church is not reduced to its sociological dimension. So much so that we cannot hope for a significant missionary advance as long as the faithful and the basic institutions of the ecclesial community—the family, the school, the parish, the diocese, the associations, the movements, etc.—have not been catechized to understand that their missionary commitment fits into God's own commitment. For these ecclesial structures embody the divine-human communion that is proper to the Church. Indeed, Christ and the Spirit dwell within them through the gift of the Word of God and of the sacraments.

From this perspective, Baptism, Matrimony, and Holy Orders appear particularly important, but nothing equals the contribution of the Eucharist, which activates and vitalizes all the ecclesial structures for the service of the mission. For the Eucharist, the covenantal mystery par excellence, is the sacrament of the Trinitarian love poured out and communicated, which constitutes the source and summit, the soul and driving force of the missionary vocations of all baptized persons. They are called to "live in God's commitment",[14] as Hans Urs von Balthasar puts it while summarizing his *theo-dramatic* perspective.[15] From this starting point, the missionary future of a synodal Church in our time opens up. Indeed, the Holy Trinity is the *Archè* [beginning, principle] of synodality, for it is communion and mission, the eternal source of the participation of the Son and of the Spirit in the communion that establishes the People of God as a sacramental reality— hence the vital importance of the Eucharist at the heart of the synodal research, for the baptized constantly receive from it the Spirit, who sanctifies them, regenerates them, and sends them to walk together in unity, organizing their spiritual worship (*leiturgia*), supporting their witness (*martyria*), and organizing the harmonization of their charisms for the good of the whole (*diakonia*).[16]

The current synodal research will be fruitful insofar as it discerns the presence and the authentic action of the Holy Spirit in every testimony or proposal that better serves the union of Christ and the Church and the missionary character of the People of God. If it is thought of as a more or less democratic method of modernizing the Church, its fruits will be minimal or ambiguous, if not bitter. If, on

---

[14] See Hans Urs von Balthasar, *Engagement with God: The Drama of Christian Discipleship*, trans. R. John Halliburton (San Francisco: Ignatius Press, 2008).

[15] Hans Urs von Balthasar, *Theo-Drama*, 5 vols. (San Francisco: Ignatius Press, 1988–1998): vol. 1, *Prolegomena*; vol. 2, *The Dramatis Personae: Man in God*; vol. 3, *The Dramatis Personae: The Person in Christ*; vol. 4, *The Action*; vol. 5, *The Last Act*.

[16] See Giuseppe Colombo, *Teologia sacramentaria* (Glossa, 1997), 126: "To proclaim Jesus Christ is not the function of the Church but strictly speaking her very nature, her very being, rooted in the Eucharist. In the Eucharist, that is, in the communion with Jesus Christ that His own body and blood gives, the Church continually rediscovers herself and hence the authenticity of her message. Her position is not 'above' the Eucharist, but 'below' the Eucharist, or better from the Eucharist, in exactly the same way that she is 'below' the word and 'from' the word of God. The movement that 'signifies' and 'realizes' God's salvific action—the sacramental movement—goes from the Eucharist to the Church and from there to all mankind, not vice versa."

the other hand, the synodal mutual listening expresses the infallible faith of the People of God journeying toward a more radiant embodiment of the Trinitarian love, then this listening to the Holy Spirit will open minds and hearts to welcome every human person, especially the poor, and also to the emergence of new charismatic and missionary movements.

The Holy Spirit of the new and eternal Covenant is on a permanent mission in history to bring about the coming of the reign of God in the Church, the Body and Bride of Christ, until the fullness of the Kingdom. In this work of sanctification, the sacraments are acts of Christ the Bridegroom that are performed in the power of the nuptial Spirit for the building up of his Bride, the Church, until the consummation of the final nuptials when God will be all in all. Without the intimate mediation of the nuptial Spirit, the ecclesial Body would be metaphorical and the Bride fleeting; with the Spirit of glory dwelling in its members, it is sacramental, that is, an embodied mediation of a grace and a charity that joins the power of the Risen Lord and the Trinitarian fruitfulness.

It must be acknowledged that in our secularized societies, the Church confronts a disaffection for the sacraments, particularly for the Eucharist and even for Baptism. There are, of course, the effects of practical materialism on mentalities and customs, which have consigned sacramental practice to oblivion or to the random fluctuations of religious sentimentalism. The causes of this disaffection are theological, too, and forgetting the Holy Spirit is part of it, inasmuch as the kerygmatic proclamation of the mystery, the celebration of the sacraments, and the *diakonia* of charity are not watered sufficiently by the fervent invocation of his vital, life-giving breath. Doesn't this lack of life in the Spirit also explain, on the one hand, why personal and communal testimonies are so unattractive, and therefore the decline in vocations?

Infatuation with the synodal process will not be able to change this, unless it promotes a renewed experience of the closeness of God in the mystery of his Covenant with a people that embodies their faith in vocational commitments. The promotion of a synodal Church is not a "public relations" or marketing operation to stir up the participation of the base and to transform the ecclesial organization. It is first and foremost the articulated exercise of ecclesial communion so that the People of God can exercise more consciously and actively their holy priesthood, which is capable of pleasing God and evangelizing the world.

In this regard, the Church's pastoral care, preaching of the kerygma, and catechesis about the Eucharist cannot do without a pneumato-logical vision that restores the attractiveness of a nuptial theology.[17] The perspective developed here becomes part of this renewed appreciation for the nuptial symbol in theology, a symbol that is omnipresent in the Bible but neglected in systematic theology despite the patristic heritage; it is waiting to be developed more amply in order to articulate harmoniously Trinitarian theology, Christology, ecclesiology, anthropology, and sacramental theology. Saint John Paul II contributed to this remarkably by his apostolic exhortations *Familiaris Consortio*, *Mulieris Dignitatem*, *Pastores Dabo Vobis*, and *Vita Consecrata*. Benedict XVI did, too, in *Deus Caritas Est*, not to mention Francis with *Amoris Laetitia*. The adoption of the nuptial symbol as an architectonic principle, with the nuances required by the analogy [*kata-analogie*], could revitalize pastoral ministry and theology itself, "which has run aground on the sandbanks of rationalism", as Balthasar said shortly after the Council. In his introduction to the commentary on *The Song of Songs* by Adrienne von Speyr, he writes: "Nothing is more relevant today than the effort to penetrate into this nuptial mystery of Christ and the Church: from this, and not from a change of institutional structures, we must expect a real reform of the Church."[18]

This orientation of theology could also resume the missionary dialogue with contemporary culture, which lacks points of reference in this regard. The bitter fruits of individualism are evident in the

---

[17] See François-Xavier Durrwell, *L'Eucharistie, sacrement pascal* (Paris: Cerf, 1980), 146: "With regard to the Church, Christ invites and attracts, offering Himself to her; He submits to the Church by granting her the privilege of possessing Him. For her, the incorporating power of the Spirit is love. The Eucharist is nuptial; here, to eat is a word from the language of love. Christ assimilates the Church by letting Himself be eaten by her. Love is characterized by eating, mutually, in a reciprocal gift of self. The impossible dream of a total union can be achieved, because the love that Christ and the Church share with each other is the Holy Spirit, who is creative omnipotence: a love which, by loving, creates the union that it desires."

[18] Hans Urs von Balthasar, introduction to *Das Hohelied*, by Adrienne von Speyr (Einsiedeln: Johannes Verlag, 1972), 8.

inability of many people to make a lasting commitment, which leads to the crisis of the basic institutions of society and of the Church. An anthropological vision magnetically drawn by communion, in keeping with the creation of man in the image of God, can attract our contemporaries, if only by contrast with the precariousness and vulnerability of human relations. An articulate Christian response, however, must fully take into account the fact that human persons are of a social nature, and that it is therefore impossible to make them happy without a fabric of harmonious relations, which at a supernatural level call for a perspective of a communion of vocations for a missionary and synodal Church.[19]

The Communion of Vocations: A Challenge for Our Times

Saint John Paul II devoted a lot of energy to the great cause of vocations, especially by his promotion of the family as a domestic church. Already as archbishop of Krakow, he supported couples in their love with his famous Theology of the Body, which has lost none of its current relevance. His pastoral care of families was inspired by the Holy Family of Jesus, Mary, and Joseph, a little trinity on earth that reveals and reflects the Trinity in heaven. Indeed, let us not forget that Jesus unites the Trinity in heaven and the one on earth in a single family. As Son of the Father and Son of Mary, he ties the two families together indissolubly. What a grace it is for a human family to love and to be loved by the Divine Child present in their midst! What a radical transformation for Mary's and Joseph's vocation to love! Their life was turned upside down. Their fully human marital love opened itself up to a virginal gift of self, in the image of their Child. Consecrated by the Spirit who comes from him, they accepted the Father's plan for their family, which was to serve as the foundation for the Church and for all human and religious families that were going to be born of their testimony.

---

[19] See the concept of the person as mission in the writings of Balthasar, who from the anthropological perspective radicalizes the essentially missionary nature of the Church in *Theo-Drama*, vol. 3, *The Dramatis Personae: The Person in Christ*. See also my thesis about the author, an excerpt from which has been published: Marc Ouellet, *L'Existence comme mission: L'anthropologie théologique de Hans Urs von Balthasar* (Rome: Pontificia Universitas Gregoriana, 1983).

This Holy Family of Jesus, Mary, and Joseph is the historical origin of the Church, but also the permanent source from which the Church springs, always accompanying the life of this family in a trinitarian communion. For in that family the communion of Divine Persons and of human persons then blended into one divine-human family. The humble figure of Joseph allows us to see between the lines the invisible figure of the Eternal Father. The ineffable intimacy of Jesus and his Mother is a garden sealed by the Holy Spirit from the first moment of the Incarnation until the Passion, death, and Resurrection of Christ.

This mysterious family is not a myth or a fleeting idea; it is a reality just as concrete as all the poor families on the planet, a family obliged to give birth in the precarious conditions of a stable, and then to emigrate in order to save the Child from Herod's fury. What dramatic moments they lived through together: the painful discovery that she was pregnant without Joseph being involved, the danger of stoning, the heavenly intervention to strengthen Joseph in his role as the adoptive father of Jesus, the loss of the adolescent in the Temple and the parents' anguish, which was the prelude to the sorrows of the Mother during the Passion. The Gospels are discreet about the hidden life of Jesus, but we can easily imagine other human situations as in any other family, in which they fought and suffered to protect the Child, to educate him, and to prepare him for his mission.

Nowadays the theology of the Incarnation ought to include more reflection on this fundamental network of human relations which was for Jesus an initial school of humanity, a sort of springboard that enabled him to deploy progressively his divine identity and his Trinitarian relations in his thirst for the love of the whole human family. Jesus labored for a long time in anonymity as a carpenter, Joseph's trade, so as to be firmly anchored in earthly realities. Then, illuminated by his baptism in the Jordan, he left his village to follow the Father's call to reveal his mystery beyond Nazareth, in the vast world in which his prophetic teaching and his witness of love unto the end would engender a multitude of vocations to love.

Every family of married baptized persons lives with Jesus at its heart, in the sight of the Father, and animated by the Spirit of love. Made up of children of God in a divine-human communion, it gives concrete form on the ground to the Church's sacramentality. When

Christian family life is lived well, it embodies a culture of love that takes care of the other person and radiates the Spirit beyond its own limits through its fraternity, hospitality, humanity, and its membership in the ecclesial community. This domestic church signals to society that the future of hope passes through this path of humanization. Is it not an invaluable resource for the missionary future of a synodal Church? This institution is more fragile and vulnerable than in the past, but it embodies Christian mission as a sacramental reality testifying that God is love and that he walks with his people.

The wider communion of vocations to the ordained ministry and the consecrated life makes a vital contribution to the missionary service of the domestic church.[20] Along these lines, I take the liberty of recalling a special manifestation of the Holy Spirit, not so much as Spirit of the Father who animates the ordained ministry or as Spirit of the Son who is the basis of the filial priesthood of baptized persons, but, so to speak, as Holy Spirit *plain and simple*, in other words, according to his personal property distinct from the Father and the Son. This very personal dimension of the Spirit is manifested particularly in the charismatic dimension of the Church, in which it is discernible by its creative and surprising way of manifesting his freedom. In this regard, it is at the origin, for example, of the lists of charisms that we find in the Pauline letters (1 Cor 12; Rom 12), but it animates in particular the whole domain of consecrated life in its many historical forms. The *sequela Christi* [imitation of Christ] according to the evangelical counsels belongs to this creative liberty of the Spirit which adds the plurality and diversity of personal and communitarian charisms to the institutional dimensions of Baptism, Matrimony, and Holy Orders.

This whole charismatic richness is yet to be discovered and appreciated in the Church, for it is a contemporary manifestation of the Holy Spirit in his personal, creative, sanctifying, missionary, and synodal liberty. The synodal transformation that is under way will be fruitful insofar as it acknowledges this charismatic richness which supports the People of God as they tend toward holiness and which awakens among baptized persons, in all states of life, a vocational awareness of ordinary

[20] See Hans Urs von Balthasar, *The Christian State of Life*, trans. Sr. Mary Frances McCarthy (San Francisco: Ignatius Press, 1983).

and extraordinary vocations, of many kinds of missionary vocations that bring the joy of the Gospel to the world.

I am convinced that the "communion of vocations", as the Holy Spirit is promoting it in our days by a spirit of communion in the Church, is a fruitful, transversal formula that is valid for all cultures and all continents. Individualism, indifference, and solitude, which are the common traits of a global culture, gain ground everywhere, even in the Christian milieu, through the influence of the media and fashions. For example, the quest for individual performance in sport or in other fields cannot bring lasting happiness to the young and not-so-young people of this era. The Spirit of Christianity should bring an element of joy, freedom, and even enthusiasm through the Good News of the Trinitarian love that is incarnate in the Church and in our humble fraternal relations. These experiences of fraternal communion at all levels of existence, as modest as they are, support the hope of peoples who face the tragedies of war, poverty, and migrations, with their increasing numbers of innocent victims. In response to these challenges, the Spirit of the Risen Christ stimulates the charity of the members of his Body for a globalization of solidarity on behalf of those who are poorer. A spirituality of missionary communion thus grows in the light of the universal charity that animates all vocations.

"Pray therefore the Lord of the harvest to send out laborers into his harvest" (Mt 9:38). Prayer together is already a "communion of vocations" that attracts others. Moreover, the great missionary challenge of a synodal Church is not so much to be better organized, to be present in the media and the social networks, to raise funds for the Church, even though all that is important; our essential challenge is to form true Christians, missionary disciples as in the early Church, who love one another according to the Spirit of the Gospel. Authentic charity is what makes the difference, both for mission work and for synodality. Mother Teresa and her Missionaries of Charity come from Asia and are spreading on all continents. They are evangelizing the West by their care for the poorest of the poor, in the public squares of our metropolises and in our slums. Several of them have paid with their blood in order to continue their community's service in countries afflicted by terrorism and war. A synodal Church that walks in real solidarity with the poor knows the Spirit of the Beatitudes but also the fruitfulness of the Cross.

The current synodal research is an opportunity that must not be missed; it should change the face of the Church for the better and profitably employ the lively forces that are available for mission work. Without diminishing the importance of the hierarchical principle in the Church, the emergence of the synodal principle supposes a new listening at the grass-roots level, more openness to dialogue and to change, as well as a generous hand outstretched to those men and women who feel excluded. In doing so, it is advisable to be prudent and to use discernment so as to prevent ideologues on the right or the left or the globalization of indifference to turn the pilgrimage of the People of God away toward paths that are contrary to the faith.

Finally, Pope Francis exhorts us not to forget the Marian principle, which he promotes in the same Spirit as the great theologian from Basel, so as to counteract the ideological menace. The Blessed Virgin Mary is more fundamental in the Church than Peter and all those who have been put in charge of ministries; she embraces in her great motherly mantle all the baptized and the ordained ministers, reminding all men and women that the two forms of participation in the one priesthood of Christ are complementary and mutually supportive for the evangelization of the world. Her universal maternal mediation encompasses all the particular mediations that God's grace multiplies in the Church, the "sacrament of salvation",[21] in other words, "sign and instrument" of communion for the salvation of humanity.[22] All these ecclesial principles must be articulated harmoniously in a synodal and missionary communion that is aware that it prolongs sacramentally the divine missions of the Incarnate Word and of the Spirit of love and truth.[23]

The missionary future of a synodal Church is open and promising, despite the clouds that are gathering in the short and middle term over

---

[21] LG, no. 48.

[22] Ibid., no. 1.

[23] The Center for Research and Anthropology of Vocations (CRAV) organized on March 1–2, 2024, a continuation of its theological and pastoral research on vocations with a two-day conference in the Synod Hall at the Vatican on the topic entitled "Man and Woman, Image of God: Toward an Anthropology of Vocations". This event was encouraged by the Holy Father, who agreed to speak at it.

the destiny of humanity. The Church has promises of eternal life from her Founder. "She goes on ahead, walking amid the persecutions of the world and the consolations of God."[24] She is all the more active in sharing the treasure of the Gospel because she received the order to distribute to all comers the heritage of the Word of God and of the Holy Spirit. The divine-human communion that she experiences does not close her in on herself; far from it. It impels her to live by "going out", because this communion is universal in quality and therefore in extension, which means that it must be proclaimed and brought to the ends of the earth, in keeping with the Gospel. Its spread depends on the Holy Spirit and on us, for we are partners in the mission of embodying the Trinitarian love.

"Pray therefore the Lord of the harvest to send out laborers into his harvest" (Mt 9:38). Let us pray for the communion of all baptismal vocations, those to marriage and family, those to the priestly and religious life, those to the lay apostolate in all its forms. Let us not forget, above all, the priesthood of the baptized in their workplace, their social life, their leisure time, in which they incarnate the Spirit of Christ in society. This Christian spirit is a breath of hope that runs through all situations, which attracts and consoles because it gives priority to the poor, to sick and abandoned persons, to migrants and refugees. This fervent practice of charity also includes the struggle against the injustices that are abundant in a world divided between a handful of rich persons who become ever richer and the masses of the poor who become ever poorer. With Pope Francis let us stand up against these scandalous inequalities that put millions of migrants on the roads, exposed to all sorts of abuse, in search of a more dignified life. These facts disturb us and challenge us, because they urge us to fight against evil without neglecting above all to do good. We will be judged on the last day by the love that we have or have not given to those men and women who are in need.

A Christian who regularly receives the Holy Eucharist and thereby is renewed at the source of the Trinitarian communion cannot fail to be interested in the fate of humanity. He is engaged in a marvelous and dramatic planetary covenant that gives him more and more to receive and more and more to distribute to those around him.

---

[24] Augustine, *The City of God*, XVIII, 51, 2.

The communion of vocations nourishes his missionary fervor at this Eucharistic source that contains the center of gravity of all human hopes and of all cultures. Following the example of Pope Francis, let us offer to young people today and to all our contemporaries a perspective on the future that supports their dreams of a more habitable earth and a more fraternal humanity.[25]

---

[25] Francis, post-synodal exhortation *Christus Vivit* (March 25, 2019), no. 299.

Chapter 7

The Reform of the Roman Curia in the Area of the Foundations of Law in the Church

The promulgation of the apostolic constitution *Praedicate Evangelium* on March 19, 2022, confirmed from the juridical perspective several changes that had already been introduced by papal decisions, by motu proprios or otherwise, in the framework of the missionary conversion of the Church that is supposed to serve the great project of Roman Curial reform that has been under way for nine years. Some rejoice in the long-awaited conclusion of the reform, but some express strong reservations following the public presentation of the text of the commission that explained the reasons for some choices. The basic reservation that emerges concerns the decision to integrate laypersons into the governance of the Curia, which would mean settling with a *fait accompli* a long-standing controversy in Church history, namely, whether or not the power of governance is necessarily linked with the Sacrament of Holy Orders. The objection is that the constitution implicitly takes the option of not considering the Sacrament of Holy Orders as the origin of the power of jurisdiction but rather of attributing it exclusively to the *missio canonica* [canonical mission] given by the pope, who as a result would confer a delegation of his own powers to anyone who exercises a governmental function in the Roman Curia, whether he is a cardinal, a bishop, a deacon, or a layman.

Some jurists point out that this position is a Copernican revolution in the governance of the Church that would not be in continuity with, or would even be contrary to, the ecclesiological development

This essay originally appeared as an article in Italian in *L'Osservatore Romano*, July 21, 2022.

of Vatican Council II. The Council, indeed, elaborated the sacramentality of the episcopate and collegiality, without however completely resolving the question about the origin of the *Sacra Potestas* [sacred power]. Experts in canon law have debated for centuries in order to identify the origin of this *Sacra Potestas* which determines the hierarchical structure of the Church and her way of governing the People of God. Is it a question of (immediate) divine will inscribed in the Sacrament of Holy Orders that establishes the powers of sanctifying, teaching, and governing? Or is it rather a question of some (mediate) determination of the Church entrusted to the Successor of Peter by virtue of his mandate as universal pastor with the special assistance of the Holy Spirit?

History furnishes evidence that can be interpreted in favor of either position. The tendency to separate the powers of order and jurisdiction is based on many papal decisions from the past that have endorsed acts of governance without the power of orders, for example, governance by certain abbesses from the medieval era until modern times, certain bishops who governed dioceses without being ordained, or else permission given by the pope to some priests to ordain other priests without being a bishop; we could extend the list of facts that show that the power to govern does not depend intrinsically on the power of order but rather on another source that is then identified as the *missio canonica* conferred by the pope.

The other canonical school (Eugenio Corecco, Munich canonists) interprets some of these facts as borderline cases or aberrations (a nonordained bishop!) and strives to demonstrate the slow realization by the Church of the sacramental nature of the episcopate and of the powers linked with it.[1]—hence the effort that matured at Vatican Council II to declare explicitly that the powers to sanctify, teach, and govern are rooted in the power of order, while leaving open for canonists to discuss the question about the basis for the distinction between the powers or order and of jurisdiction and for their union. Would the new constitution go further than canon 129, §2, which declares: "Lay members of Christ's faithful can cooperate in the exercise of this same power [of governance] in accordance with the law"? How can we reconcile the facts alleged in history with the current

---

[1] *LG*, no. 21.

Code of Canon Law reflecting the new sacramental awareness of the Church? More broadly, how can we explain theologically the foundation of the unity of these two powers while acknowledging that they are distinct and effectively complementary?

If we follow the reasoning by Eugenio Corecco, the position of Father Ghirlanda and of the Jesuit school is positivistic and does not integrate the advances made by Vatican Council II. He argues that the Council affirmed the unity of the *Sacra Potestas* and therefore the sacramental root of the *tria munera* [threefold office]. What then would the canonical mission add to the power of order if the latter already contained the foundation for jurisdiction? The contribution of Klaus Mörsdorf, the great master of the Munich School, is his affirmation that the Sacrament of Holy Orders already confers the foundation of suitability (*l'idonéité*) for the threefold office, even though the canonical mission adds to it effective inclusion in the College of Bishops by means of simultaneous appointment to responsibility for a particular Church. Mörsdorf has reflected, studied, and published more than anyone else on this question which, in his view, deserves special attention in order to avoid schismatic tendencies. He makes sure to distinguish, without separating them, the two powers that are intrinsically bound up with the sacramental identity of the bishop who is tied to a particular community. He acknowledges, however, that as yet there is no multidisciplinary research—historical, dogmatic, sacramental, canonical—to give an account of the foundation of this *Sacra Potestas* which is multiple and yet one.

Without claiming to settle the canonical debate, which has its own methods and criteria, I wonder however about several pneumatological considerations that could help clear the way to resolve this set of problems in light of a Trinitarian and sacramental ecclesiology.

A preliminary remark. We are in the field of law, in other words, of the science about the order that exists or should exist because of the nature of matters of faith. The things under discussion here are the relations between the nature of the Church as a divine-human institution and the structures that enable her to carry out her mission in the service of the world's salvation.

Now the nature of the Church is sacramental; this is the fundamental achievement of the Second Ecumenical Council of the Vatican. Before being a juridical society immersed in the cultures of this world, it is a mystery of communion, a community inhabited and unified by the communion of the Divine Persons.[2] Its internal juridical relations are rooted in the Trinitarian communion, which is given in a participatory way through the sacraments, particularly Baptism, Holy Orders, and the Eucharist.

According to its sacramental nature, ecclesial communion involves a hierarchical dimension that corresponds to the Trinitarian mystery as it was revealed to us. The Father is the source of the Trinitarian processions: one generates the *communio*, the other confirms or regulates it; the two converge on the Father, the *Archè* [principle] of the *communio*.

The hierarchical dimension of ecclesial communion consequently reflects participation in the identity of the Father and of the Son, which the Holy Spirit opens up to the members of the community through faith and Baptism, and also through the sacraments of Holy Orders and the Eucharist. The gift of the Divine Persons to the members of the Mystical Body of Christ through the sacraments establishes new relations between human persons, relations of communion according to a certain order that the Holy Spirit guarantees in various ways according to his own personality as Spirit of the Father and of the Son. Thus, he grants to some the filial identity and attitude that belongs to the baptismal character and to the grace of participating in the divine filiation; to others he grants the paternal identity and attitude that corresponds to the character and the grace of the Sacrament of Holy Orders. The power to teach, to sanctify, and to govern that belongs to the latter group [of ordained Christians] thus deploys the energies of grace, that is, the power of the Holy Spirit in their relations of authority and service with regard to the People of God as a whole and, concretely, in the presence of the community for which they are responsible as ministers.

Does this mean that the power of governance must depend necessarily and exclusively on the power of order? Historical facts deny this. How then can we salvage the sacramental principle at the origin of the power of jurisdiction unless by the detour of the canonical mission that proceeds from the supreme authority of the Church, in other words, a bishop invested with the universal pastorate? The foundation of the inseparable unity between the power of order and

---

[2] *LG*, nos. 1–4.

jurisdiction is the figure of the Successor of Peter as head of the College of Bishops, who possesses in communion with them the maximal
unity of the power of order and jurisdiction, and consequently can
apply their effects in all directions, both in the sacramental domain
and in other juridical or administrative domains. He can also delegate
his power of jurisdiction and thus make members of the People of
God share in it.

Those who tend to separate the two powers harden the distinction between the sacrament and the canonical mission, forgetting that
Holy Orders incorporates a man into the episcopal College, the Head
of which possesses the supreme jurisdiction that extends to all areas of
the Church's life. This is why the power of governance that is attributed to female religious orders and to their authorities is always
formally confirmed and accompanied by the papal authority and
therefore is not exercised independently of the power of order. In
this case, the authority is not exercised by an ordained minister but by
a charismatic figure who is recognized as such and is associated with
the ordained ministry by the hierarchical structure of the Church.

Those who tend to maximize the union of the powers of order
and of jurisdiction for every exercise of the power of governance run
the risk of perpetuating the face of a clerical Church, and as a result
they promote clericalism, to the detriment of the charismatic dimension of the Church, which is now recognized as co-essential alongside the hierarchical power, while being subject to its discernment.[3]
We are still at an initial stage of this recognition which canon law
has not yet integrated and which necessarily has consequences in its
domain following the doctrinal progress officially recognized by the
Congregation for the Doctrine of the Faith. For this purpose I think
it is legitimate to set forth several lines of pneumatological reflections
that might help to untie the knots caused by binary rationales that
lack, it seems, a Trinitarian basis.

For example, while maintaining the principle of the unity and the
distinction between the two powers, which are inseparable for the exercise of the ordained ministry in all its degrees, shouldn't we recognize

---

[3] See Congregation for the Doctrine of the Faith, Letter *Iuvenescit Ecclesia* to the Bishops of
the Catholic Church regarding the Relationship between Hierarchical and Charismatic Gifts
in the Life and Mission of the Church (May 15, 2016) (hereinafter *IE*).

a third power of communion, authority, and service that does not proceed from the Sacrament of Holy Orders as such but rather from the freedom of the Holy Spirit? To express this hypothesis is to take seriously the theological fact that the Father governs his saving plan by means of the two divine missions of the Word and of the Spirit. This third power of governance would be exercised not only by virtue of the authority of the Father and of the Son through the Sacrament of Holy Orders (*Sacra Potestas*), but specifically by virtue of the authority of the Spirit. The latter is never totally independent of the former, since it proceeds from it, but it does however involve its own identity, which can be pinpointed ecclesially; otherwise, we would implicitly deny the proper Personhood of the Holy Spirit. In the life of the Church this authority of the Spirit is manifested in the diversity and the unity of the charisms and is not detached from the ordained ministry, for it seeks its recognition and its confirmation from the latter; it is exercised however by virtue of its own charismatic gift, even in the case where the charismatic community is directed by an ordained minister. This line of reflection ought to advance the theology of the consecrated life and at the same time make it stronger when faced with the acknowledged but limited prerogatives of the ordained ministry. When we think of Francis of Assisi or Mother Teresa, we immediately recognize the imprint of a gift of the Spirit that imposes, as it were, a line of government. The power of jurisdiction in this case is founded on the charism, even though it is authenticated by the pope or an ordained minister.

How can we explore in even greater depth the unity and the distinction between the powers of order and of jurisdiction in their operational deployment as well? Another pneumatological line of reflection would be the Trinitarian nature of ecclesial communion and therefore the participation of the faithful of all categories in the Trinitarian relations. Klaus Mörsdorf approaches this perspective when he distinguishes between the "word" and the "sacrament", and when he seeks to explain the functional diversity of the two powers by means of two principles: the *principium generans* [generative principle] for the Sacrament of Holy Orders and the *principium dirigens* [directive principle] for the canonical mission; these principles complement and strengthen one another. However, he does not seem to manage to distinguish the divine missions of the Word and of the Spirit at the basis of these principles, which act in the sacramental and administrative order of the ecclesial community and become involved in it so as to guarantee its growth and unity.

In fact, the authority of Christ as the Father's representative is communicated to the Church through the Sacrament of Holy Orders so that his filial identity, given to the baptized to share through the Sacrament of Baptism, will be nourished and strengthened by the proclamation of the Word and the mediation of the Holy Spirit, who ensures the "sacramental" communion of the ministers and the faithful. The good order of the "communion" between the two groups is guaranteed by the Spirit, who pours out charity into their hearts, thus perfecting the ecclesial relations that are founded on the structural and sacramental differences between the one group and the other.

The power of order incarnates Christ's authority in the Church, an authority that generates the sacramental life, thus structuring the community and referring all its members to the source of obedience to the Father from whom all paternity derives its name. The power of jurisdiction incarnates the authority of the Holy Spirit, which is in charge of maintaining the order of love in the Church, which presupposes the concrete fulfillment of the commandment of love but also law, discipline, decision, and correction, an authority that refers by itself to the Father of the only Son who is the source of the whole divine plan and of its management until the fullness of the Kingdom.

Engendering eternal life in souls, on the one hand, and on the other hand accompanying this life, protecting it, and making it fruitful, are aspects of the unfolding of the two divine missions of the Word and of the Spirit, which are at the twofold yet single foundation of the *Sacra Potestas*. The latter implies that the Divine Persons themselves are manifested in certain ecclesial subjects equipped with specific powers that can be pinpointed socially. Its efficacy can always be attributed in the first place to the Divine Agent who acts personally according to a twofold modality, Christological and pneumatological, as a power of order that gives divine life or as a power of jurisdiction that ensures the order of love in all the extremely diversified dimensions of the ecclesial communion that is involved in human history—hence the importance of the ministry of Peter, who possesses the unity of this twofold power for the unity of the Church according to the Petrine charism, and hence, too, the charismatic authority, subject to the discernment of the Successor of Peter, while it does not proceed directly from the ordained ministry but from the freedom of the Holy Spirit.

In this light, the apostolic constitution *Praedicate Evangelium* can very well integrate laymen and laywomen, and also men and women religious, in the governance of the Church, without upsetting the hierarchical structure of the Church but by actualizing and balancing it with the help of pneumatology, which unfortunately is all too absent from canonical controversies, whereas it holds the key to a reform of the Church in this hour under the sign of the times: synodality. Providentially a universal pastor who comes from the charismatic domain of the Church could introduce discreetly and peacefully this reform of the ecclesial government that does not relativize the importance of the *Sacra Potestas* but rather integrates it better into the broader framework of the Trinitarian and sacramental ecclesiology of the Second Ecumenical Council of the Vatican. The reservations that have been expressed and the debates currently in progress should make possible a more in-depth, pneumatological investigation that is essential for the continuity and the creativity of the authentic ecclesial tradition.

Chapter 8

Unity and Distinction between the Powers of Order and of Jurisdiction in Exercising the *Sacra Potestas*

How can we justify the participation of laypersons in the exercise of the *Sacra Potestas* belonging to the pope and the bishops? Since 1983, canon law foresees a possibility of laypersons collaborating in a subordinate position,[1] but the recent promulgation of the apostolic constitution *Praedicate Evangelium* on the reform of the Roman Curia broadens this possibility to include the assignment of leading positions in the dicasteries of the Roman Curia.[2] The fact that baptized persons who have not received the Sacrament of Holy Orders are thus associated with the governance (*munus regendi*) of the supreme pontiff has not easily won the approval of a certain fringe of the Curia, as well as other circles beyond. Their reservations stem from the vexed question concerning the origin and articulation of the power of order and of the power of jurisdiction that has stirred up controversy in

---

This essay is based on a lecture given at the symposium "*Triplex munus*. Prêtres, prophètes et rois dans la vie de l'Église", Institut Catholique de Toulouse, France, January 19, 2024.

[1] See can. 129, §1: "Those who are in sacred orders are, in accordance with the provisions of law, capable of the power of governance, which belongs to the Church by divine institution. This power is also called the power of jurisdiction"; can. 129, §2: "Lay members of Christ's faithful can cooperate in the exercise of this same power in accordance with the law."

[2] Francis, Apostolic Constitution on the Roman Curia and Its Service to the Church in the World *Praedicate Evangelium* (March 19, 2022), pt. 2, no. 5 (hereinafter *PE*): "Each curial institution carries out its proper mission by virtue of the power it has received from the Roman Pontiff, in whose name it operates with vicarious power in the exercise of his primatial *munus*. For this reason, any member of the faithful can preside over a Dicastery or Office, depending on the power of governance and the specific competence and function of the Dicastery or Office in question."

the Church since the Middle Ages.[3] Might the pope have tried to settle the question by an arbitrary, partisan decision? Wouldn't this initiative go against the doctrinal development of Vatican Council II concerning the unity of the Sacrament of Holy Orders (*Sacra Potestas*) with its three levels of exercising the powers of teaching, sanctifying, and governing (*tria munera*), in the episcopate and the presbyterate and to a lesser degree in the diaconate? Does this endanger the foundation of the distinction between clergy and laity and the prerogatives of the ecclesial hierarchy? These many questions oblige us to start over in examining the relations between the sacramental and juridical dimensions within the framework of the current search for more synodal structures.

When the document was promulgated, the controversy, which is primarily of interest to canonists, was made known to the general public, too, and theologians had the opportunity to shed some light on it. For my part, I formulated a hypothesis that aims to reconcile the divergent positions about the origin and articulation of the *Sacra Potestas*.[4] Starting from a radically theological perspective, I suggested appealing to the complementary character of the missions of the Word and of the Spirit so as to distinguish and unite the two dimensions of pastoral authority in the Church: the one that comes from the Sacrament of Holy Orders and the one that proceeds from the canonical mission given by the pope. This complementarity, founded on revelation, allows us to explain the relation between the powers of order and of jurisdiction, by distinguishing the Christological aspect of the power of order and the pneumatological aspect of jurisdiction, since the first is manifested as the aspect that generates the life of the sacraments and the second as the aspect of ecclesial authority that regulates the communion.

This theological hypothesis attempts to take into account both poles, without confusing them or separating them as two independent

---

[3] See Riccardo Battochio, "Note storiche e teologiche sul dibattito attorno alla distinzione fra potestas ordinis e potestas iurisdictionis", in Associazione Theologica Italiana, *Autorità e forme di potere nella Chiesa* (Milan: Glossa, 2019), 125–54.

[4] See Marc Cardinal Ouellet, "La riforma della Curia romana nell'ambito dei fondamenti del diritto nella Chiesa", *L'Osservatore Romano*, July 20, 2022, https://www.osservatoreromano .va/it/news/2022-07/quo-164/la-riforma-della-curia-romana-nell-ambito-dei-fondamenti -del-di.html.

powers. For, on the one hand, the canonical approach is conditioned by its historical method and tends to separate the two powers;[5] on the other hand, an overly rigid interpretation of the theological findings of Vatican Council II tends to increase the power of order and to reduce jurisdiction to a purely administrative regulation.[6] The initiative by Pope Frances obliges us go back to the drawing board with the theology of law and the sacramentary so as to find the reasons for an overture that is meant to be synodal and adapted to the changing time in which we live. This search must be at the same time ecumenical and respectful of the Catholic tradition, open to the new promptings of the Spirit and creatively promoting the missionary awareness of the Church.

These parameters require a more in-depth theology of law, which for a long time has been a *desideratum*, particularly at the instigation of Antonio Maria Cardinal Rouco Varela,[7] and which would be less influenced by the heritage of Roman law or by an extrinsicist approach to the relations between nature and grace.[8] In this regard, the famous diagnosis by the Protestant theologian Rudolf Sohm, radically separating the juridical domain from the sacramental

---

[5] See Gianfranco Ghirlanda, "L'origine e l'esercizio della potestà di governo dei vescovi: Una questione di 2000 anni", *Periodica* 106 (2017): 537–631.

[6] See Eugenio Corecco, "Natura e struttura della 'Sacra Potestas' nella dottrina e nel nuovo Codice di diritto canonico", *Communio* 75 (1984): 24–52; Eugenio Corecco, "Nature and Structure of the Sacra Potestas from the Point of View of Doctrine and in the New Code of Canon Law", *Eugenio Corecco*, https://www.eugeniocorecco.ch/scritti/scritti-scientifici /canon-law-and-communio/canon-law-and-communio-10/. For a good overview of Msgr. Corecco's position, see Jacques Bagnous, *Charismes et Mouvements selon Mgr Eugenio Corecco* (Paris: Chora, 2020), 40–42, 61–84.

[7] See Antonio Maria Rouco Varela, "Fundamentacion teologica del Derecho canonico: Nuevas Perspectivas", translated into Spanish from the original German: "Theologische Grundlegung des Kirchenrechts: Neue Perspektiven", *AFKKR* 172 (2003): 23–27. The cardinal encourages the Church "to open up the ecclesial space to the presence and charismatic action of the Holy Spirit for the ordinary and extraordinary paths that He freely chooses in order to lead the Church toward an increasingly vital union with her Lord and Spouse" (p. 15).

[8] See Antonio Maria Rouco Varela, *Teologia e Derecho: Escritos sobre aspectos fundamentales de Derecho Canónico y de las relaciones Iglesia-Estado* (Madrid: Cristiandad, 2003), 262–306. "The internal essence of Canon Law consists fundamentally in the **relatio** produced by interpersonal unions, for which the Church appears at the local level as the true and apostolic *communio* in the Word and the sacrament of Jesus Christ; and at the universal level as the apostolic *communio Ecclesiarum* [communion of Churches] in the same Word and sacrament of Jesus Christ." Ibid., 284 (translated from Spanish).

domain, is unacceptable in Catholic theology. Nevertheless, it provoked an examination of conscience which revealed that the Catholic juridical method suffered to a lesser extent from the same schizophrenia.[9] Vatican Council II played an important role in this theological development, although the 1983 revision of the Code of Canon Law [CIC] did not arrive at a unified, decisive juridical vision, considering the vexed question about the origin and the articulation of the powers of order and jurisdiction.[10] The severe critique by Eugenio Corecco in this regard, however, forgets that the ambiguity of the Code only reflects the state of the controversy, which was not settled by the Council.

The debate remained open, indeed, concerning the central question treated in the *nota praevia* of the dogmatic constitution *Lumen Gentium*, which stipulates that incorporation into the college of the successors of the bishops is effected by episcopal consecration, which gives the power of order "and by hierarchical communion with the head and members of the College", which depends on the canonical mission given by the pope to each ordained man. The specific weight to be assigned to each element is a matter of debate, but both are essential to the constitution of the *Sacra Potestas*: (1) the power of order and (2) jurisdiction, in order to be full-fledged members of the College of Bishops with the corresponding empowerment for the ministerial exercise of the *tria munera* (three-fold office), which is distinguished essentially from the *tria munera* exercised by baptized persons.

In order to make explicit the theological hypothesis formulated earlier concerning the unity and distinction between the powers of order and of jurisdiction, it will be useful first to show how the divine missions are related to the overall sacramental and juridical structure of the Church; second, to set forth the differentiated application of these missions to the specific field of the *Sacra Potestas*; and

---

[9] See ibid., 65–80.

[10] See Corecco, "Natura and Structure of the Sacra Potestas": "In the name of technical and juridical efficiency, inspired by a criterion of modernity, the Code has unfortunately manifested a deplorable theological regression in such a vital ecclesiological sector as the '*potestas*'"; see also "Fondements ecclésiologiques du Code de Droit Canonique", *Concilium* 205 (1986): 19–30. Corecco is right to deplore the absence in the 1983 Code of Canon Law of any reference to the charismatic dimension in the Church.

third, to draw from this several conclusions for the renewed exercise of authority in a more synodal Church.

The Divine Missions of the Word and the Spirit in the Sacramental Structure of the Church

Let us recall at the outset the perspective of Saint Thomas Aquinas, who considers God's action *ad extra* as the prolongation of the processions of the Word and the Spirit, whether in creation, the Incarnation, or else the Church and the sanctification of souls.[11] Extending this theological view, which is based on Sacred Scripture, we can show more precisely the complementarity of the missions of Christ and of the Holy Spirit in the sacramental structure of the Church. Indeed, God the Father gives to the Church his own Son, his Word, with the help of the Holy Spirit, who stirs up faith in him and engenders sons and daughters of God through Baptism—hence the filial and fraternal relations of baptized persons, who are constituted legal subjects by virtue of the sacramental character of Baptism and also by the gifts of grace that are bestowed on them as members of the Body of Christ. Even prior to the relations instituted by the exercise of the *Sacra Potestas*, therefore, there is this fundamental correlation between the Word and faith into which the two Persons and divine missions enter: the first for the objective aspect of the Word and Sacrament, the second for the subjective aspect of faith; without both there is no ecclesial community. This complementarity is revealed by Sacred Scripture, which must be mentioned at least briefly here in order to justify the application to the exercise of the *Sacra Potestas*.

Biblically, it appears that, without being clearly distinguished, the Word and the Spirit work in synergy from the very beginnings, when God creates through his Word (Gen 1), but not without the Spirit, who hovers over the waters accompanying him with his power

---

[11] Thomas Aquinas, *STh* I, q. 44, art. 2, ad 1; q. 45, art. 1; art. 2, ad 1; *Summa Contra Gentiles*, bk. IV, chaps. 1 and 11; *In I. Sent.*, Prologue: "Sicut trames procedit extra alveum fluminis, ita creatura procedit a Deo extra unitatem essentiae, in qua sicut in alveo fluxus personaru continetur." "As a road proceeds alongside a riverbed, so creation proceeds from God outside of His unity of essence, in which the flow of Persons is contained as though in a channel." *Q.D. de Potentia*, q. 2, art. 5, ad 6.

(Gen 1:2). "Even in the Old Testament, once the term 'spirit' has become usual, word and spirit remain fundamentally linked: word is primarily the content and particular application of God's command, and spirit [designates] the divine power with which God executes what He has determined."[12] Without construing inappropriately a doctrine of the Trinity in the Old Covenant, we can still discern some preparation in the events of salvation history from the days of Abraham, Melchizedek, and Moses, as well as in the retrospective and prospective interpretations that the prophets make later on: "In the post-exilic period,... the Spirit is associated with Israel's past or—even more—projected into Israel's messianic future: the king of the end-time will be equipped with all the gifts of the Spirit (Is 11); indeed, the Spirit will be poured out on the entire nation (Joel 3:1–2)."[13]

Notwithstanding certain clues, the personalization of the two missions remains latent and indiscernible; it will be necessary to wait for the personal revelation of the Incarnate Word and of his bond with the Spirit, particularly at his baptism in the Jordan, completed by the testimony of the disciples after the Resurrection, in order to distinguish and unite the two missions. Both are creative, both reveal the divine wisdom, both sanctify the ecclesial community; the two missions accompany and follow one another according to the stages of God's plan. The decisive stage is obviously the Incarnation of the Word in the whole extent of the process that runs from the first instant of the virginal conception until the Resurrection of Christ; the Holy Spirit then takes charge and continues the incarnation of the Trinitarian love by imprinting upon it his own modality of "communion"; this causes the Church to emerge in her sacramental and nuptial nature, along with her hierarchical structure and her synodal dynamic that is animated by the charisms. This is an initial, very succinct insight into the articulation of the two missions, whose complementarity must be made explicit in the Church.

I introduce into this framework a special consideration about the figure of the Virgin Mary, who is the theological locus par excellence of this synergy and this complementarity of the missions of the Word and the Holy Spirit. For in her, the Servant of the Word, the Spirit

---

[12] Hans Urs von Balthasar, *Theo-Logic*, vol. 3, *The Spirit of Truth*, trans. Graham Harrison (San Francisco: Ignatius Press, 2005), 63.

[13] Ibid., 64.

brings about subjective adherence to the Word, who takes flesh of her flesh. The Virgin Mary thus acquires a "supra-sacramental" status, so to speak, because of the Word of God, who becomes incarnate in her womb through the working of the Holy Spirit; *he was conceived by the Holy Spirit.* In her the two aspects of the Word and the sacrament are combined in the unity of her response in the Spirit, which simultaneously brings about the Incarnation of the Word and the nuptial and maternal existence of the Church. When Hans Urs von Balthasar speaks about the Marian principle that prevails over the Petrine principle in the Church, he takes as his point of departure this *fiat* of the Virgin Mary in the Holy Spirit which accompanies faith in the Word and the sacramental life everywhere in the Church; by this permanent *fiat*, the Virgin Mary envelops the whole sacramentality of the Church, including the dimensions of the hierarchical ministry.

The two missions are reciprocally immanent (i.e., mutually inclusive); however, this does not prevent us from distinguishing them and seeing their operative functionality in the foundation of the Church and the constitution of the structures of the new People of God on their pilgrimage toward the Kingdom. The one Mediator of salvation gives a glimpse of the eschatological horizon by his preaching about the Kingdom of God, which becomes plain at the moment of his Pasch, but the Spirit is the one who will introduce the disciples into this fullness: "I will ask the Father, and he will give you another Counselor, to be with you for ever" (Jn 14:16); "When the Spirit of truth comes, he will guide you into all the truth" (16:13). The latter "will not speak on his own authority, but whatever he hears he will speak.... He will glorify me, for he will take what is mine and declare it to you" (16:13–14)—hence the radical continuity between the mission of the Word and that of the Spirit by virtue of the Trinitarian logic: "All that the Father has is mine; therefore I said that he will take what is mine and declare it to you" (16:15). Being the interpreter of the Son, as the Son interprets the Father,[14] the Spirit will not lack originality in his mission, since he will crown the order of

---

[14] Ibid., 70: "If, in Johannine terms, truth means the 'making known' (1:18) of God (the Father) by the incarnate Son, then he who makes this truth known can rightly be called the 'Spirit of truth' (14:17; 15:26; 16:13), at various levels: he utters the truth and can 'witness' to it because he knows it; and he knows it because he is internal to it, that is, internal to the relationship between the Father (who allows himself to be made known) and the Son (who makes him known)."

love in the economy of salvation as he eternally crowns the glory of the love between the Father and the Son in the Holy Trinity.[15] He will be the final Agent, the Defender, the Master of the work of Trinitarian communion in the Church-sacrament.

His appearance on the scene according to his own hypostasis coincides with the Resurrection of Christ, who confirms the victory of the Trinitarian love over sin and death. For through his power, the Father raises up the Christ from among the dead in response to his loving obedience unto death (Rom 1:4). The Holy Spirit then brings to a successful conclusion the mission of Christ the Redeemer, making it visible and operative through the sacraments for the benefit of all humanity. He therefore prolongs the economy of the Incarnation according to a new, properly pneumatological modality, a communional modality, under the sacramental form of the Church, the Body and Bride of Christ—hence the axiom formulated earlier that the Church's communion is the Incarnation continued in a sacramental-pneumatological modality.

This ecclesiological view is not new; it can be identified with the school of Johann Adam Möhler (1796–1838) and with the encyclical *Mystici Corporis* (1943), but the pneumatological accent is new. It proceeds from the Trinitarian, paschal, and nuptial logic that emanates from the Resurrection of Christ. Indeed, that is the moment when the Holy Spirit ties all the mysteries together: the Trinitarian gift of the Spirit confirms that Christ is the Son of the Eternal Father, who truly fulfilled the New Covenant in his blood, that he is therefore fully established as the eschatological Bridegroom whose fertility engenders the Church-Bride; from there the Holy Spirit, who is received from the Father, is poured out as the Spirit of the New Covenant, the Spirit of peace, truth, reconciliation, and communion, a nuptial Spirit who is diffused from the Eucharistic gift of Christ the Bridegroom. This is where the hierarchical structure of the Church is born from the authority of the Spirit of the Father, who raises up Christ and confers on him all power in heaven and on earth: "Receive the Holy Spirit. . . . Forgive the sins of any" (Jn 20:22–23). This Trinitarian, paschal, and nuptial articulation constitutes the sacramental

---

[15] Ibid., 74: "We must always remember that the Spirit is simultaneously the (objective) attesting of this love between Father and Son (as the third Person, dogma would say) *and* the inner fruit of this reciprocal (subjective) love; thus he can be called the Spirit of love of the Father and of the Son (cf. Rom 8:9)."

framework and the heart of the Spirit's mission in the Church, where he must bring to completion the incarnation of Trinitarian love— hence the summary formula that designates the Church's communion as the pneumatological modality of the Incarnation.

For the Incarnation that prolongs Christ's humanity presupposes a bodily, visible continuity but also a new modality that corresponds to the Holy Spirit's property of being a Person-communion.[16] This is accomplished in the highest degree in the relation of the Eucharist to the Church in which the Bridegroom and the Bride commune in the same divine life through the twofold epiclesis over the offerings and over the community. The Spirit constitutes the Church by prolonging what he did in Mary: the Incarnation of the Body after that of the Head. He joins the glorified humanity of Christ the Bridegroom with the redeemed humanity of the Church, his Bride. This begins at Baptism and continues with all the other sacraments, which are wedded to the stages and conditions of human life following Christ. It should be noted that the sacramental order is fundamentally Christological, for the Spirit develops all that comes from him, including the *ex opere operato* dimension of Christ's sacramental acts; he manifests himself, however, by a new dimension of sacramental efficacy *ex opere operantis*, which emanates from the communion and is expressed by charity, witness, authority, charisms, apostolate, etc. From the beginning of *Lumen Gentium*, Vatican Council II brought out this new paradigm of sacramentality based on the communion that radiates from the loving response of the Bride to the Bridegroom, the sacramentality of holiness. In short, the Holy Spirit inaugurates this new sacramental paradigm of communion that takes up and crowns the efficacy of the Word and of the sacraments in the overall sacramentality of the ecclesial communion as participation in the Trinitarian communion.[17]

---

[16] Saint Thomas does not use these terms, but he does set up road markers concerning the Holy Spirit that point in this direction. See Jean-Pierre Torrell, "Yves Congar et l'ecclésiologie de Saint Thomas d'Aquin", *Revue des Sciences Philosophiques et Théologiques* 82, no. 2 (April–June 1998): 213–18. Torrell comments: "We must insist more on the second divine mission, that of the Spirit, for from it the work of the Incarnate Word preserves today its salutary efficacy for eternal life" (p. 213).

[17] Balthasar, *Theo-Logic*, 3:357–58: "If Church can be defined as *communio*, her 'constitutive elements' must be 'totally immanent in each other' in such a way that they 'cannot be separated from one another....' It is this reciprocal immanence of elements, themselves structurally distinct and unconfused, that makes Christ's Church a reflection of the Trinity; thus, too, it renders the operation of the Holy Spirit in her a valid and salvific interpretation of the unity

One immediate consequence of the sacramental incarnation of the ecclesial communion is that Christ's priestly, prophetic, and royal mediation is made universal. This mediation is conferred on baptized persons first, who become the *subjects* of it, then on those who are called and graced with specific charisms, who become the *ministers* of it. Thus, the prophetic, royal, and cultic mission of the priestly people is carried out with the help of all the baptized and the ordained ministers, a differentiated, sacramental, and existential participation in the one priesthood of Christ the Priest, Prophet, and King. In specifying the essential difference and the articulation of this exercise, we must never lose sight of the primordial importance of the existential participation of the baptized, which during the time of the economy of salvation had the ministerial participation at its service.[18] This presupposes a fundamental perspective that highlights the relation between the exercise of the threefold office by the baptized and the exercise of these *tria munera* by those who through their reception of the Sacrament of Holy Orders are holders of the *Sacra Potestas*. A question like this requires an adequate explanation of the arrangement of the divine missions of the Word and of the Spirit in the hierarchical communion of the Church with the help of the new pneumatological paradigm applied to the sacramentary and to Church law.

Divine Missions and *Sacra Potestas*

To speak about law and sacraments in ecclesiology nowadays is to invoke the fundamental distinction established by Klaus Mörsdorf between *Word* and *sacrament* as fundamental elements of the ecclesial identity that are reflected in the binomial order-jurisdiction.[19] The juridical structure of the Church is distinguished from civil societies

---

and distinction between the Father and his incarnate Son, in which God shows his nature as love, and love is manifested as the 'law of grace.' "

[18] See Marc Cardinal Ouellet, ed., *A Fundamental Theology of the Priesthood*, 2 vols. (Mahwah, N.J.: Paulist Press, 2023). The main task of the Roman Symposium in February 2022 was to articulate this complementarity of the two participations in the one priesthood of Christ.

[19] See Arturo Cattaneo, "La complementarità di ordine e giurisdizione nella dottrina di Klaus Mörsdorf", *Cuadernos doctorales* 1 (1983): 383–438, esp. p. 403: "The resulting difference finds its most significant expression in the duality of the ecclesiastical hierarchy. Power of jurisdiction and power of order correspond to Word and Sacrament."

by its foundation, the Word of God in Christ, who calls us to faith and who, according to the economy of the Incarnation, takes concrete form in the sacrament—hence the Christian initiation structured by the sacraments of Baptism, Confirmation, and Eucharist, which incorporate the baptized person into the Body of Christ and configure the person as a member who is ontologically incorporated into Christ the Priest, Prophet, and King, and therefore qualified to participate in divine worship, prophetic witness, and the royal service of charity in all areas of human, apostolic, or professional activity. This basic structure of the Church is completed by the hierarchical principle which is constituted by the Sacrament of Holy Orders according to its three degrees—episcopate, presbyterate, and diaconate—which manifests the duality of the *power of order* accompanied by *jurisdiction* as a complementary and irreducible determination of the *Sacra Potestas*.

The scholar from Munich (i.e., Mörsdorf) by his positive studies in history identified two characteristics that make explicit the distinction between the word and the sacrament at the level of the *Sacra Potestas*; on the one hand, to use his terminology, it concerns a *potestas generans* (generative power) that corresponds to the sacrament, the essential function of which is to constitute Christian or ministerial identity; and, on the other hand, it is about a *potestas dirigens* [directive power] corresponding to the authority who directs and therefore determines the exercise and the concrete modalities of mission in the case of ordained ministers. Therefore, it is a question of a complementary regulative word (*dictio*) that is not on the same order as the sacramental word yet has a real effect on the juridical level.[20] Mörsdorf failed only to identify the theological root of these two inseparable and irreducible principles of the *Sacra Potestas*: the synergy of the Persons and missions of the Word and the Spirit, who can give a better account of the operational unity and irreducible distinction of these two powers at the heart of the *Sacra Potestas*.

Vatican Council II did not broach the question about the origin of the *Sacra Potestas* and of the unity of its two dimensions, sacramental and jurisdictional. It upheld the two elements, sacramental and extra-sacramental, in treating the question about membership in the

---

[20] Ibid., 401–3. "The power of order as a vital principle of the Church needs the regulative hand that can order [i.e., arrange] its growth", citing Mörsdorf at note 62, p. 401.

College of Bishops without further defining one element in relation to the other. This work is left to the theologians. The explanatory hypothesis of the missions of the Word and the Spirit, the Father's two hands (Irenaeus), considers the power of order as the Christological dimension and jurisdiction as the pneumatological dimension. This hypothesis confirms each of the dimensions as being irreducible to the other and invites us to consider them in a way that is more theological than historical, ecumenical, or political. This means explaining the difference and the unity between them by the divine missions, their specificity, and their mutual relations, as we did earlier, and also by their ability to resolve some conundrums.

Now, theoretical positions in ecclesiology range from an affirmation that these powers are separate and complementary, to the tendency to relativize as much as possible the power of jurisdiction in favor of the power of order. This second tendency identifies with Vatican Council II and its unified vision of the Sacrament of Holy Orders, acknowledging the full sacramentality of the episcopate. In the final analysis, jurisdiction then would be an administrative coordination with no possible comparison to the sacramental power, for the latter comes immediately from God (divine law), whereas the jurisdiction granted by the pope has only the weight of a human mediation (ecclesial law), although it is recognized that it has the assistance of the Holy Spirit. For some thinkers, this latter approach justifies the demand for decentralization vis-à-vis the Roman Curia in the name of the power of order, a sacramental power that jurisdiction cannot annul even though it can suspend the exercise thereof. Such decentralization supposedly would stimulate the identity of the local churches and their own initiatives, thus promoting their synodal and missionary dynamism. Let us note this thesis without however addressing the question about its merits.

The famous *nota praevia* at the end of the constitution *Lumen Gentium* maintains that, in addition to the power of order, hierarchical communion with the head of the College and its members is an essential element for full membership in the College of the successors of the Apostles. Of these two elements, we must acknowledge the preponderance of episcopal consecration on the basis of the order of the Trinitarian processions, with the Christological dimension (divine law) preceding the pneumatological dimension (ecclesial law); however, we must not exaggerate the difference, because the pneumatological element is also divinely ordained, which suggests that we should not degrade jurisdiction (ecclesial law) to the level of mere human administration with the help of the Holy Spirit. The two powers are derived from the same divine source insofar as the action of the Word and the action of the Spirit are of the same nature while having differentiated institutional particularities. Due to the influence of civil law on canon law and the lack of a sacramental vision of the Church as communion, the exercise of ecclesial authority was depreciated and eventually modeled on the standards of civil society.

The principle of sacramentality as a pneumatological modality of the Incarnation, expounded earlier, obliges us therefore to make a more nuanced contrast between divine law and ecclesial law, because both come from the divine will and the second builds up in a special way the ecclesial communion that is the purpose of the complementary missions of Christ and the Spirit. Consequently, let us admit humbly that ignorance of the pneumatological dimension of ecclesial law diminished our appreciation and exercise of the ordained ministry and exposed it to the logic of civil authority. We claim to avoid this in theory, but we are still dependent on it in practice, for lack of an adequate theological vision of pastoral authority.

Therefore, we must rethink the distinction of powers in a way that recognizes that the canonical mission, the regulation of the exercise of the power of order, is not just an administrative appendix to episcopal consecration—we say this in all respect for the primacy of the Christological dimension but without forgetting the pneumatological dimension that is closely associated with it. Otherwise, we would have to say that the Risen Christ is sufficient to found the sacramental order and that the Holy Spirit has a role that is only subaltern, if not fleeting. Whereas in fact the glorified Christ acts through his Spirit in the Word, the sacraments, the law, and all the spheres of the Church's life. The most obvious example is the Eucharistic transubstantiation, which is an act of Christ carried out by the Spirit, in perfect harmony. By giving himself up even to death for love of his Church, Christ left room for the Holy Spirit and abandoned himself to him in a kenotic-eucharistic mode for what was to happen next. The Spirit reciprocated by raising him from the dead and by integrating his entire work with its specific causality in his own mission of sanctification and of bringing about the Kingdom of the Trinitarian communion in the Church.[21] Thus, the close and complex collaboration of the two divine missions achieves the fundamental purpose of the sacraments in general and of the *Sacra Potestas* in particular: the sacramental participation of the *ecclesial communion* and of the *communion of churches* in the Trinitarian communion with very important input from the *canonical mission* at all levels, while dependent on the fullness of the Petrine charism.

This pneumatological sacramental participation is manifested at the level of action among the baptized with their *tria munera* which are exercised according to the filial grace of their common priesthood, whereas the *tria munera* are exercised also at another essentially different level by the ordained ministers according to the paternal grace of their hierarchical priesthood.[22] The Council explains that the two forms of the one priesthood of Christ are ordered to each other and that the ministerial priesthood (*Sacra Potestas*) is at the service of the priesthood of the baptized. This confirms from a different perspective the fact that the Christological sacramental dimension has its ultimate purpose in the pneumatological dimension of communion. This articulation is already present at Baptism, which is completed by Confirmation. It fits also into the configuration of the *Sacra Potestas* with the twofold powers of order and of jurisdiction, which complete the overall sacramental structuring of the Church-communion as a "sign and instrument" of the Trinitarian communion that is shared with humanity as a gift. It should be noted once again, however, that Christ's redemptive work is confirmed, achieved, and crowned by this communion in the Holy Spirit, who glorifies the Father and the Son.

This pneumatological kind of juridical-sacramental perspective should be understood as being beyond the logic of *ex opere operantis* and on this side of the logic of *ex opere operato* in the Christological

---

[21] See Jn 16:14: "He will take what is mine and declare it to you." The Spirit can dispose of Christ's goods and show their actual relevance for all generations of believers precisely because he is the agent of the Resurrection, in other words, of the exaltation of Christ at the right hand of the Father with his whole glorified life.

[22] See Marc Cardinal Ouellet, "The Holy Spirit and the Priesthood of Christ in the Church", in *Fundamental Theology of the Priesthood*, 1:113–37.

dimension. For these common categories do not quite express the rich nuances of pneumatological sacramentality, which include the factor of human freedom and therefore the limits resulting from sin and resistance to grace. The Holy Spirit, poured out into hearts by grace and conferred on ministers as a charism of authority, carries out his work of unification and communion by liberating and respecting human freedom, which is fallible and sometimes rebellious. This is true at all levels of the Church's life, from the chief pastor to the least of the laity. Therefore, it is necessary to acknowledge that the exercise of the pastoral authority of the supreme pontiff over the whole Church far surpasses the level of mere "sacramentals" and is registered in the sacramental sphere of communion under the prompting of the Holy Spirit for the unity of the Church. By virtue of his Petrine charism, which gives him a universal and immediate jurisdiction over the whole Church, the pope performs acts of discernment and makes decisions under this sacramental prompting of the Holy Spirit which builds up the missionary communion of the Church *ex opere operantis* but with a valence that is increased by the importance of his responsibility and his charism. This does not mean a discount sacramentality compared with the efficacy of Christ's sacramental gestures but rather a sacramentality of another order, of a nuptial sort, founded on the Person-communion of the Spirit, the model for which is not the minister's act *ex opere operato* but rather the Marian *fiat* prolonged in every act of faith and of ecclesial obedience.

Upon reflection, we must acknowledge that the sacramentality of the ecclesial communion still remains to be discovered because of the ditch that has been dug between the sacramental dimension and the juridical dimension of the Church. Since we have confined sacramentality to the Christological dimension of the seven sacraments and reduced the exercise of doctrinal or pastoral authority to the administrative level, we do not have the resources and the adequate categories with which to articulate the sacramentality of the ecclesial communion. For that, a pneumatological approach is necessary that structures the ecclesial communion in terms of the bond between the Eucharist and the Church. Indeed, the Church's sacramentality lives on the Eucharistic communion and effectively radiates into the world through fraternal charity and missionary zeal. From the very first lines of the dogmatic constitution *Lumen Gentium*, Vatican II pointed out this sacramental and missionary horizon of the Church-communion as Church-sacrament, "sign and instrument" of communion with God and of the unity of the human race.

In this pneumatological sacramental perspective, the *ecclesial communion* founded upon Baptism and the Eucharist, and enlarged and amplified by the *communion of bishops*, leads finally to the universal sacramental importance of the *communion of churches*. The Spirit of the Father is conferred to the minister of Christ, the Head and Bridegroom, qualifying him to build up the communion of churches starting with the upbuilding of his own Church, in hierarchical communion with all the other bishops, *cum et sub Petro* (with and under Peter)—hence the peaceful, evangelical witness of the Church, which in all the dimensions of her being, her juridical structure, and her mission is inhabited by the Spirit of the Trinitarian communion. To acknowledge in this way the pneumatic and pneumatological dimension of the Church is to think in terms of the efficacy and authority of the communion and not only in terms of the efficacy of certain juridical acts, like those of a worldly power. The crisis of the hierarchical ministry obliges us to overcome a worldly vision of power that obscures the sacramental dimension by counting more on constraint than communion. Forgetfulness of the Holy Spirit has caused the exercise of authority in the Church to drift toward worldly ways of thinking, whether political, ethnic, or cultural—hence the abuses of power, the negative public image, and the difficulty of developing a mystique of service as a nuptial kind of pastoral charity, according to the Spirit of the Covenant between God and his people. It is to be hoped that Pope Francis' call to synodal conversion will open up the pneumatolocial path of communion, which will give rise to the welcoming and integration of charisms, and consequently an increased participation and a renewed practice of pastoral authority.

A New Sacramental and Juridical Paradigm for a Synodal Church

The thesis of a new paradigm starts with the nature of the Church, when it is finally grasped in its sacramental specificity as a missionary communion. The *Christo-monistic* model (Congar) that predominated for centuries causes the hierarchical institution to prevail, to the detriment of the mysteric and dynamic character of the People of God, thus obscuring in a way their participation in the Trinitarian communion in the Holy Spirit, which is the new emphasis and the Copernican revolution of the Council.

Along this line of communion, it is certainly necessary to affirm the power of order as the element that determines membership in the College of Bishops. It is significant that the ordination of a bishop normally requires at least three bishops as a sign of the College into which the sacrament incorporates the recipient. It is the decisive, Christological element; although when the head of the College determines the concrete place and manner of exercising the new authority, this adds an essential dimension at the functional level. Theology does not offer a ready-made solution for the canonical adjustments that will be necessary for this pneumatological integration of the *Sacra Potestas*, but it does furnish a foundation that is capable of calming the controversy, because it is in keeping with the doctrinal development of Vatican Council II and springs directly from the mystery of the Church as Body and Bride of Christ.

What are the advantages of this pneumatological vision for the exercise of the bishop's *tria munera*? On the one hand, the affirmation of the primacy of the power of order reinforces the element of universality of his membership in the College of Bishops, which as a result increases his sense of responsibility for the Universal Church *cum et sub Petro*; on the other hand, the pneumatological sacramental dimension of the *canonical mission* conferred by the supreme pontiff reinforces his organic tie to the local Church that is entrusted to his care, which strengthens his creativity and fatherhood. The ecclesial communion is thus fortified horizontally and vertically, which awakens the dynamism of the charisms and promotes the growth of the missionary and synodal subjectivity of the local Church. The baptized are stimulated by it in the exercise of their *tria munera*, which unfold at their level and in their filial and fraternal style, in a Spirit of ecumenical openness and universal fraternity. In this way the ecclesial communion grows in quality and in extension, stimulated by the missionary awareness of the faithful and of their pastors both at the level of worship in spirit and in truth (*leiturgia*), and also at the level of the witness given to the truth (*martyria*) and at the level of the royal service of charity and peace (*diakonia*).

How are these considerations pertinent with regard to the conundrums in the history of the *munus regendi* (office of governing) in the Church? Do they have sufficient practical relevance to settle the controversy about the origin and the articulation of the power of order and of jurisdiction? Are they sufficiently coherent and pertinent to integrate the coessentiality of the charismatic dimension into the missionary development of a synodal Church and to stimulate the co-responsibility of the laity for it?

First of all, the theological approach consolidates the distinction and the operative unity of the *Sacra Potestas*, without unduly favoring one aspect at the expense of the other. This means a twofold power in the sense of an ability to act, but the two powers are different and complementary in nature: the power of order generates life; the power of jurisdiction regulates the order of love in the missionary community that is the Church.[23] It has been proved historically that this distinction is here to last; attempts to reduce the importance of one aspect or the other on the historical level have failed. The most recent reform of the Roman Curia by Pope Francis confirmed its importance by opening up the possibility of a layman becoming prefect of a Roman dicastery, thus taking up a practical position in favor of the possibility of a certain extra-sacramental origin of the power of jurisdiction, while leaving the theological question open.[24] We have attempted to discuss it in greater depth by appealing to a broader sacramentality that integrates the sacraments into an overall pneumatological vision of sacramentality. Moreover, the points for reflection that we have provided concerning the divine missions, their manner of acting and cooperating in the implementation of the Father's plan, lead to a better understanding of the sacramental structure of the Church and of the unified and differentiated exercise of the *Sacra Potestas*.

---

[23] See Balthasar, *Theo-Logic*, 3:354–55: "[The law of the Church] is the only guarantee that the Church cannot and must not be anything other than the community of that love which is shown to us in Christ and given to us in the Holy Spirit."

[24] See Sergio F. Aumenta and Roberto Interlandi, "La Curia romana secondo *Praedicate Evangelium*: Tra storia e riforma", *Subsidia Canonica* 40 (2023): 61: "This, however, must not lead us to conclude that Pope Francis wanted to settle once and for all the vexed question of the origin of the power of governance, which remains open to this day."

This still does not resolve all the conundrums, but a pathway is now open to completing, if not reforming, the canonical methodology whose habits of thinking are more characteristic of civil law and historical cultures than of the newness of grace and pneumatology. The divine missions of the Word and of the Spirit are acknowledged right away and affirmed in the birth, the constitution, and the mission of the Church with her sacramental and canonical dimension. But in practice, pneumatology has often been forgotten, even in Christology and in the domain of grace, and so it is not surprising that it has been neglected even more in canon law. This is not a question of appealing to the Holy Spirit as a *Deus ex machina* who resolves enigmas; his role cannot be arbitrary or interpreted artificially under pressure from cultural movements or new ministerial needs; it must be registered with all theological rigor in the economy of the Incarnation and as an integral part of the mysteric nature of the Church—hence his specific contribution that emanates from his *tropos hyparxeos* (way of subsisting) in the Trinitarian communion, a Person-communion who operates at the level of being and of acting in a way that justifies the hierarchical and missionary articulation of the Church-communion.

Having thus identified more precisely the theological origin of the *munus regendi* in the mission of the Holy Spirit that constitutes a new sacramental order including the Christological sacramental order, the way is now clear to develop the charismatic dimension of the Church, land that has been lying fallow, if not awaiting delivery in the tradition, because of the unilateral development of the institutional Christological dimension. Admitting in principle the pneumatological origin of the *munus regendi* sets free the reception and recognition of the charisms and paves the way for a better integration of their multiple and varied gifts into the development of communion and mission. For these charisms proceed from the generosity of the Holy Spirit ("the wind blows where it wills"), and it is consistent that the discernment of charisms and the management of their integration should be guaranteed by a function of the hierarchy that emanates from a specific assistance of the Holy Spirit. Having acknowledged a charism capable of participating in the *munus regendi*, the ecclesial authority respects its value and proper authority and determines its place and mode of service to the common good of the community.[25] In general, this jurisdictional dimension of the discernment of charisms gets too little attention from pastors because of a lack of sensitivity to communion and insufficient attention to the presence and the concrete manifestations of the Holy Spirit in the community.

We would have to add a whole chapter on the coessentiality of the charismatic dimension as a counterweight and complement to the hierarchical dimension of the Church, because history reveals not only a distrust and a dismissal of charismatic developments but also a strict discipline and a certain monopoly of the ecclesial institution at the expense of Christian freedom and missionary creativity. The charismatic dimension has fortunately flourished in the area of consecrated life; its contribution to communion and to the Church's mission was effectively coessential in fact before being recognized now on the doctrinal level.[26] This is a late acknowledgment, which speaks volumes about how slowly human beings perceive the signs of the Spirit and reform themselves radically along the lines of synodality. This means listening not only to the faithful at the grass-roots level but also to those men and women who receive particular charisms for the good of the community. This means furthermore accepting the fact that the integration of these charisms modifies the dynamic of ecclesial relations and thus the exercise of the *Sacra Potestas*, opening up larger spaces of consultation and participation in decisions that concern the community as a whole.

By way of example, the concrete situations of the Christian communities in the Amazon, where the shortage of priests limits their sacramental life, demand a new appreciation of the charisms that the Holy Spirit offers to the community. Deacons, catechists, leaders of base communities, men or women who organize prayer groups and

[25] In this light we understand the decisions by Pope Francis to entrust top-level responsibilities to laypersons or women religious who are endowed with a special charism for the direction of a particular dicastery of the Roman Curia. Moreover, some charisms offer a foundation for a subordinate but real exercise of authority. Recall the example of the major religious orders in the Church that are governed by the authority of their charism.

[26] See *IE*. See also Hans Urs von Balthasar, *Theo-Logic*, 3:356: "This charism, too, since it is given by God, has a specific right to pursue its own task—once it has been tested by the appropriate Church authority. We see this in the great charisms of the religious orders and in the influence of particular saints in whom the Spirit shines forth. It shows how the Spirit's operation in the Church transcends the 'legal' division into clergy and laity."

the many charitable services to the sick, the poorest of the poor, the victims of exploitation—a whole series of witnesses to the faith in a wide variety of areas could receive a certain ecclesial recognition of their role with the corresponding mission to organize the community. This already exists and could be intensified in collaboration with itinerant pastors, whether the latter are priests or deacons of a diocese or else members of missionary teams that are duly recognized in that territory. Creative arrangements based on the real co-responsibility of the laity and the recognition of charisms could arouse a new movement of evangelization that is less dependent on presbyteral resources alone. The paradigm shift inspired by a pneumatological approach gives priority to the service of charity and of the Word, which involves first the baptismal resources of the community, which the Eucharist then comes to crown at more distant intervals according to the availability of the ministers.

Frequency of the Eucharist does not automatically create an evangelizing dynamism in the community, as we see in our secularized societies where what makes the difference is not primarily the possibility of the Eucharist but rather the faith experience and a passion for fraternal communion. The faith is transmitted more by personal witness than by institutional channels, even if they are liturgical. Communities with a shortage of priests demonstrate this and should make us more sensitive to the real dynamics of evangelization, which proceed above all from the quality of the disciples even more than from the multiplication of the ministers. The future of the synodal Church ought to be built more on the basis of the baptismal and charismatic dimension that is well integrated into the organic communion of the various members of the ecclesial Body, animated by the Holy Spirit. Please God that such an orientation might create by itself, through an outpouring of the Holy Spirit, a new springtime of religious and ministerial vocations!

We started from a theological hypothesis in order to reconcile the contrasting positions concerning the unity and the distinction between the powers of order and of jurisdiction in the history of the *Sacra Potestas*. The solution proposed in order to resolve the controversy obliged us to modify the frame of reference of the sacramentary by prolonging the Christological vision of the sacraments in general, and of the power of order in particular, toward a pneumatological vision of the Church's sacramentality. In doing so we followed the Trinitarian logic of the divine missions of the Word and of the Spirit, whose common and differentiated action, in the mystery of the Incarnation and of the Church, communicates to humanity a real participation in the communion of the Divine Persons. The Christological dimension of the seven sacraments thus leads ultimately to the pneumatological dimension of the Church-communion, which becomes the fundamental category of the sacramentary. We are talking about a new paradigm that appreciates the efficacy and the finality of the sacraments for the purpose of ecclesial and missionary communion. This leads, incidentally, to a better understanding of the major axes of the action of Pope Francis: the importance of universal fraternity, the communion of churches, global solidarity for our common household and peace, the powerful attraction of the saints for the efficacy of evangelization.

Within this ecclesiological perspective that emerged from Vatican Council II, it becomes possible to show the unity and the distinction between the powers of order and of jurisdiction, thanks to pneumatology, which enables us in the first place to bring together the sacramental and juridical dimensions that for too long have been separated and considered heterogeneous. This emerges, obviously, from the exercise of the *Sacra Potestas* by the supreme pontiff, which enables us to see that his "administrative" decisions, with their multiple juridical consequences, proceed from a fullness of the Holy Spirit that is given to him by the Petrine charism, in order to serve the unity of the Church as the supreme pastor in all the areas pertaining to this unity.[27] The fullness of the power of order that he possesses as head of the College of Bishops is prolonged by a plenary power of jurisdiction that comes not from an analogy with earthly authorities but rather from the sacramentality of the Holy Spirit, the purpose of which is communion according to the proper nature and mission of this Divine Person who is involved in all the dimensions and structures of the Church.

The principal advantage of this pneumatological approach to sacramentality is the revalorization of the pastoral ministry *ex opere*

---

[27] Think of all that it means for the Petrine ministry to convoke a council or a synod, to write an encyclical, to intervene in season and out of season in problems and dramatic situations, etc.

operato by the fruitfulness *ex opere operantis* of the ecclesial relations of communion that emanate from a sacramental vision *sui generis* of the *munus regendi*. Moreover, in this expanded framework of pneumatological sacramentality, the domain of the charisms receives not only a right of citizenship but also a grateful and enthusiastic openness according to the Spirit of communion and mission. As a result, finally, the exercise of the *Sacra Potestas* will certainly be facilitated by the addition of new resources and by a renewed esteem for the hierarchical communion of the Church, even if the cost is a synodal conversion that presupposes authentic listening to the Holy Spirit at the grass roots, a sharing of decisions and responsibilities, a greater Spirit of love and service. I believe more firmly now that the stakes are high: the Church's mission in our time passes by way of this change of sacramental and synodal paradigm.

Part III

Charism

Chapter 9

The Spirit and the Bride Say "Come!"

The Spirit and the Bride say, "Come." And let him who hears say, "Come." And let him who is thirsty come, let him who desires take the water of life without price.

—Revelation 22:17

Dear friends: bishops, priests, and deacons,

I bless the Lord for having gathered us once again during the paschal season, after the great encounter at the Chrism Mass that allowed us to renew our promises of fidelity to Christ the Shepherd and to his Church. In this paschal season, which is rich in hope because of Christ's Resurrection, I am happy to greet you with the traditional formula that is customary in many churches: "Christ is risen, Alleluia!" "Yes, he is truly risen, Alleluia! Alleluia!"

During the first assembly of the clergy in which I participated last year, I shared with you some reflections on the priesthood in a message in which I expressed my wishes for the Church of Quebec that the Lord is calling me to love and to serve. I would like to prolong the reflection on one way of spiritual and pastoral sharing, guided by the Lord's words to his Apostles: "No longer do I call you servants;... but I have called you friends, for all that I have heard from my Father I have made known to you" (Jn 15:15). The friendship of the Lord that unites us as brothers in the priesthood presupposes shared trust and

This essay is based on a conference given at the Annual Assembly of the Clergy in Quebec, May 19, 2004.

closeness. May the Holy Spirit help us to make progress in this friend-ship which builds up the Church by the unity of the *presbyterium*.

The theme of the Paschal Mystery that we have chosen for today repeats in a way the reflection begun at the celebration of my cardi-nalate in Saint Roch: *Starting anew in Christ*, which is the great theme proposed by John Paul II at the beginning of the third millennium in *Novo Millennio Ineunte*. I will not address this theme academically but rather in terms of our pastoral life and our spirituality as ordained ministers in the service of the People of God. I will call your attention in passing, however, to several suggestive passages from the encycli-cal *Ecclesia de Eucharistia* and from the apostolic exhortation *Pastores Gregis*, about the bishop, the servant of the Gospel of Jesus Christ for the hope of the world. These teachings help us to think and to live as Church, in a spirit of ongoing formation for a new evangelization.

Maranatha

"The Spirit and the Bride say, 'Come.' And let him who hears say, 'Come.'" This verse from the Book of Revelation that I have selected as a motto neatly explains the paschal dynamic that we are experienc-ing, which is in the first place the object of a desire and a prayer on our part. Together with the Spirit and the Bride we implore the Lord of history, the One who lives on our paths, to come and consum-mate his work: "*Maranatha!* Come, Lord Jesus! May Your Kingdom come!" We ask less for his "return" than for his "coming", because "return" rather suggests the earthly Jesus, whereas the coming of his Kingdom accentuates more the newness of the Lord. Together in the love that unites the Spirit and the Bride, we therefore beg the Risen Christ to give us a new inspiration and fresh hope. Who does not need this in order to confront the challenges of the present hour?

For my part, I found valuable help and encouragement in the recent teachings of the Holy Father John Paul II on the Eucharist and the bishop, servant of hope. Besides nourishing my spirituality as a friend of the Bridegroom by his developments in nuptial ecclesiol-ogy, the Holy Father never ceases to amaze me and to edify me by his personal dedication to the ministry, despite his declining health and the fact that he has passed his eighty-fourth birthday. What a witness for the whole world! What a consolation for elderly persons! What an example for us!

He writes: "Each Bishop is configured to Christ in order to love the Church with the love of Christ the Bridegroom, and in order to be in the Church a minister of her unity, enabling her to become 'a people gathered by the unity of the Father, of the Son and of the Holy Spirit.'"[1] I recall two features of this text, which neatly portrays the bishop's ministry of unity: its Trinitarian foundation and its nuptial symbolism. These two fundamental features can nourish our spirituality of communion, both at the level of the ecclesial community as a whole and also at the level of the *presbyterium*, which is a particular structure of communion at the service of the whole.

Then, I was thrilled to see confirmed in the document the idea proposed last year that the Sacrament of Holy Orders refers to the mystery of the Father and to his sacramental presence in the Church. The Church lives on the living, active presence of the Divine Persons, who give her a share in their communion in Christ. For the bishop, who is an image of the Father, a sacramental mystery like this involves imitating the Good Shepherd, the Bridegroom of the Church, who gives his life for his sheep, drawing after him all the faithful, and in the lead the priest, consecrated persons, deacons, and the many men and women who labor for the Gospel. For all of them the bishop is, after God's image, "father and mother", the document tells us, perhaps recalling John Paul I, who had dared to express himself this way in speaking about God.

Priests participate abundantly in this spiritual fatherhood, at their subordinate level but quite truly, when they joyfully accept the holiness of their state of life by praying to the Spirit, whom they received at their ordination. This year I had the great joy of ordaining three priests—two religious and one diocesan—and also three deacons who will soon be diocesan priests for the service of our Church. Three permanent deacons also are added to this fine harvest that revives our hope. We thank God for this blessing; we pray and we ask others to pray for new vocations to the diaconate and the priesthood. "In

---

[1] John Paul II, Post-Synodal Apostolic Exhortation on the Bishop, Servant of the Gospel of Jesus Christ, for the Hope of the World *Pastores Gregis* (October 16, 2003), no. 13 (hereinafter *PG*).

raising this prayer to the Father of lights, from whom comes every good endowment and every perfect gift (cf. James 1:17), the Church believes that she will be heard, for she prays in union with Christ her Head and Spouse, who takes up this plea of his Bride and joins it to that of his own redemptive sacrifice."[2]

At the Heart of the Paschal Mystery

In order to deepen our own spirituality of communion at the source of the Paschal Mystery, let us follow the example of Moses, which John Paul II reminded us of by inviting us to enter "the dark yet luminous cloud of the mystery of the Father, Son and Holy Spirit".[3] Like Moses courageously leading his people and guiding them through the Red Sea, the bishop and the priest are pastors of a pilgrim people, by being interpreters of the Word of God for them and mediators of the Covenant. They are ministers of Christ, the New Moses, who fulfills all the prefigurations of the Old Covenant in his own Paschal Mystery.

At the heart of this mystery, God the Bridegroom, who aspires to the loving response of his Bride, inaugurates a New Covenant in Jesus, the Paschal Lamb who was sacrificed. This wedding of the Lamb, celebrated between heaven and earth on the glorious Cross, displays the totality of God's gift with the initial response of the Church, who in the Spirit becomes Body of Christ and Bride of the Risen Lord. Even though the Church's communion with Christ the Bridegroom still remains imperfect, it is no less real and definitively established, to the point where it founds a radically new lifestyle. Consecrated persons and ordained ministers, indeed, witness by their life to this eschatological newness that is already present and active at the heart of the vicissitudes of human history. The Holy Father writes, "In the reality of the Church and the world today, the witness of chaste love is, on the one hand, a form of spiritual therapy for humanity and, on the other, a form of protest against the idolatry of instinct."[4]

---

[2] John Paul II, Encyclical Letter on the Eucharist in Its Relationship to the Church *Ecclesia de Eucharistia* (April 17, 2003), no. 43.

[3] *PG*, no. 12.

[4] Ibid., no. 21.

Although they are aging, the religious communities that I have had the good fortune to visit are still vibrant at the mention of this nuptial mystery that is the foundation of their happiness and their commitment in the Church. Nowhere have I heard the prayer of the Spirit united so intensely with that of the Bride for the eschatological coming of the Kingdom. The Church of Quebec can count on this wealth of praise, adoration, and supplication, which corresponds to the ministry of the priests and supports my hope. The Paschal Mystery shines through these testimonies of prayer, suffering, and joy. Let us not forget, dear friends, to acknowledge openly and to proclaim proudly the extraordinary contribution made by these women and, in particular, by female and male religious communities to the development of the spiritual and cultural patrimony of our people. Our blessed founders and our blessed foundresses have not ceased to build up the future by means of our spiritual, liturgical, and cultural memory.

At the Inspiration of the Spirit

This effort to remember is not a nostalgic retreat into the past. It is a form of obedience to the Spirit that is a memory of the origins resolutely oriented toward the future, by plans aiming to meet the young generations. How can we fail to mention here the 19th World Youth Day, on Palm Sunday 2004, which confirmed the fruitful insights of our youth ministry with the enthusiastic participation of more than six hundred young people? What an extraordinary moment of fraternity and creativity! Do you know what these young people remembered as being most significant when they evaluated the day? Their personal encounter with the priest during the communal celebration of forgiveness with individual confession and absolution. This experience of grace touched the young people, who then went out into the streets, happy to declare their faith and to celebrate it enthusiastically at the Palm Sunday Eucharist in the cathedral.

A rejuvenating wind is blowing on our Church, which inspires new initiatives at several levels, which I cannot describe in detail, although I notice them here and there while making pastoral visits. Some old movements are being renewed, the Movement of Christian

Workers has just held here a very important international assembly; catechetical experiments are multiplying; volunteers persevere in their apostolate despite a certain age-related shortness of breath and the difficult situation of workers and families. As pastors on the ground, you encourage the celebration of anniversaries of parishes and communities; you support charitable activities and sacramental initiations, of which you are the artisans. All this deserves to be emphasized here: the intense and not always easy work of the pastoral teams, with fewer resources and on more extensive territories, thanks to the invaluable aid of the episcopal vicars and the regional teams, which are effectively coordinated by the director of pastoral care and the moderator of the archdiocesan Curia.

I observed the evangelical fruitfulness of the *Brebis de Jésus* [Jesus' Sheep] who are developing an excellent formula for catechization that is very much at home here. I rejoice over the fresh start that we gave to the Institute on the Family by the appointment of two competent persons who are renewing the partnership of the archdiocese with this highly meritorious institute at the service of the family. Several important developments can be foreseen in this area, and also in denominational religious instruction in the schools, which we still need for the basic religious instruction of the great majority of families in Quebec. What memories I have of the meeting of families at [the parish of] Christ-Roi de Lévis (nine hundred people!), which gave me a glimpse of what is perhaps the most promising development of our long-term pastoral programs.

As the first pastor of the archdiocese, I plan to offer, starting in September, several regularly scheduled hours when I will be available at the cathedral to anyone who comes, without appointment, for a brief personal meeting, counseling, an opportunity to confide, and even for sacramental confession. This initiative is meant to express a desire for direct contact with all the faithful and especially with the poor, who desire to confide something to their pastor or to receive from him a word of encouragement, a blessing, or even individual absolution. These symbolic moments of meeting with the bishop will be seconded by other ministers at set, regularly scheduled hours, so as to take another step toward improving communication and a renewed appreciation of the Sacrament of Reconciliation in its ordinary form.

The paschal experience has a glorious side that revives hope, but it also involves a sorrowful side; pastoral visits sometimes enable me to put my finger on it. For example, preparations to close the church in Bienville on the southern bank [of the St. Lawrence River], several weeks before Easter, allowed me to share in the pain of a community on the point of losing the use of their parish church. I felt, during a Sunday Mass, the sorrowful sacrifice of this community, which from now on will have to combine with other assemblies in the area. Moments like these make you realize the human and spiritual identity of a parish. A Christian community is not an anonymous crowd; it bears a name and has a history, and both deserve respect.

This pain made me share your sufferings and stirred me more deeply by your invaluable friendship at the major turning points of pastoral life. Despite the difficulties connected with pastoral rearrangements and the changes of mentality demanded by new catechetical approaches, you willingly accept the necessary adaptations, notwithstanding the aging of the volunteers and the decline of their health. I must salute you for your generosity at work and your openness to an in-depth rethinking of the place and role of parish structures in the Church's mission.

The Paschal Witness of the Presbyterium

I just mentioned a few salient facts among so many others in the life of the archdiocese that have nourished and stimulated my hope and my pastoral charity, and that of my immediate collaborators, I think: the auxiliary bishops, the episcopal vicars, and the priests, assisted by the deacons. I feel that it is my duty in charity to thank you all for the loyal, generous collaboration that you offer to a young bishop who is still an apprentice and grappling with multiple challenges. The Paschal Mystery of Christ thus runs through the network of our presbyteral and pastoral relations in the service of the Church. We are presently living through a particularly significant moment in this regard. The rich episcopal tradition of the Archdiocese of Quebec continues to provide bishops for other dioceses.

Dear friends, I no longer call you servants; I call you my friends, because all that I learned from my Father I have made known to you. The Paschal Mystery of Christ still contains many mysterious sides, in the inner recesses of our lives, which we could share. The preceding reflections revealed some very fragmentary aspects of my first year and a half of pastoral experience in Quebec; I gave a more detailed account of it elsewhere. You can tell that this effort of communication with you and with the faithful, despite my limitations and my mistakes, is meant to serve the new evangelization and the friendship with the Lord that unites us in one and the same pastoral mission. Faced with the current challenges, we sometimes feel weary and in danger of throwing in the towel. I too experience the same feelings and the same temptations. This is why I invite you to pray for me and for one another so that we might all live up to our call to holiness.

The apostolic exhortation *Pastores Gregis* insistently recommends that the bishop be faithful to his personal apostolic prayer, to the Liturgy of the Hours, which is a song that the Bride addresses to the Bridegroom, to the exemplary practice of the evangelical counsels, which are "a reflection of the life of the Trinity in every believer".[5] Could you please help me, dear friends, by your prayer and by the example of your virtues, to be the holy pastor who reflects the face of Christ for the whole people, "the face of poverty, meekness and the thirst for righteousness; the merciful face of the Father and of the peaceful and peacegiving man; the pure face of one who constantly looks to God alone."[6] For my part, I pledge to support you as well as I can with God's grace.

By way of conclusion, allow me to tell you again the joy it gives me to be the friend of the Bridegroom and your friend by the grace of God. The nuptial ecclesiology of the Holy Father seems to me to complement very well the pre- and postconciliar ecclesiology of the Body of Christ and the People of God. The developments along these lines in *Pastores Gregis* bring out the reciprocity of the Church-Bride with regard to Christ her Bridegroom, which is a better foundation for the man-woman partnership in the Church and for the vocational fruitfulness of gratuitous love, which remains an enchanting sign in

[5] *PG*, no. 18.
[6] Ibid.

a disenchanted world. May we find takers and caretakers [*preneurs et entrepreneurs*] of a culture of vocations for the renewal of Christian communities in the service of our society. *Duc in altum!* [Put out into the deep water!]

The Spirit and the Bride say, "Come." And let him who hears say, "Come." And let him who is thirsty come, let him who desires take the water of life without price.

Chapter 10

The Beauty of Being Christian

The word *beauty* spontaneously evokes a landscape, a work of art, an athletic feat, a loving gesture, or else other symbols that attract and move the heart and the energies of men. "Beauty is what pleases and attracts", Plato once wrote. Beauty evokes harmony, singularity, and even uniqueness, and at the same time it implies diversity because you cannot appreciate the uniqueness of a gesture or of a work except in terms of a whole in which this gesture or this work detaches itself and stands out with the character of a splendid exception, in a word, a miracle. Think of Michelangelo's *Pietà* or the Jupiter Symphony by Mozart.

The beauty of the loving relation between a mother and her child stands out against the background of multiple social relations of exchange, sharing, and service that do not have the intimacy, the permanence, and the intensity of the mother-child relationship. The same goes for a wedding, which despite the increasing difficulties in our times remains one of the most beautiful symbols of human life, both by the loving relationship that it presupposes and by the meaning of life that it celebrates. God makes preferential use of it to express his covenantal mystery with the creation that has come from his hands.

At the theological level, the perception of beauty (glory) depends on divine revelation and conditions that it sets and presupposes in order to be grasped by the human mind. Hans Urs von Balthasar thinks that the manifestation of God in history appears in its absolute specificity precisely from the perspective of beauty. God's action

This essay is based on a conference given at a meeting of the ecclesial movements and new communities at the request of the Pontifical Council for the Laity, 2006.

directed toward mankind in Christ, he writes, "is credible only as love—specifically as God's own love, the manifestation of which is the glory of God"; Christianity, in its reflection on itself, "can be interpreted . . . solely in terms of the self-glorification of divine love".[1]

The conditions for perceiving this love require, in the language of Saint Thomas, a certain connaturality between subject and object. In order to perceive the divine love in its specific glory, more is needed than the natural capacity to admire the beauty of things, of works of art, or of human relations. It takes a gift of the Holy Spirit that arouses faith in a human being, the faith of the Church, a divine and catholic faith. A faith that is not merely the assent of the mind to abstract truths or an emotional surge of pure trust in the mystery. A Christological faith that participates in Jesus' way of seeing, in his fundamental attitude of accepting the Father's will and obeying in love to the end. Such a faith is not acquired by imitation but by the gratuitous communication of the Holy Spirit. It is a gift springing from the beauty of Christ, from his Resurrection from the dead.

For Christ's Resurrection is the splendor of the Trinitarian glory. It testifies to an excess of love at the heart of the Trinity that bursts into history. Responding to the gift of the Father, who engenders his Son and hands him over by love, and to the gift of the Son in return, the Holy Spirit causes the glory of God to manifest itself as absolute love and to shine in the flesh of Christ. The radiance of this glory on the face of Christ announces at the same time the success of the Covenant between God and man, the birth of the Church as Bride and Body of Christ, and her evangelizing mission that embraces the whole universe.

They assigned me the topic of *the beauty of being Christians*, in the plural, because the Christian identity is never purely individual; it always implies others, since we are created and re-created in Jesus Christ, in the image and likeness of the Triune God. This theme is fascinating but rarely discussed and formidable, because people traditionally prefer to present Christianity from the perspective of truth and goodness rather than from that of beauty. I could not address it without introducing it, as I just did, by mentioning at least the glory of God manifested in the Resurrection of Christ.

---

[1] Hans Urs von Balthasar, *Love Alone Is Credible* (San Francisco: Ignatius Press, 2004), 10.

But is esthetics really a fruitful approach for the Church today? Kierkegaard warned against the superficiality of the *esthetic* stage of life, the stage of the dilettante who does not commit himself personally in a deep and lasting way. In some aspects, might not contemporary Christianity, detached from its life-giving roots, run the risk of remaining stuck in the past, a cultural residue from another era? Does beauty have enough weight to start up the work of evangelization again in a world that is thirsting for values but has turned away from God, assuming that it knows him although in fact it is ignorant of his Word and his face? I ask this question as a challenge that confronts us all and brings into play not only a social commitment to a cause but a dramatic response of the whole person and of the whole Church to the absolute love manifested in Jesus Christ.

I venture to say, however, as a hypothesis or a bet, that the path of beauty, understood in this radical sense, seems to be the one taken by the ecclesial movements and the new communities. At the start of the third millennium are we not called to set out again from the beauty of Christ? Don't we owe our verve and our attractiveness to a new perception of Christ's beauty? Following the example of Saint Francis in the Middle Ages, who set about repairing the beauty of the Church after his encounter with the Crucified Lord in San Damiano! I am very honored and deeply grateful to have the opportunity to participate in this congress. May it mark a new stage in the growth of the ecclesial movements and the new communities in the service of the Church's mission.

Is the Beauty of the Church a Program?

From the outset I would say that the theme of beauty, the framework for the reflection of this assembly, is valid as a recapitulation and a program, all the more so because it was taken from the first homily of our beloved Holy Father Benedict XVI.

Validity as a recapitulation because it presupposes the findings brought to light during his magisterial intervention at the 1998 Congress. His theological lesson on the charisms in tradition served then to situate more accurately the movements and the new communities and to gain universal recognition for their identity and their original contribution. The road signs that he set up are still of capital importance in bringing to fruition the reform and the current renewal in the Church along the conciliar lines of a "hermeneutic of continuity".[2]

In his first encyclical, Benedict XVI chose to count on beauty by discussing the harmony between divine love and human love. The very positive response that he received indicates the pertinence of his choice, which intends "to call forth in the world renewed energy and commitment in the human response to God's love".[3] We are therefore urged by him to live under the banner of the beauty of love and to communicate the joy of believing that fills us. But we should not call that a program, because it has to do with a grace, the grace of holiness. The Holy Spirit gives it to whomever he wants, and he does not refuse it to someone who humbly prays for it every day.

To Behold and to Be Delighted by the Face of Jesus Christ

Hans Urs von Balthasar meditated at length on Christian revelation from the perspective of beauty. His theological esthetics in seven volumes was written while in Rome the Fathers of Vatican Council II were experiencing the great Pentecost that he called *the council of the Holy Spirit*. Balthasar chose to envisage Christian revelation from this angle, with the firm conviction that the perspective of glory (the theological name of beauty) is the most comprehensive and makes it possible to show the originality and the attractiveness of the Christian experience: "Whoever sneers at her name," he writes, "as if she were the ornament of a bourgeois past—whether he admits it or not—can no longer pray and soon will no longer be able to love."[4]

His central insight is summed up in the little book entitled *Love Alone Is Credible*, in which he shows how the path of beauty meets the deepest aspirations of the human heart, while aiming, beyond

[2] *SaC*, note 6, and Benedict XVI, Address to the General Assembly of the Italian Episcopal Conference (May 24, 2012). Cf. Benedict XVI, Address to the Roman Curia (December 22, 2005), where the pope comments about a "hermeneutic of discontinuity and rupture", as well as the "hermeneutic of reform".

[3] Benedict XVI, encyclical *Deus Caritas Est* (December 25, 2005), no. 1.

[4] Hans Urs von Balthasar, *The Glory of the Lord*, vol. 1, *Seeing the Form*, trans. Erasmo Leiva-Merikakis, 2nd ed. (San Francisco: Ignatius Press, 2009), 18.

its emotional and rational needs, at the deepest dimension of being in which the person responds to the call of gratuitous love manifested in Jesus Christ. Let us follow him along this path, starting with two other preliminary considerations, one of a methodological sort, and the other of a historical sort, in order to situate our argument within the current context of secularized cultures. Von Balthasar introduces his aesthetic method as follows: "If all beauty is objectively located at the intersection of two moments which Thomas calls species and lumen ('form' and 'splendour'), then the encounter of these is characterized by the two moments of beholding and of being enraptured."[5]

To behold the figure of God's glory on the face of Christ and to be delighted by its brilliance to the point of going out of oneself, of being dispossessed and enlisted in the service of the Trinitarian love in the Church—this, in a few words, is the Christian experience of beauty, which consists in a perception and a delight springing from a genuine personal encounter. As Benedict XVI writes in his first encyclical, "Being Christian is not the result of an ethical choice or a lofty idea, but the encounter with an event, a person, which gives life a new horizon and a decisive direction."[6] This fundamental statement, in the very first paragraph, gives his encyclical an orientation that is resolutely esthetic in the strongest theological sense, which invites us first to adoration, but also includes the total gift of self in imitation of Christ, the *diakonia* that can go to the point of *martyria*.[7]

Today it is urgent to explore this path of beauty, because the perspective of truth and goodness is less agreeable and less vital to contemporary man, who is imbued with skepticism and relativism. Indeed, it seems to him, rightly or wrongly, that the affirmation of the truth historically gave rise to intolerance and that the imposition of a universal moral good is incompatible with his freedom. The harmony between truth, goodness, and freedom is disrupted, and it is

---

[5] Balthasar, *Glory of the Lord*, 1:10.

[6] *DCE*, no. 1.

[7] See ibid., no. 25: "The Church's deepest nature is expressed in her three-fold responsibility: of proclaiming the word of God (*kerygma-martyria*), celebrating the sacraments (*leitourgia*), and exercising the ministry of charity (*diakonia*).... For the Church, charity is not a kind of welfare activity which could equally well be left to others, but is a part of her nature, an indispensable expression of her very being."

the task of Christians today to restore this harmony, starting with the living encounter with Christ, which awakens the person's heart and gives meaning to his life by opening him to all of reality.[8]

The most serious problem affecting secularized cultures is the narcissistic turning in on oneself that vitiates authentic human relations and pollutes the general atmosphere of society. It is enough to note, for example, the disintegration of customs, morals, and laws concerning the family to estimate the social and cultural consequences of breaking the living relation with the God of Jesus Christ.

This brings me to another consideration of a historical sort, so as to approach the topic of the beauty of being Christians starting from their condition in the world. This condition is dramatic; it involves a never-ending struggle with the spirit of the world. The *Letter to Diognetus* describes it for us in a way that has lost none of its relevance. Externally, the condition of Christians is identical to that of their contemporaries, but interiorly they often find themselves in a situation of tensions and conflicts with the surrounding world:

> Christians love all men, but all men persecute them. Condemned because they are not understood, they are put to death, but raised to life again. They live in poverty, but enrich many; they are totally destitute, but possess an abundance of everything. They suffer dishonor, but that is their glory.... (Christians) live in the flesh, but they are not governed by the desires of the flesh.... The Christian is to the world what the soul is to the body.... Christians love those who hate them just as the soul loves the body and all its members despite the body's hatred.[9]

And the author concludes with a statement that sums everything up: "God has assigned them this illustrious position, which it were unlawful for them to forsake."[10]

Having thus cleared the ground a bit, let us come now to the heart of the subject, to the heart of the beauty of being Christians, in the plural, while being aware that this plural is not opposed to

---

[8] This is the set of problems analyzed by the encyclical *Veritatis Splendor* (August 6, 1993) by John Paul II.

[9] "The Christians in the World: From a Letter to Diognetus", Holy See, https://www.vatican.va/spirit/documents/spirit_20010522_diogneto_en.html.

[10] Ibid.

uniqueness, because the divine love that shines on the face of Christ and of the Christians who are his disciples makes each one unique and original. It awakens the *I* of every man and every woman in his or her most personal and freest dimension.

Let us say even more. The uniqueness of Christianity in comparison to any other religion consists of the paradoxical fact that in a way it makes each person's *I* absolute by relativizing it, that is, by making it fully relational. Let me explain. The Trinitarian image of God in man, already perceptible in natural family relations, calls persons in communion to an ever-greater mutual donation. This mutual love tends to cause person and love, self-gift and self-realization to coincide to the maximum extent—a Trinitarian *noblesse oblige!*[11] The *I* is found by being lost in the *we*, where it rediscovers itself in a more substantial form than by itself. Ask people who are in love what they feel when they are compelled to separate and to renounce an impossible love. They prefer death. Tristan and Isolde, Romeo and Juliet are famous expressions of this.

Let us return, however, to the heart of the matter. It has a proper name, a name that is singular but at the same time universal, a name to which Christians individually and as a group are indebted. A name venerated by other religions who also aspire to a fullness that we Christians are happy to call Grace and are conscious of doing so: Full of graces!

The Woman Filled with Graces

"From generation to generation," Benedict XVI writes,

> the wonder evoked by this ineffable mystery [of the Incarnation] never ceases. St. Augustine imagines a dialogue between himself and the Angel of the Annunciation, in which he asks: "Tell me, O Angel, why did this happen in Mary?" The answer, says the Messenger, is contained in the very words of the greeting: "Hail, full of grace" (cf. Augustine, *Sermon* 291, 6). In fact, the Angel, "appearing to her," does not call her by her earthly name, Mary, but by her divine name, as she

[11] See Marc Ouellet, *Divine Resemblance: Toward a Trinitarian Anthropology of the Family*, trans. Philip Milligan and Linda M. Cicone (Grand Rapids, Mich.: Eerdmans, 2006).

has always been seen and characterized by God: "Full of grace—*gratia plena*," which in the original Greek is *kecharitomenè*, "having been fully graced," and the grace is none other than the love of God; thus, in the end, we can translate this word: "beloved" of God (cf. Lk 1:28). Origen observes that no such title had ever been given to a human being, and that it is unparalleled in all of Sacred Scripture (cf. Origen, *In Lucam* VI, 7). It is a title expressed in passive form, but this "passivity" of Mary, who has always been and is for ever "loved" by the Lord, implies her free consent, her personal and original response: in *being loved*, in receiving the gift of God, Mary is fully *active*, because she accepts with personal generosity the wave of God's love poured out upon her. In this too, she is the perfect disciple of her Son, who realizes the fullness of his freedom and thus exercises the freedom through obedience to the Father.[12]

Next, mentioning the Letter to the Hebrews, the pope highlights the beauty of the spousal structure of the New Covenant: "When Christ came into the world, he said ...: 'Here I am, I have come to do your will, O God' (Heb 10:5–7). Before the mystery of these two 'Here I am' statements, the 'Here I am' of the Son and the 'Here I am' of the Mother, each of which is reflected in the other, forming a single *Amen* to God's loving will, we are filled with wonder and thanksgiving, and we bow down in adoration."[13]

Kecharitomenè in Greek, *Gratia plena* in Latin: The Woman Filled with Graces. Why did we choose this name as central to our approach? Because in it we find the beauty of "the whole in the fragment", to repeat another title by the great Swiss scholar. The whole, that is, God, the Church, humanity, the family, in a woman preserved from all original sin, perfectly transparent to the divine love, crowned with stars in the midst of the pains of giving birth to eternal life in us. A woman, Mary of Nazareth, Mother of God and Mother of the Church, who lives in us, her children, and pours out on us her incomparable beauty.

Mary's beauty, the beauty of being Christians in unity with her, for what she possesses as a unique privilege she distributes to us

---

[12] Benedict XVI, Homily at the Ordinary Public Consistory for the Creation of New Cardinals (March 25, 2006).

[13] Ibid.

entirely by her perfect correspondence to the Trinitarian Spirit dwelling within her. The Holy Spirit is, in God, the glory of love (Saint Gregory of Nyssa). He gives himself in a self-effacing way between the Father and the Son in order to glorify their mutual love. Thus Mary, the Daughter of Zion, lives in the unity of the Church, in perichoresis with the People of God, since she was elevated to her status as Bride of the Lamb by her standing at the foot of the Cross. Mary then communed profoundly in the night of faith, in the abandonment of the Son of God, thus becoming associated to his abandonment and therefore fruitful in him and through him, bringing forth all the graces that proceed from the Cross and are poured out upon souls.

The beauty of being Christians in the plural thus passes from her into us by osmosis, less by imitation than by childbirth, for the reproductions of her Christian beauty (which we are) are such through her efficacious mediation, which is the work of the Holy Spirit. This unique experience of Mary, an archetypical experience,[14] is the living response of her Immaculate Heart to the grace of love for God: "The response of the 'Bride', who in grace calls out, 'Come!' (Rev 22:17) and, 'Let it be to me according to your word' (Lk 1:38), who 'carries within the seed of God' and therefore 'does not sin' (1 Jn 3:9), but 'kept all of these things, pondering them in her heart' (Lk 2:19, 51). She, the pure one, is 'placed, blameless and glorious' (Eph 5:26–27; 2 Cor 11:2) before him, by the blood of God's love, as the 'handmaid' (Lk 1:38), as the 'lowly servant' (Lk 1:48), and thus as the paradigm of the loving faith that accepts all things (Lk 1:45; 11:28) and 'looks to him in reverent modesty, submissive before him' (Eph 5:24, 33; Col 3:18)."[15]

Mary's immaculate, unlimited *fiat* accompanied the event of the total Incarnation of the Son of God, in other words, all his mysteries from his conception, birth, Passion, and death to his Resurrection, his gift of the Holy Spirit, and finally his Eucharist, which

---

[14] The notion of archetypical experience is developed at length by Balthasar in *The Glory of the Lord*, 1:293–355; it implies the idea of model but also that of mediation: "The archetype, by its very nature, has a maternal form and under its 'protective mantle' it embraces the progeny that will imitate it" (ibid., 1:332).

[15] Hans Urs von Balthasar, *Love Alone Is Credible*, trans. D. C. Schindler (San Francisco: Ignatius Press, 2004), 77–78.

engenders his ecclesial body. The *Woman filled with graces*, the pure and fruitful Virgin, is made passively available and actively offered by the prevenient action of the Holy Spirit, who makes his divine fruitfulness pass from Christ into her and from her into us. In all these mysteries which she weds and ponders in her heart, Mary is "expropriated ... for the benefit of all", "Mary's whole experience ... is an experience for others—for all.... 'Behold, there is your son!'"[16]

The Church's Beauty—Communion, Fullness of Humanity

Over the centuries, the Christian experience of beauty has been expressed in countless works of art, whether architectural, pictorial, or musical, but it has been embodied above all in prayer and action, through gestures, ways of life, personal and communitarian vocations, in a word in the Church-communion, whose mission is to witness to the hope that dwells within it. The martyrs and saints give this witness by their fidelity to the original, archetypical form of testimony in the Church.[17] This original form is Trinitarian, Christological, and Marian: "By this my Father is glorified, that you bear much fruit, and so prove to be my disciples. As the Father has loved me, so have I loved you; abide in my love" (Jn 15:8–9).

Three complementary moments in Mary's life show this form in action and the nuptial paradigm that characterizes the relations between God and his people: (1) the fact of being loved and of accepting the divine will; (2) the experience of fruitfulness in the Holy Spirit; (3) active accompaniment of the Incarnate Word throughout his earthly trajectory and his heavenly life. The saints reproduce in a way this model that illumines the whole life of the People of God and shows the impact of faith on the meaning and beauty of human existence.

---

[16] Balthasar, *The Glory of the Lord*, 1:332.

[17] Balthasar, *Love Alone Is Credible*, 75–82. He explains in this way "The conditions for man's perception of divine love: (1) the Church as the spotless Bride in her core, (2) Mary, the Mother-Bride, as the locus, at the heart of the Church, where the fiat of the response and reception is real, (3) the Bible, which as spirit (-witness) can be nothing other than the Word of God bound together in an indissoluble unity with the response of faith" (pp. 78–79).

Communion in the mysteries of the Incarnate Word, indeed, sheds a decisive light on the beauty and joy of human existence—God at the heart of human life, the light of love that confirms and fulfills the humanity of man and woman, after the example of the Holy Family in Nazareth. What good news for our world, which is on the path of dehumanization! How beautiful it is to respond to the call of love in every state of life and thus to be fully human! How beautiful it is to love in a Christian way without turning in on oneself, to study, to work, to marry, to give oneself to God in the priesthood and the consecrated life, to devote oneself to the poor, the sick, the afflicted. Saint Gianna Beretta Molla confided to her husband, while paging through a magazine about beautiful, fashionable clothing, shortly before her final sacrifice, that she wanted a pretty dress, if, however, she survived her ordeal. The saints are close to the little things in life. The mystery of the Incarnation protects them from esoteric spiritualities. For all realities of human life are illuminated, nourished, and transformed by the presence of Jesus in our midst and by the splendor of his Eucharistic mystery: God with us, the Bridegroom who comes to consecrate all human reality and to gather all in the unity of one Body and one Spirit.

One of the tasks of the ecclesial movements and the new communities present right now in the world and in the Church is to educate: to educate people to an authentically human life; to educate them to a fullness of humanity that begins with the family, which involves integral respect for the human person and solidarity with all humanity, which is saved in Jesus Christ. How many lay saints, saintly couples, and saintly families are required for this great mission!

Beauty to Be Restored: Christian Unity

The Apostle Paul writes to the Ephesians: "I therefore, a prisoner for the Lord, beg you to walk in a manner worthy of the calling to which you have been called, with all lowliness and meekness, with patience, forbearing one another in love, eager to maintain the unity of the Spirit in the bond of peace. There is one body and one Spirit ..., one Lord, one faith, one baptism, one God and Father of us all, who is above all and through all and in all" (4:1–6).

The ecclesial movements and the new communities exist and develop for the sake of this growth in unity, as the Holy Father John Paul II
recalled on Pentecost of the year 1998—to work in unity to witness to the God of love who became Word and sacrament in the
Church; to work in unity through the sign of mutual love by which
the disciples of Jesus are recognized. This love unites and reconciles;
it is an ecumenical task and responsibility, while respecting legitimate
differences and repenting for the wounds caused by the division of
the churches.

I would like to share with you a memory of the visit by a delegation from the Greek Orthodox Church to Rome in March 2002, the
first official visit in a thousand years, which I had the good fortune
to welcome and to accompany at the Vatican for a week. We could
not pray together, because from a strictly Orthodox perspective, one
does not pray with heretics. But after the audience with the Holy
Father John Paul II, we went to visit the magnificent *Redemptoris
Mater* chapel, the chapel of unity. When the six members of the delegation saw and recognized the Eastern saints, their saints, with the
Western saints, flanking the Mother of God in the center, they were
delighted and started to sing with us a Marian hymn that I will never
forget. It was the high point of the visit! Isn't this an invitation to seek
unity through the beauty of the ecumenical movement, reenergized
in the school of the saints and primarily in the school of Mary, the
Mother of unity?[18]

A Pedagogy of Beauty: The Example of the *Brebis de Jésus*

Before concluding, allow me to summarize by giving an example of
a pedagogy of beauty by describing a movement founded in Quebec
twenty years ago, which is spreading now in about twenty countries:
the movement of the *Brebis de Jésus*, founded by a Franciscan nun,
whose testimony I quote here.

---

[18] It is remarkable that among the most significant ecumenical documents of recent years,
two concern the Virgin Mary; one was produced by the Dombes Group in 1997 and the other
by the official Anglican-Catholic dialogue in 2005; both conclude by acknowledging that the
veneration of the figure of Mary cannot be considered an obstacle to unity.

Come, you matter to me, you are valuable in my sight and I love you.

Come! In the beginning there is a call, the call of Love. At each meeting, a Sheep of Jesus hears herself called by this name by her Shepherd. Everything originates in God's heart. He is the one who takes the initiative. Come! There is an invitation here. The response to this invitation makes a person enter into the beauty of love that is its inspiration.

You matter to me. Every child is called personally by his name, tenderly. He is known by God. The person accompanying is invited to pronounce the child's name in Christ's own name. Each time, he asks Christ for the following grace: that while pronouncing his name, he might call forth the best that is in that child. That he might bring to birth what is unique about him, his profound identity as a creature and child of God. Every child is an "original." The beauty of love is expressed in uniqueness.

You are valuable in my sight, very precious, the price of the ransom that clothes the person with a glorious splendor, a marvelous beauty. The Sheep of Jesus is invited to look at herself through the eyes of the Good Shepherd Himself who gave His life for her. It is a long journey. You must not be surprised if one of the fruits of the meetings is the conversion of one's own way of seeing oneself. The child says: "I love myself more, I have more self-confidence."

I love you. Opening herself to the love with which she is loved is the primary objective of the pedagogy of Jesus' Sheep. This declaration of love runs through the whole Bible and desires to run through the life of every person.

Everyone who looks to Him will shine. They will no longer be shame-faced.

All the meetings of Jesus' Sheep rely on the Word of God, a Word that is heard, accepted, shared, experienced. Guided by the Holy Spirit, the one who accompanies makes himself the servant of the Word. His manner is self-effacing so that the Word may give Itself to the child and produce in him the fruits of the Kingdom. It is a school of looking, of becoming less self-centered so as to allow the light from on high to illuminate the depths of one's being. Iconography always tries to express the light of the resurrection. Thus the baptized person, one of Jesus' Sheep, is called to become an icon of Christ. This is the greatness and the beauty of his divine vocation.

How beautiful she is, the Sheep of Jesus all lit up by the light of love! To reflect this light is her responsibility, too. There is a stage in the journey that is called "being received as a Sheep of light." It is at the same time such a difficult struggle. One must live in personal fidelity in order to keep one's lamp lit. Many obstacles arise along the way that might extinguish its light. You train my hands for war, and my fingers for battle [Ps 144:1]. There is a beauty in this struggle. It is the beauty of fidelity, or of infidelity forgiven, of abandonment, of constantly handing oneself over to God in trust.

There is also this commitment to radiate the light, to share it, despite the trials along the way. The Christian is in the world and is no longer of this world. There are Sheep of Jesus who serenely accept being laughed at because of their faithfulness to the meetings. They say: "If they laugh at me, it is because they do not know Jesus. If they knew the love of Jesus, they would come to the meetings, and maybe they would be more fervent than me." There is a beauty in this look at the other, made up of forgiveness, understanding, bringing hope. Several Sheep of Jesus already experience a mystery of persecution. Christ scourged and crowned with thorns is divinely beautiful. Only love can contemplate this beauty.

For the big Sheep of Jesus who persevere, one main idea guides them. They hear the beating of the Heart of the Lamb who invites them to follow Him. This intimacy puts them in profound communion with our Holy Mother the Church. They hide in her bosom so as to be nourished, forgiven, enlivened. They do not judge the Church; they love her and give themselves up with her. They are among the little ones to whom the mysteries of the Kingdom are revealed. They do not make noise, but their daily offering, united with Christ's, raises up the world and hastens the return of Jesus. They experience the beauty of Eucharistic life made possible by the sacrifice of the Lamb.

This is the testimony of the *Brebis de Jésus*, taken as one example out of a thousand, which no doubt verifies, modestly, the pedagogical experience of several ecclesial movements and new communities. All fruitful evangelization occurs by way of a personal and ecclesial appropriation of the Word-made-flesh, which transforms the believer's way of looking at God, at others, and at himself. This real transformation always starts by a true encounter with Jesus and by prayer, personal prayer, liturgical, lay, and monastic prayer; when its beauty is experienced and renewed again and again, it bears many fruits of peace, conversion, and hope. This transformation is nourished above all by the Eucharist, the source and summit of evangelization and of the Church's life.

And prayer opens the heart to the poor and the walking wounded in life, who then become not only the beneficiaries of our charity but also our benefactors and even our masters. Since the beginnings, the poor have been the wealth of the Church, according to Saint Lawrence. Do they not silently reveal to us the face of the Crucified, his call to compassion, and the path of the first Beatitude?

"As the Father has loved me, so have I loved you; abide in my love" (Jn 15:9). To be loved by God in Jesus, to abide in his love and in this way to bear much fruit so as to give God joy: this is the beauty of being Christians. The love of Jesus is given abundantly and in a great variety of ways to the ecclesial movements and the new communities, in the joy of the Holy Spirit, so as to testify together to the beauty of Christ and of the Church. Dear friends, by your generous response to the universal call to holiness, by your firm and serene support for the Church's Magisterium, and by your enthusiastic willingness to evangelize, you are a big, beautiful sign called to grow and to spread throughout the world. May your particular charisms develop in unity and peace, with a lively awareness that the ever-greater divine love summons us to a vibrant testimony that is trustworthy!

The beauty of being Christians is a grace that follows from the beauty of Christ and of Mary-Church through the gift of the Holy Spirit. Saint Francis summed up the grace of his life in two words: Jesus and Mary! This grace is also a responsibility, a mission, the mission to evangelize, which becomes in today's world the priority of all priorities. To evangelize by radiating the light of love through prayer, action, passionate commitment, and also through reason and through art, as the recently departed Don Luigi Giussani gave such fine witness—to evangelize by the witness of faith and by the example of a fully human life; to evangelize also in persecution and trials, for our Christian and apostolic maturity is measured by our willingness to suffer for the Name of Jesus. Love is not just a feeling; it is a Person, a vision and a commitment in a Covenant mystery. This is why the beauty of being Christians always culminates in the Eucharistic mystery of the Church and is unceasingly replenished in it.

"We are busily refashioning and improving this Church according to the needs of the times, the criticisms of our opponents, and our own models," Balthasar writes again. "But do we not lose sight in all this of the only perfect criterion, that is, of the archetype? Should we not keep our eyes fixed on Mary in all of our reforms—not in order to multiply Marian feasts, devotions, or even definitions in the Church, but simply in order to remain aware of what Church, ecclesial spirit, ecclesial conduct really are?"[19]

The place in his plan that God has appointed for Christians is so beautiful that they cannot desert their post, even at the cost of sharing in the Lord's Passion so as to enter into his glory. Let us therefore remain at our post, let us work together in charity and unity, and in order to grow in Eucharistic splendor, let us open ourselves even more profoundly to the Holy Spirit so that his grace, given abundantly, may be poured out again by the Church, the sacrament of salvation, on humanity as a whole. As Saint Basil marvelously says in his treatise on the Holy Spirit, and I conclude with this excerpt: "From the Spirit comes foreknowledge of the future, understanding of the mysteries of faith, insight into the hidden meaning of Scripture, and other special gifts. Through the Spirit we become citizens of heaven, we are admitted to the company of the angels, we enter into eternal happiness, and abide in God. Through the Spirit we acquire a likeness to God; indeed, we attain what is beyond our most sublime aspirations—we become God."[20]

---

[19] Hans Urs von Balthasar and Joseph Cardinal Ratzinger, *Mary: The Church at the Source*, trans. Adrian Walker (San Francisco: Ignatius Press, 2005), 123–24.

[20] Basil the Great, *On the Holy Spirit*, quoted in *The Liturgy of the Hours*, 2:976.

Chapter 11

The Golden Rule

If we love one another, God abides in us and his love is perfected in us.

— 1 John 4:12

Dear friends, recently appointed bishops,

The Word of God, proclaimed in this Eucharist that precedes our audience with Pope Francis, speaks about love, the essential ingredient of our life and of our episcopal ministry. "Over all these put on love, which binds everything together in perfect harmony", Saint Paul writes to the Colossians (3:14). And the Gospel of Luke puts us in the presence of Jesus teaching the crowd: "I say to you that hear, Love your enemies, do good to those who hate you" (6:27). We receive this solemn word in the place where the Apostle Peter shed his blood for the love of the Lord and of his people, and not far from the place where the Apostle Paul gave the same testimony of blood.

Dear friends, this Word that we receive, in a form that has been proclaimed and incarnated to the point of martyrdom, speaks to us about our own identity as bishops, disciples of Christ, and successors to the Apostles. "Put on then, as God's chosen ones, holy and beloved, compassion, kindness, lowliness, meekness, and patience" (Col 3:12). These are the qualities of love in the disciples of Jesus, to which Paul adds forgiveness, fraternal correction, thanksgiving,

Homily given during the Mass at Saint Peter's Basilica concluding the initial formation session of new bishops, September 2019.

and praise. This exhortation to love cannot possibly concern us more directly. For above all, dear brother bishops, we are disciples of Christ, and because of our call to ministry, we must become his disciples more and more. Otherwise, the episcopal ministry, which has become ours as a grace and a responsibility, runs the risk of being diverted from its purpose and of serving our own worldly interests.

Humble love, nourished by the prayer of thanksgiving and praise, keeps us in close friendship with the Lord, who chose us *to be with him*, in other words, to belong totally to him, abiding with him in disinterested love, and not only by the exercise of our ministry. "Whatever you do, in word or deed, do everything in the name of the Lord Jesus, giving thanks to God the Father through him" (Col 3:17). This formula by Saint Paul applies both to disciples and to ministers. It unifies in us the fullness of the baptismal priesthood, in other words, the totality of our life that must radiate the Holy Spirit, and the fullness of the ministerial priesthood, the specific powers of which consecrate us to the service of the ecclesial communion as representatives of Christ the Head and Bridegroom of the Church.

Our episcopal identity is therefore entirely defined by love, the love of the Father, who chose us, the love of Christ, who united us to his priesthood, and the love of the Holy Spirit, who fills us with peace and joy by allowing himself to be distributed by us in all that we are. This Trinitarian dimension of our identity was highlighted by the post-synodal apostolic exhortation *Pastores Gregis*, of which Pope Francis, then cardinal archbishop of Buenos Aires, was the linchpin at the Ordinary Roman Synod in 2001. I invite you to reread paragraph 7, which speaks about the configuration of the bishop to the Trinitarian mystery.

"If we love one another, God abides in us and his love is perfected in us" (1 Jn 4:12). This Gospel refrain resounds in a special way in our hearts today. It resounds as a grace and a requirement, the grace of being God's dwelling place through our episcopal communion as successors of the Apostles. If the distinctive sign of Christians is their witness of mutual love, then as a result, this requirement is doubled for us bishops, for the mutual love among bishops! This is the first requirement of episcopal collegiality: that we love one another in all truth, without calculation and unconditionally. That we live in an authentic communion that is human, and divine, affective and effective, which is expressed on this precise occasion through our repeated promise of fidelity to our episcopal communion, *cum et sub Petro* [with and under Peter]. Is this not the DNA of a Church that desires to evangelize "by attraction"?

A bishop's love for God and for his people is expressed by his fidelity to the Gospel, by his loyal and sincere support of the Successor of Peter, by active solidarity among bishops for the service of the poor and of the local churches, by their watching over the flock and their peaceful struggle to safeguard Church unity in our times when those who sow division have powerful media at their disposal. Let us beware of being co-opted by the great Divider and Accuser of our brethren.

"Be merciful, even as your Father is merciful" (Lk 6:36), Jesus emphasizes in this solemn speech in which nothing smacks of worldliness or populism. "Judge not, and you will not be judged; condemn not, and you will not be condemned; forgive, and you will be forgiven" (Lk 6:37). These words of our Master challenge us mightily at the dawn of our episcopal ministry, since we are in a way, in Christ, icons of the Father, witnesses of the Risen Lord, and Apostles of mercy. May we thus be effective artisans of a synodal Church that is built up by trust in the Holy Spirit more than by our organizational genius. The Holy Spirit unceasingly pours out his gifts and charisms on the People of God to build up the Body of Christ in the love that surpasses all understanding and human achievement.

While offering together on this joyful and moving occasion the paschal sacrifice of the Lamb, who was slain and yet is victorious, let us humbly ask for the grace of fidelity to the love that calls us and sends us, fidelity to the mutual love that includes first and foremost the grace of fidelity to the Successor of Peter. Amen!

Chapter 12

Servants of Ecclesial Communion

"Each particular Church, as a portion of the Catholic Church under the leadership of its bishop, is likewise called to missionary conversion. It is the primary subject of evangelization, since it is the concrete manifestation of the one Church in one specific place, and in it 'the one, holy, catholic, and apostolic Church of Christ is truly present and operative'."[1]

Dear friends, Pope Francis repeated this beautiful ecclesiological formulation by the Second Ecumenical Council of the Vatican in his major programmatic exhortation *Evangelii Gaudium*, to invite the whole Church, but first of all the bishops, to a missionary conversion. This exhortation concerns us directly and invites us to seek ways to respond to it now, by reason of our new mission and the current needs of the Church and of the world. The Holy Father adds: "To make this missionary impulse ever more focused, generous and fruitful, I encourage each particular Church to undertake a resolute process of discernment, purification and reform."[2]

What might this missionary conversion mean for us and for the particular Church to which we are sent? The quotation that serves as a point of departure, taken from the decree *Christus Dominus* on the pastoral office of bishops, presents the Church of Christ as a universal subject present and active in her concrete manifestations, the particular churches. It does not speak about the Church in terms of a collective or a federation of local communities but rather as a unique,

This essay is based on a conference given during the initial formation session for the new bishops, September 2015.

[1] *EG*, no. 30, quoting Vatican Council II, Decree on the Pastoral Office of Bishops *Christus Dominus* (October 28, 1965), no. 11.

[2] Ibid.

universal subject, present and active in a concrete place. What is our place and our role in this Church which is inseparably universal and particular? Pope Francis writes, "The bishop ... will sometimes go before his people, pointing the way and keeping their hope vibrant. At other times, he will simply be in their midst with his unassuming and merciful presence. At yet other times, he will have to walk after them, helping those who lag behind and—above all—allowing the flock to strike out on new paths."[3]

We have grown accustomed to the Holy Father's original metaphors, which accompany his gestures and arouse enthusiasm. I recognize in his suggestive description his own way of exercising the Petrine ministry, which challenges us: What sort of bishop and pastor do we want to be and perhaps must we become in this hour of reform in the Church? This is the major question that preoccupies us, which we want to discuss within the framework of this initial formation session near the tombs of the Holy Apostles Peter and Paul. We are all familiar with models, bishops with whom we are acquainted or who have inspired us in Church history. For my part, I know a Colombian bishop who greatly edified me when I was rector of his Major Seminary of Manizales. A model bishop because of his sense of the Church, his doctrine, and his way of governing, he served in three dioceses and then continued to serve in an exemplary fashion as a bishop emeritus. At the age of ninety-six, he recently celebrated sixty years of his episcopate; maybe you have recognized him: I mean His Eminence José de Jesus Pimiento Rodriguez, archbishop emeritus of Manizales, whom Pope Francis has just created a cardinal. A great man of the Church, whose wisdom and pastoral prudence I salute.

Some bishops see the Church the way a manager might look at her; they are sensitive to her structures, her organization, and her output, considering themselves good administrators and even moderators of a good consensus between priests and faithful. Other bishops see the Church as a people ruled by the golden rule of charity, particularly with regard to the poor and suffering and marginalized persons; they are concerned about the community experience and social questions, while seeking to be a significant presence in the communications media. Finally, other bishops promote above all the sanctification of

---

[3] Ibid., no. 31.

the faithful, the sacramental life, popular piety, priestly and religious vocations, and they preferably view themselves as hosting a spiritual program. These different ways of exercising the episcopal ministry correspond to one dimension or another of the mission that we have received. None of them is foreign to the nature of the Church. But a one-sided emphasis on one or another can cause some essential aspects of the episcopal mission to suffer.

The Bishop and the Church

I will not pursue further this initial sketch of the episcopal ministry, because in order to frame our reflection appropriately I think that it is helpful and even necessary to introduce our exchanges of ideas and our dialogue with a sort of "meditation on the Church", to quote the title of a well-known work by Father Henri de Lubac.[4] Any reflection on the figure of the bishop presupposes a vision of the Church of which he is one of the essential pillars, as a successor of the Apostles. The bishop is called to feed his flock, God's Church, by exercising the threefold office of *priest, teacher, and pastor* according to the specific modality of his episcopal ordination. His way of exercising this ministry depends in large measure on his way of looking at the Church, a view conditioned by his spirituality, his particular formation, and his previous ministerial experiences. Because of God's call, confirmed by the Church, this view must now be broadened to the dimensions of the Universal Church. What a challenge for a bishop who has scarcely been ordained to go beyond his own geographical, cultural, and even spiritual horizon so as to assume a universal responsibility! What a qualitative leap is required to go from the exercise of a particular ministry to a universal missionary responsibility! Does he not have to have a powerful grace so that his heart and mind may be open to what is beyond his limits and his familiar loyalties?

I know no better example of missionary conversion than what you have been experiencing since your episcopal ordination. For the

---

[4]Henri de Lubac, *Méditation sur l'Église* (Paris: Éditions du Cerf, 1956). The Dogmatic Constitution on the Church, *Lumen Gentium*, is largely inspired by this masterful, serene work, written while the theologian was going through a time of trial caused by suspicions about his orthodoxy.

fullness of the priesthood that you received by ordination commits you to watch over (*episcopè*) the unity of the People of God for whom you are jointly responsible. This ecclesial responsibility consists above all in watching over the communion of the Universal and particular Church, which means much more than supervising the observance of the canonical discipline in one's diocese. I highly recommend on this subject an excellent article in the June 2015 issue of *La Civiltà Cattolica* that explains the figure of the bishop in the teachings of Pope Francis.[5]

To introduce our dialogue on this major question, I therefore propose a meditation on the Church with the help of the ecclesiology of communion that resulted from Vatican Council II. This ecclesiology of the People of God will reveal the sacramental nature of the Church and her symbolic figure as the Body and Bride of Christ; this ecclesiological consideration will finally bring us back to the figure of the bishop as a *servant of ecclesial communion*. In doing so, I will formulate several questions aimed at furthering our personal reflection and integrating our own experience. The point of departure could be the following questions: "Church of Jesus Christ, what do you say about yourself?" "And how do we, successors of the Apostles in the third millennium, look at the Church?"

The Church, the Pilgrim People of God

The Second Ecumenical Council of the Vatican is widely recognized as an ecclesiological council. The Dogmatic Constitution on the Church, *Lumen Gentium*, clarified the sacramental nature of the Church and her hierarchical constitution, including the historically late dimension of episcopal collegiality; furthermore, the document recognized its charismatic dimension and promoted it at the

---

[5] Diego Fares, "La figura del vescovo in Papa Francesco", *La Civiltà Cattolica*, June 13, 2015, 433–49. Fares states, "What I want to emphasize is this peculiar depth of *watching over* [*vegliare*] as compared to a more general form of *supervision* or as compared to a more specific vigilance. *Supervision* [*Sorvegliare*] refers more to a concern for doctrine and customs, while *watching over* alludes instead to making sure that there is salt and light in people's hearts. *Vigilance* [*Vigilare*] speaks about being alert to imminent danger, while *watching over* speaks about bearing patiently with the processes through which the Lord furthers the salvation of His people" (p. 434).

service of communion and mission. The Pastoral Constitution on the Church, *Gaudium et Spes*, for its part, sketched the anthropological and social vision that explains and articulates the Church's role in the modern world, particularly with respect to the major questions about marriage and the family, economic-social and political life, and safe-guarding peace among nations.

The immediate postconciliar period, as we know, experienced tur-bulence and dubious interpretations in some milieus, particularly in the fields of liturgy, ecclesiology, and social justice; these however do not negate the important advances in ecumenism and interreligious dia-logue, as well as in the Church's social teaching. Now, fifty years after the conclusion of the Council, we observe that its documents have not aged and that the new missionary inspiration that it channeled is more than ever at the center of attention.

Everyone remembers the first gesture made by Pope Francis on the balcony of Saint Peter's in Rome on the evening of his election: he bowed to the People of God, asking for their prayers and inviting them to travel together toward the Kingdom. The pope thus sym-bolically evoked his vision of the Church, the pilgrim People of God within history, guided by the Word of God and inspired by the Holy Spirit. Anyone who wishes to see in this a resurrection of the "spirit of the Council" promoted apart from the documents, and a new edition of liberationist ecclesiology, should be reminded of how fervently the Holy Father repeats a typical Ignatian expression: "Our Holy Mother, the hierarchical Church", thus setting aside all sociological reductions and integrating his ecclesiology of the People of God into the concil-iar vision as a whole. We will return to this later on.

At the turn of the year 2000, on the occasion of the Great Jubi-lee, Joseph Cardinal Ratzinger took stock of the reception of the conciliar ecclesiology, and he recalled in a timely fashion that it had been interpreted superficially at first, which gave rise to interminable debates about structures, to the detriment of its theological newness as *People of God* rooted in mystery of the Trinitarian communion.[6] The beautiful formula from the constitution *Lumen Gentium* that concludes the description of the Holy Spirit's mission in the Church

[6] Joseph Cardinal Ratzinger, "The Ecclesiology of the Constitution *Lumen Gentium*", reprinted in Joseph Cardinal Ratzinger, *Pilgrim Fellowship of Faith: The Church as Communion*, trans. Henry Taylor (San Francisco: Ignatius Press, 2005), 123–52 at 126–27.

testifies to this: "Thus, the Church has been seen as 'a people made one with the unity of the Father, the Son and the Holy Spirit.'"[7] The future Benedict XVI then reminded us vigorously that the conciliar ecclesiology is founded on God and must be interpreted theologically if we want to avoid the ideological manipulations that equate the ecclesial community with dominant cultural models.

One of the major turning points of the conciliar ecclesiology in the chapter on the People of God is that it discussed first the common priesthood of the faithful as the foundation of the dignity of the People of God: "Christ the Lord, High Priest taken from among men (cf. Heb 5:1–5), made the new people 'a kingdom and priests to God the Father' (cf. Rev 1:6; 5:9–10). The baptized, by regeneration and the anointing of the Holy Spirit, are consecrated as a spiritual house and a holy priesthood, in order that through all those works which are those of the Christian man they may offer spiritual sacrifices and proclaim the power of Him who has called them out of darkness into His marvelous light (cf. 1 Pet 2:4–10)."[8] This editorial choice restored and highlighted the fundamental dignity of the *royal priesthood* in the People of God, without thereby diminishing the specificity of the hierarchical or ministerial priesthood. Moreover, the Council did underscore the fact that the two forms of priesthood are correlative and complementary, because "each of them in its own special way is a participation in the one priesthood of Christ."[9]

It is important for the bishop to be able to contemplate the priestly identity of his people, because the episcopal, presbyteral, and diaconal ministry exists with a view to the conscious, fruitful exercise of this *royal priesthood*. This consideration is essential to the unity of the particular Church and to the missionary influence of its Christian communities. The latter are all the more vital and missionary because the communion between pastors and faithful is founded on the same priestly dignity and experienced as an exchange of gifts that are both "hierarchical and charismatic"[10], with which the Spirit provides the Church so as to adorn, rejuvenate, and lead it "to perfect union with its Spouse".[11]

---

[7] *LG*, no. 4, quoting Saint Cyprian, *De Orat. Dom.* 23 (PL 4, 553).
[8] Ibid., no. 10.
[9] Ibid.
[10] Ibid., no. 4.
[11] Ibid.

What are the fruits of a harmonious mutual relation between the two essentially different and complementary kinds of participation in Christ's priesthood? Absent the interference of foreign factors, we observe an abundance of charisms that the Holy Spirit pours out on the People of God, raising up vocations to the priesthood and the consecrated life, households that are united and fruitful, personal and communal testimonies of ecumenical openness, and commitment to justice, social peace, and safeguarding creation. If this communion is lacking, then the soil is favorable to the development of secularization, sectarianism, and religious indifference. On the other hand, where the two forms of Christ's one priesthood are mutually enriching, the Church evangelizes "by attraction" by "receiving the sacraments, in prayer and thanksgiving, in the witness of a holy life, and by self-denial and active charity".[12]

In circles where a mentality of power-seeking, rivalry, and ideological division is predominant, we observe the decline of Christian joy, anemic or sterile pastoral work, sometimes accompanied by destructive media campaigns. Pope Francis never stops denouncing the spiritual worldliness or just plain worldliness that undermines the credibility of the Church and her pastors. What is needed then is an authentic conversion of her ministers to the Lord's humility and merciful compassion so as to rekindle hope among baptized persons and to help communities to start out again together in a Spirit of conversion and reconciliation. The People of God ecclesiology that Francis lives and teaches is essentially missionary and profoundly theological; it is "a mystery rooted in the Trinity",[13] and is built on "the primacy of grace".[14] He writes: "Being Church means being God's people, in accordance with the great plan of his fatherly love. This means that we are to be God's leaven in the midst of humanity."[15] What are the resulting spiritual and pastoral requirements for us bishops, who walk with the People of God "amid the persecutions of the world and the consolations of God"?[16]

---

[12] Ibid., no. 10.
[13] EG, no. 111.
[14] Ibid., no. 112.
[15] Ibid., no. 114.
[16] LG, no. 8.

Sacrament of Trinitarian Communion

We mentioned at the start the challenge to move from a priestly mission at the service of a diocese to an episcopal mission at the service of the Universal Church. The widening of perspective that this presupposes has a geographical dimension because of a bishop's status as a member of the episcopal college who shares responsibility for the Universal Church; but it also involves a sacramental dimension rooted in the mystery of the ecclesial communion of which the bishop is a major expression. From its very first lines, the dogmatic constitution *Lumen Gentium* brings into play the notion of sacrament, which specifies the profound nature of the Church and as a result renews its relation to the world: "This Sacred Synod gathered together in the Holy Spirit eagerly desires ... to bring the light of Christ to all men, a light brightly visible on the countenance of the Church." The Church, for its part, "is in Christ like a sacrament or as a sign and instrument both of a very closely knit union with God and of the unity of the whole human race".[17] We see here the notion of sacrament as "efficacious sign of grace" converge with the notion of "communion" (*koinonia*);[18] they coalesce together in "one complex reality [made up of] a divine element and a human element".[19]

The notion of sacrament is applied to the Church, the Body of Christ, with the help of the analogy of the Incarnate Word: "As the assumed nature inseparably united to Him, serves the divine Word as a living organ of salvation, so, in a similar way, does the visible social structure of the Church serve the Spirit of Christ, who vivifies it, in the building up of the body (cf. Eph 4:16)."[20]

The notion of communion is applied in a very nuanced, cautious way to mark out the path for ecumenism without sacrificing our own vision of Catholic truth: "This Church, constituted and organized in the world as a society, subsists in the Catholic Church, which is governed by the successor of Peter and by the Bishops in communion with him."[21] This, essentially, is the affirmation of the identity of the

---

[17] Ibid., no. 1.

[18] See Jean-Marie Tillard, s.v. "communion", in *Dictionnaire critique de théologie*, ed. Jean-Yves Lacoste (Paris: Presses Universitaires de France, 2007), 285–93.

[19] *LG*, no. 8.

[20] Ibid.

[21] Ibid.

Catholic Church, expressed in such a way as not to exclude other ecclesial entities. The Council adds: "Many elements of sanctification and of truth are found outside of its visible structure. These elements, as gifts belonging to the Church of Christ, are forces impelling toward catholic unity."[22]

The Church offers to the world the light of Christ through her proclamation of the Word of God and the sacraments, which structure its participation in the Trinitarian communion. This sacramental communion is nourished above all by Christ's paschal sacrifice, which transcends and traverses the centuries, diachronically and synchronically, conveyed by communities that are guided by the communion of the successors of the Apostles *cum et sub Petro*. This participation in the Trinitarian communion follows first of all from the sacraments of Christian initiation; it is then extended and consolidated by the other sacraments, and also by the variety of charisms that are conducive to the Church's unity and missionary dynamism.

Concretely, the grace of Baptism confers on the child of God his filial identity; the grace of Confirmation strengthens this filial identity by the seal of the Holy Spirit with a view to personal testimony; the grace of the Eucharist gathers the children of God around the sacrificial offering of Christ to his Father, obtaining for them the outpouring of the Holy Spirit on the assembly and on all creation.

This Trinitarian structure of Christian initiation is extended and perfected by the other sacraments, each of which contributes in its own way to building up the Church, the Body of Christ. The Sacrament of Matrimony confers on the human couple, who are created in the image of God, a likeness to the Trinitarian love that transforms the family into an ecclesial reality, like an icon of the Holy Trinity. "Christ the Lord ... comes into the lives of married Christians through the sacrament of matrimony" and "He abides with them."[23] He makes his own the loving relationship and community of life between the man and the woman, really and not just symbolically expressing in it his own love for the Church, his Spouse, thus conferring on the institution of the family an authentic identity and ecclesial mission.

Furthermore, for decades now much ink has been spilled about the two different and complementary kinds of participation in the one

[22] Ibid.
[23] GS, no. 48.

priesthood of Christ, either to justify or to criticize this firm doctrine of the Catholic Church. Here, as in other areas, a more in-depth, Trinitarian view enables us to resolve the unhealthy tensions and to overcome envy and rivalry between clerics and laypeople. Indeed, the Council clearly affirms the essential difference—not just one of degree—between the two kinds of priesthood, but it leaves it up to the theologians to provide the explanation.

For my part, I think that the common or royal priesthood of baptized persons lies in their participation in the priesthood of the Son inasmuch as he offers himself as a sacrifice to the Father for us, in love, and obtains for us in return the gift of the Holy Spirit. As for the ministerial or apostolic priesthood, I see it as being essentially different, founded on the fact that Christ is the One sent by the Father and represents the Father, speaking with his authority and obeying him in everything. He is in a way "the Apostle of the Father", since this apostolic dimension is added to and completes his filial priesthood. This "apostolic" dimension of his one priesthood becomes more visible in the economy of salvation on Easter evening when the Risen Lord appears to the Apostles, breathes the Holy Spirit upon them, and thus confers on them the power to forgive sins in the name of the three Divine Persons.

It follows from this that the Apostles and their successors are endowed and sent by him in this way to prolong his *apostolic* or *ministerial* priesthood—hence their reference to the figure of the Father and their experience of the spiritual paternity that belongs to bishops and, to a lesser extent, to priests. From this Trinitarian perspective, which the post-synodal apostolic exhortation *Pastores Gregis*[24] also speaks about explicitly, emerges a more evident articulation of the fact that hierarchical ministers are ordained in order to promote the royal (filial) priesthood of the baptized. In light of this, any rivalry or conflict between the members of the two forms of priesthood is shown to be contrary to the Spirit of Christ. For this Spirit confirms their unity, each making the other fruitful in the life of the Church, just as he confirms the unity of the Father

---

[24] *PG*, no. 7: "Christ is the primordial icon of the Father and the manifestation of his merciful presence among men and women. The Bishop, who acts in the person and in the name of Christ himself, becomes in the Church entrusted to him a living sign of the Lord Jesus, Shepherd and Spouse, Teacher and High Priest of the Church."

and the Son in the Trinity. Just as the Father and the Son coexist in the Spirit of their eternal love, so, too, pastors and the lay faithful edify each other mutually by their reciprocal love, enriched by their blessed difference and priestly complementarity.

The Church, the People of God, therefore participates in the communion of the Divine Persons through the grace of Baptism and through all the sacramental articulations that make the Church "a sign and instrument both of a very closely knit union with God and of the unity of the whole human race".[25] Thus, she carries out her mission through the exercise of the priesthood of Jesus Christ, which spreads Trinitarian love throughout the world. Through the proclamation of the Gospel and the celebration of the sacraments of Christian initiation and through their extension in her hierarchical and charismatic structure, the Church of Christ, founded and inhabited by the Trinitarian love, thus becomes more and more missionary, a "sign and instrument" of communion, a pure service to the love of Christ, in short, *Sacramentum Trinitatis* [a Sacrament of the Trinity].

How is the Church's sacramentality integrated into our ecclesiological views? What impact does it have or should it have on the exercise of the episcopal ministry? Is our ecclesiology of communion fundamentally Eucharistic? What is its relation to episcopal collegiality and to ecumenism?

"Our Holy Mother, the Hierarchical Church"

Our look at the Church has included so far her sociological, visible dimension as the pilgrim People of God and her Trinitarian and Eucharistic dimension, hidden beneath the notion of communion, with a sacramental significance. Now we continue our contemplation of the light of Christ that shines on the face of the Church, so as to reflect it as much as possible for our contemporaries. The preceding discussion reveals it partially but does not exhaust its richness. The Council took care to list various biblical images, which warn us to avoid any worldly reduction of the mystery of the Church. I mention here one of them that deserves our attention because it is

---

[25] *LG*, no. 1.

both suggestive and uncommon. I am thinking of the Ignatian expression that is heard often on the lips of Pope Francis: "Our Holy
Mother, the hierarchical Church".

The expression is rather paradoxical and at first glance seems old-
fashioned or outmoded, something belonging to a bygone age. For
this expression synthesizes two dimensions which at first glance seem
to be mutually exclusive. On the one hand, the Church's motherhood, and on the other hand, her hierarchical structure. The first
recalls the Virgin Mary; the second makes us think of the bishops.
How can they be integrated in a balanced ecclesiological vision?

Francis answers this question with the help of Hans Urs von
Balthasar, by noting, as he does, a hierarchy between what he calls
the Marian principle and the Petrine principle of the Church.[26] "In
the Church, Mary is more fundamental than Peter", they both affirm,
because Mary embodies the immaculate faith by which the Church
welcomes the Incarnate Word and gives him to the world. In the
most important hierarchy, the hierarchy of faith and love, Mary
reigns and holds the highest rank, since her fruitfulness confers on
her a universal motherhood that wraps all the members of Christ's
Body in her great mantle. Peter represents ministry in the Church; he
is the principle of her visible unity since he is her universal pastor as
Bishop of Rome and head of the College of Bishops. He can exercise
his ministry of representing Christ, the Head and Bridegroom of the
Church, because the Church, the Body and Bride of Christ, is already
constituted by the immaculate faith of Mary. In this respect let us
listen to an echo in a conciliar document:

> The Church, further, "that Jerusalem which is above" is also called
> "our mother" (Gal 4:26; cf. Rev 12:17). It is described as the spotless
> spouse of the spotless Lamb (Rev 19:7; 21:2, 9; 22:17), whom Christ
> "loved and for whom He delivered Himself up that He might sanctify
> her" (Eph 5:25–26), whom He unites to Himself by an unbreakable
> covenant, and whom He unceasingly "nourishes and cherishes" (Eph
> 5:29), and whom, once purified, He willed to be cleansed and joined
> to Himself, subject to Him in love and fidelity (cf. Eph 5:24).[27]

---

[26] See Hans Urs von Balthasar, "The All-Embracing Motherhood of the Church," in *The Office of Peter and the Structure of the Church*, 2nd ed., trans. Andrée Emery (San Francisco: Ignatius Press, 2007), 195–238.
[27] *LG*, no. 6.

To continue our meditation on the Church in greater depth, I call attention to this nuptial symbolism that runs through the Bible, from Genesis to Revelation, with the Song of Songs at the center as the hermeneutical key to the relation between God and his people, between Christ and the Church. Ecclesiology has not yet thoroughly integrated this symbolism, which allows us to appreciate from another perspective the unity and personality of the Church. An in-depth look at the Church, Spouse and Mother, in light of pneumatology and of Mariology, can refine and even transform the relations among her members, particularly between the bishop and his faithful.

Let us recall in passing that the biggest conciliar debate had to do with how the Virgin Mary would be considered in relation to the Church. Should the Council issue a separate document in order to exalt her preeminent figure, or should it dedicate to her a chapter within the Dogmatic Constitution on the Church? The debate was dramatic, and the resulting vote was quite close, for the conciliar assembly truly was divided between two widely represented tendencies. The second opinion prevailed, thank God, thus curbing the exaltation of Mary's privileges over the Church and reinstating her as a member—"the most excellent" member but a member nonetheless—as a model and typical realization of the Church. In this way, the conciliar ecclesiology was enriched with a chapter on Mariology that is very dense without being exhaustive, crowning a harmonious overall vision, even though it remained excessively discreet with regard to the Church's nuptial and maternal character. The pontificate of Saint John Paul II, lived out under the banner of Mary at the foot of the Cross, confirmed the Council's hermeneutic, which Paul VI decided to balance on the last day by declaring the Virgin Mary "Mother of the Church"—hence the relevance of Francis' ecclesiological formula: "Our Holy Mother, the hierarchical Church", which encourages us to regard the Church as a person, a subject, and not just as an organization, a people, a communion, but above all as a Spouse and a Mother, a "mystic Person", as Saint Thomas Aquinas puts it.[28]

What can be the importance of this nuptial view for a pastor who intends to be ahead of his flock, in the midst of it, and sometimes even behind it? Is it not enough for him to have devotion to the

[28] STh III, q. 48, art. 2.

Virgin Mary and to invoke her often when faced with challenges to his pastoral work? If the pastor sees Mary exclusively as a model or a mediatrix in heaven, and if he does not see her discreet, active presence in the midst of the People of God, how will he integrate the popular piety that reveals Mary's preferential option for the poor? Moreover, if the principle of Church unity that is Peter, as head of the College of Bishops, is not understood within the principle of unity that is Mary, as the intimate form of ecclesial communion, what kind of ecclesial communion will be promoted and by what means? Won't the juridical and disciplinary aspects run the risk of replacing the pastoral attitude and the mystagogical dimension? And what about ecumenism with the Orthodox?

The bishop's view of the Church will be evident in all his personal and communal relations, on the local and universal level. Depending on the depth of his view, he will have a different way of setting his pastoral priorities and of experiencing the vertical and horizontal communion of the Universal Church in his particular Church. If he takes to heart Jesus' words to his beloved disciple at the foot of the Cross, he will welcome the Mother of the Savior as his Mother, the New Eve, the Bride of the Lamb once slain and now victorious. Won't his apostolic fruitfulness be multiplied in proportion to his union to this Immaculate Virgin, Mother of the Church? In short, just as the Church is not mother without being spouse, can pastors be truly paternal without looking at the Church in a spousal way?

The Bishop, Servant of Ecclesial Communion

Our meditation on the Church started with an evocation of the particular Church, the first subject of evangelization, in which the one, holy, catholic, and apostolic Church of Jesus Christ is present and active. Having contemplated her mystery in the reality of the People of God, and having explained its sacramental nature as a communion of persons participating in the communion of the Divine Persons, we return now to the figure of the bishop at the junction between the Universal Church and the particular Church.

Whether it is planted in Rome, Jerusalem, Montevideo, Sydney, or Kampala, the Church is always universal and particular at the same time, since this twofold dimension characterizes her as a mystery of communion with a missionary tendency toward union with God and the unity of all humanity.

The bishop to whom a particular Church is entrusted must take care to safeguard the universality of the Church in his particular Church and the particularity of his Church in the Universal Church. The two dimensions are essential, and the bishop, by virtue of his membership in the College of Bishops, is the concrete bond that welds one to the other sacramentally. Consequently, the bishop cannot limit himself to taking care of the specific flock of which he is the proper pastor. He must feel that he shares responsibility for the Universal Church and thus for all the other particular churches entrusted to his colleagues in the College of Bishops. The exercise of this responsibility, obviously, involves precise markers and conditions that are determined by canon law. But the essential thing is still his ecclesiological view, his adherence to the papal Magisterium, his participation in the effective or affective expressions of episcopal collegiality, his interest in the missionary conversion that is required of each particular Church.

Being a *servant of ecclesial communion* consequently means, for a bishop, being aware of the universal nature of the Church, in the service of which he organizes his particular community so that it lives in this openness and does not close itself off within its own geographical, ethnic, or cultural horizon. The holiness of a particular Church radiates by its contribution to the universal communion of the Church; this contribution obviously includes its participation in papal charities, but it is above all qualitative, by the holiness of its members, their missionary dynamism, and their witness of unity.

The bishop is the principle of unity who guarantees the communion and the mission of a particular Church, but he is also the essential link of communion between this Church and all the other particular churches of the past or the present, since the Church's communion embraces the continuity of generations in tradition as well as the present-day solidarity of all the particular churches *cum et sub Petro* [with and under Peter].

It is remarkable that the conciliar Decree on the Pastoral Office of Bishops, *Christus Dominus*, discusses in the first place the responsibility of bishops with regard to the Universal Church as a member of the College of Bishops before discussing his pastoral responsibility with regard to a particular Church. To be *servants of ecclesial communion* therefore presupposes that bishops have a profound awareness of their own sacramental mystery that unites them as members of the College of the successors of the Apostles, thus becoming collegially co-responsible for the Universal Church, even though their pastoral activity binds them above all to the service of the particular Church that is entrusted to their care.

With regard to his own portion of the Universal Church, the bishop is her pastor "with the help of his presbyterium". Consequently, his absolute priority will be the unity of this presbyterium, because the fruitful service of the royal priesthood of the baptized demands a witness of unity that makes more credible the presence of the Risen Lord in the ecclesial community and in its pastors.

Certainly, this witness depends on everyone's good will and on their sincere search for holiness. It will rely more and more on the golden rule of mutual love in the Spirit of Jesus, but it will be greatly promoted by a theology of vocation and of the states of life that shows their complementary, harmonious relations within the framework of a Trinitarian ecclesiology.[29]

Within this framework the universal call to holiness is achieved as the perfection of charity in all the states of life. Considered as a participation in the Trinitarian love, this perfection of charity promotes the mutual fructification of vocations to the priesthood and to the consecrated life, in the service of the first and most fragile cell of the Church, the family.[30] The bishop, servant of ecclesial communion, fixing his eyes on Christ and the Church, his Spouse, will not fail to promote the communion of all the states of life in service of the family, the domestic church, which is called more than ever to radiate the light of Christ in a disoriented world.

Dear friends, at the Holy Father's invitation, we have the grace of starting our episcopal ministry with an experience of sacramental

---

[29] On this point I highly recommend Hans Urs von Balthasar, *The Christian State of Life*, trans. Sister Mary Frances McCarthy (San Francisco: Ignatius Press, 1983). Italian edition: *Gli stati di vita del cristiano* (Milan: Jaca Book, 1966); French edition: *L'état de vie chrétien* (Fribourg: Johannes Verlag, 2015).

[30] Balthasar, *Gli stati di vita del cristiano*, 330–35.

fraternity in Rome, near the tombs of Saints Peter and Paul, at the dawn of the Great Jubilee of Mercy. The episcopal ordination and the pastoral mission that you have received certainly awaken within you feelings of gratitude, but also a salutary fear in the face of the responsibility and the missionary conversion that they involve— hence the increased demand for prayer that we feel, accompanied by an insistent, daily supplication to the Holy Spirit that he might produce in us openness of heart and mind to the universal and particular dimensions of our episcopal mission.

Whatever our previous talents and experience may have been, the service of ecclesial communion that is demanded of us surpasses our abilities and presupposes on our part a daily vigilance so that as pastors we might be attentive to the needs of the People of God, contemplatives of the Trinitarian mystery that shines through the ecclesial communion, and friends of the Bridegroom who have taken to heart the look that Jesus gives to the Church, his Bride. Episcopal ordination has divested us of ourselves so that we now belong totally to him, but this grace must also be acquired through spiritual and missionary conversion. For in order to go forward, in the midst of and behind the people who have been entrusted to us, we must closely follow the one Pastor and with him faithfully watch over the unity of the Universal and particular Church for which we are jointly responsible.

Pope Francis shows us the way of a missionary conversion that launches evangelization again "by attraction".[31] May we be touched by his witness, and may we seek to serve, as he does, the Trinitarian communion that shines on the face of the Church. As bishops of the one, holy, catholic, and apostolic Church, in the particular portion that has been entrusted to us, let us ask for the grace to follow Christ the Lord worthily, in profound communion with the Successor of Peter and all our confreres, so that the world might believe that God has given it his only Son and eternal life.

[31] EG, no. 14, quoting Benedict XVI, Homily at Mass for the Opening of the 5th General Conference of the Latin American and Caribbean Bishops (Aparecida, Brazil, May 13, 2007), AAS 99 (2007): 437.

Chapter 13

Communion and Synodality

In the Spirit of the Apostolic Constitution
Praedicate Evangelium

The reform of the Roman Curia demands attention to, and appreciation for, yet another aspect of the mystery of the Church. In her, mission and communion are so closely united that we can say that the purpose of mission is precisely that of making everyone know and live the *new* communion that the Son of God made man has introduced into the history of the world.

— *Praedicate Evangelium,* no. 4

Speeches on synodality abound and confirm that at the beginning of the twenty-first century, we are at an epochal turning point in the history of the Church. Pope Francis set this synodal enthusiasm in motion with his famous Address during the Ceremony Commemorating the 50th Anniversary of the Institution of the Synod of Bishops on October 17, 2015, right in the middle of the Synod on the Family. Since then, many diocesan or national synods have been held, as well as the Roman Synods on the Amazon region and young people, which followed those on the family. The most original is the Synod currently in preparation that deals precisely with synodality. This may give the impression of circling around an ill-defined concept that is served with all sorts of sauces, but we should expect more surprises from the Holy Spirit, who is at work in this synodal search.

This essay is based on a conference given to the Plenary Assembly of the Pontifical Commission for Latin America, May 23–27, 2022.

What can be said, then, to go beyond the clichés that promote neither theology nor the Church's mission? Some serious studies already
exist, in particular, the contribution of the International Theological
Commission.[1] In Latin America, this synodal dynamism should make
it possible to appreciate the originality of the continent and the contribution of the local churches that are experiencing trials because
of the pandemic and the consequences of the war in Ukraine. The
Pontifical Commission for Latin America wants to participate in this
urgent task, and it is especially well positioned to observe and intervene under the benevolent watch of the first Latin American pope.
In tune with our dear Pope Francis, I chose to take as my inspiration the new apostolic constitution on the Roman Curia, which will
come into force on Pentecost Sunday, June 5, 2022. Although it is
a legal text, this constitution is presented under the banner of synodality, and I would like to draw your attention to several principles
that serve as an inspiration and framework for this constitution. My
considerations will not be very practical at first, but they could have
important consequences for the synodal practice of the Church and
especially for her synodal face at the dawn of the third millennium.

Therefore, I will attempt a sounding to determine the depth of
the missionary reform of the Church, which the new apostolic constitution on the Roman Curia intends to serve, by commenting on
the statement that the mystery of the Church combines "mission"
and "communion" in such a way that the former has meaning only
in terms of the second, in other words, that the purpose of mission is
precisely to make everyone know and experience "the new communion" that has entered into history with the Son of God made man.

Along this line of reflection, I could say at the outset that the synodal practice of the People of God is the dynamic dimension of their
communion, provided, however, that we specify the nature of this
communion and the articulation of this dynamic. For we could easily
stop at the organizational aspect of the ecclesial communities, which
certainly is important but does not state the essential thing. How then
should we define the essential dimension of synodality? Let us quote
again the text of the new constitution: "This life of communion

---

[1] International Theological Commission (ITC), *Synodality in the Life and Mission of the
Church* (March 2, 2018).

makes the Church *synodal*; a Church marked by reciprocal listening, 'whereby everyone has something to learn. The faithful people, the College of Bishops, the Bishop of Rome: all listening to each other and all listening to the Holy Spirit, the Spirit of truth (cf. Jn 14:17), in order to know what he says to the Churches (cf. Rev 2:7)'."[2]

"This life of communion" *gives to the Church the face of synodality*. What a beautiful expression, which favors personalist vocabulary rather than functional language. For communion concerns the life of persons and not only their tasks, plans, and aspirations. In this vein the document adds right away the idea of learning from one another thanks to listening—a kind of listening that involves everyone, at all levels: person to person, between the pope and the bishops, everyone listening to each other and everyone listening to the Holy Spirit, the Spirit of Truth.

At this point here we are already on the threshold of a deeper theological and existential consideration. We must dare to pose major questions: Who is this Spirit of Truth? What does this listening signify in order to know what he is saying to the churches? What does this Spirit want to tell us by this "walking together" in a spirit of synodality? How and on what conditions could we arrive at a renewed, synodal, joyous ecclesial mentality, accompanied by an imperative missionary consciousness? What is keeping the joy of the Gospel that fills our chief pastor from spreading throughout the ecclesial body? How can we contribute more to this synodal and missionary spirit in Latin America? Until now we have renewed structures: the reform of CELAM [Episcopal Conference of Latin America], the creation of CEAMA [Bishops' Conference of the Amazon], the convocation of a continental ecclesial assembly: fine initiatives that favor the organizational approach. But don't we have to arrive at a deeper level of synodality, one that is perhaps less spectacular but closer to the concrete conditions of families and of women, and to the increasing poverty of an immense majority of our Catholic faithful?

Far be it from me to devalue the current research and the fine initiatives that it creates; certainly, it is necessary to promote organic participation in the structures that are in place, but in the hope of eliciting the inner spirituality that springs from the Word of God and

---

[2] *PE*, no. 4, quoting Francis, Address during 50th Anniversary of Institution of Synod of Bishops.

responds to the vital and vocational needs of our communities. For this necessary personal interior life makes believers open to communion and more sensitive to justice and social solidarity. Sometimes in our Catholic circles we tend to pit religious concerns against social causes, as though the faith were foreign to the world, as though faith exiled us from social reality, whereas the gift of faith in the Risen Christ immerses us in real history at its most profound level of reality. The reason for this is that an authentic Christian lives at the shifting frontier between history and the Kingdom, and already in this present life, his faith makes him tip over into eternal life. The faith that he professes does not cause him to say farewell to this history, as though it were a fleeting existence that must be surpassed so as to be interested in the next world exclusively. For a Christian—like his Master who wins life and death in his triumph—carries with him into the Kingdom the whole fabric of relations that he has developed over the course of his earthly journey, a sacred history worthy of having been lived because it is crisscrossed by beauty and grace. In short, our Pasch, our resurrection, like the Passover of Christ, is neither an evasion nor a leap into the inaccessible next world, but rather is an assumption, a taking-up of our earthly reality into the Kingdom of Love, the Kingdom of the Spirit of Truth.

Might we be digressing from the topic for our reflection, synodality? Maybe, if we think only in operational categories on the sociological level; no, if we want to reach the aforementioned level of the interior life. *Praedicate Evangelium*, in speaking about the *new communion* that has entered world history through the Son of God, quotes the post-synodal apostolic exhortation *Christifideles Laici*, which refers precisely to the Trinitarian communion: " 'That which we have seen and heard we proclaim also to you, so that you may have fellowship with us; and our fellowship is with the Father and with his Son Jesus Christ' (1 Jn 1:3)."[3]

Here the real question comes up: How can synodality be rooted in the mystery of the Trinitarian communion? Is it realistic to ask a question like this? Wouldn't we be dreaming or sinking into myth? The Holy Trinity transcends world history and at first glance does not seem very functional, unless as a generic model of communion for various esthetic representations that we can make for ourselves. But is it possible to think about the Trinity's relation to the world as

---

[3] *CFL*, no. 32.

a dramatic interplay of freedoms that meet each other, a sort of theo-drama, in other words, an encounter and even a confrontation of the divine freedom with the human free wills on the historical scene? Hans Urs von Balthasar dared to unfold his *Theo-Drama* in five large volumes of his immense trilogy on the subject. The drama of God with his world is to manage to make concrete humanity, made up of sinful human beings, enter freely into his infinite interior space of communion. For this purpose, the Father sends his Son as Mediator, who becomes incarnate and walks along the roads of history, doing good and drawing everything into the eschatological center of gravity of his Cross and Resurrection. The fruit of his Paschal Mystery, in other words of his mediation (his priesthood), is the outpouring of the Holy Spirit on all flesh, communicating the eternal life of the Father and the Son to every creature that consents to believe and to receive his salvation from Christ. Now this salvation is nothing other than humanity's participation in the Trinitarian communion already in this life and for all eternity.

Well, since the communion of Divine Persons is truly offered to the communion of human persons through faith in Christ, let us try to sketch in broad strokes the major axes of this encounter of the Trinitarian communion with humanity in Christ and the resulting dynamic for human relations. The conciliar constitution *Lumen Gentium* speaks about the mystery of the Church as a community of "theandric" relations, in other words, of divine-human relations, an interpenetration of mutual relations between the Trinity and humanity in which the Holy Spirit plays a key role that we must now explain so as to grasp the importance, the nature, and the ramifications of it.

The point of departure for such an explanation is the sacramental reality of the Church, which Vatican Council II developed beyond all expectations, well beyond the seven sacraments, but while integrating the seven sacraments as fundamental articulations of the Church's sacramentality. The Church is communion, a communion that is the sacramental sign of the communion which is the Holy Trinity.[4] That means that this communion really contains with it, invisibly, the communion of the Divine Persons of which it is the

---

[4] See *LG*, no. 1: "The Church is in Christ like a sacrament or as a sign and instrument both of a very closely knit union with God and of the unity of the whole human race."

sacrament. *Lumen Gentium* forcefully declares that the unity of the People of God participates in " 'the unity of the Father, the Son and the Holy Spirit' ".[5] Let us see, therefore, how the grace of the Trinitarian communion, which is the basis for the synodal dynamic, is articulated concretely in the Church.

The point of departure is Baptism: "I baptize you in the name of the Father, and of the Son, and of the Holy Spirit." To be baptized means to be plunged into the infinite love of the three Divine Persons. By this immersion, the Holy Spirit confers on each baptized person the grace of divine filiation, a configuration of the human subject to the Person of the Incarnate Word that effects an indestructible identification, even in those cases in which the child of God who has been graced and configured in this way ends up consciously denying his membership in Christ. The gifts of God are indisputable; they do not depend on the degree of consent of the person who is sanctified by Baptism. Even in the situation of an apostate's refusal, a certain presence of the Son of God continues to dwell within the baptized subject, calling and moving him to conversion. This is expressed by the classic theological concept of the sacramental character. Consequently, a baptized person never acts alone in the world; he is in a way inhabited and possessed by the Son of God, who shed his blood for him and activates him by ties of love that are constantly renewed and active, so that in the actions of a believer who lives out his membership in the community of baptized persons one can see the action of the Son of God—hence his charity, which is the virtue par excellence and the unsurpassable testimony to communion with the Father in the Spirit. This is why the new commandment of love, left to us as a testament by the Lord Jesus, is the touchstone of fidelity to the synergy that the Holy Trinity dreams of sharing with all humanity so as to make it one great family of children of God: *Fratelli Tutti*.

Baptism thus gives the filial grace that establishes the New Covenant between the Trinity and humanity. This is the first fruit of the Incarnation of the Word and of the gift of the Spirit of the Son: an authentic participation in the divine filiation of the Incarnate Word. This gift of filiation draws another one after it; it is inseparable from closeness to the divine paternity in Jesus: "He who sees me sees him

---

[5] Ibid., no. 4, quoting Saint Cyprian, *De Orat. Dom.* 23 (PL 4, 553).

who sent me" (Jn 12:45). "He who hears you hears me,... and he who rejects me rejects him who sent me" (Lk 10:16). "He who believes in me will also do the works that I do;... because I go to the Father" (Jn 14:12). Such a personal presence of the Father in the Son continues to be perceptible, by divine institution, in the sacramentality of the Church. This is the gift of the Sacrament of Holy Orders, which identifies some subjects who are chosen and called with Christ inasmuch as he bears within himself the Father's witness. Christ is the Son of the Father, and he is also his envoy, his messenger, his Apostle, his minister; his Holy Spirit (the Spirit of the Father this time) can communicate a sacramental participation in this "ministerial" identity of Christ the Lord, the High Priest of the New Covenant. This is the vocation of the ministers who are ordained to the different degrees of the ministerial priesthood—hence the paternal traits of the priestly identity and the corresponding spirituality of the Good Shepherd who gives his life so that the sheep might have life and have it abundantly. Through this identification of the ordained ministers with Christ the Priest, Shepherd, and Bridegroom, through the Spirit of the Father, the Church is constituted in her hierarchical structure. This structure embodies the Trinitarian communion inasmuch as it gives a sacramental participation in the relation between the Father and the Son, a participation which then becomes the beneficiary of the dynamic of ecclesial relations between the community of the baptized and the *diakonia* of the Lord's ministers. One and the same Spirit guarantees the unity of these relations inasmuch as he is communicated as Spirit of the Father and Spirit of the Son. We already sense that for the nature and the exercise of synodal communion, the awareness of such a configuring grace and of such a participation in the Trinitarian relations can awaken energies and synergies that in another way are more significant and effective than the dynamisms identifiable by the human sciences. However, let us not create oppositions where there should be none; let us just root the sociological elements in the theological elements.

Let us go further yet, much further in the surprises that God's grace has in store. We have identified the graces of participation in the divine filiation and to a certain extent the participation of the ordained ministers in the divine paternity through the effect of the outpouring of the Spirit of the Father and of the Son in the sacraments of

Baptism and Holy Orders. These two sacraments, we should add, are joined marvelously in the Eucharistic celebration of the Paschal Mystery. The Sacrament of the Eucharist is in effect the locus par excellence of the New Covenant between the Trinity and humanity, the place of the admirable exchange between the offering of the Son of God *pro nobis* [for us] through which he draws all humanity with him toward the Father, an offering that the Father welcomes and to which he responds by pouring out abundantly the Spirit of love in the Eucharistic Communion. The latter as a result builds up the *communio sanctorum* [communion of saints] in the ecclesial community that has gathered. In short, through the mediation of the ministers who celebrate the sacrament and through the offering of the baptized persons who unite themselves to and participate in Christ's offering, the Church is constituted in her sacramental reality as Body of Christ, which proceeds from the Eucharistic Body, and also in her identity as Bride of the Lord, who lives by the constant reception within her of the fruitfulness of her divine-human Bridegroom.

Now the fruitfulness of the divine-human Bridegroom, living and interceding for us at the right hand of the Father, is the Holy Spirit of God, fruit of the exchange of love between the Father and the Son, the consubstantial, infinite kiss that becomes, in the economy of salvation, the kiss of resurrection taking in all humanity in its merciful embrace. The Holy Spirit is the quintessence of the divine fruitfulness that is poured out in this way, the dawn of the new creation, the Spirit of Truth who inaugurates and brings to its glorious completion the coming of the Kingdom, a Kingdom of justice and mercy, of love and peace. At the heart of the Church as she makes her pilgrim way along the roads of history, this Spirit of gratuitousness, unity, and liberty is manifested also in a way that is proper to it, complementing the personal manifestations of the Father and the Son that we spoke about earlier. This is a fundamental point that I wish to insist on, because it holds one of the keys, if not the master key, to the synodal nature of the Church. The personal manifestation of the Holy Spirit is displayed in particular in the charismatic dimension of the Church, a dimension that had been neglected for centuries until Vatican Council II once again brought it to the fore: it concerns very specifically the Sacrament of Matrimony, consecrated life (both contemplative and active), the apostolic and missionary movements, the prophetic and mystical gifts, the associations, in short, everything that helps to stimulate the holiness and unity of the Church, the beauty of her communion and the ever-widening influence of its mission.[6] Saint Paul draws up several lists of charisms that he had experienced, which he developed and disciplined in the early days of the Church. These lists are far from exhaustive, and we must avoid thinking of charisms as extraordinary phenomena designed for an elite. The Holy Spirit pours out his gifts abundantly on all baptized persons for the service of the common good and the building up of the Body of Christ. Some are more spectacular, others are scarcely visible, but all are given to build up communion and to serve missionary work.

Let us take stock of our argument, which seeks to root the synodal practice of the Church in the Spirit of the Trinitarian communion. We described the involvement of the Trinitarian communion in the articulations of the ecclesial communion in such a way as to go beyond the "esthetic" model that is generally utilized. For we have not been talking about a reference model, but rather about a dramatic entrance upon the scene of the Divine Persons in the ecclesial relations that are founded on the sacramental structure of the Church. Paternity, filiation, and fruitful liberty are the properties of the Divine Persons that are manifested in the sacraments of Baptism, Holy Orders, and the Eucharist, and also in the multitude of charisms that adorn the believing community because of the freedom of the Spirit of the Father and of the Son, poured out in history. According to this theo-dramatic vision, God walks with us in history; he walks on a human level, so to speak, disguising his majesty in the humility of his love, working in unity and for unity, so as to restore and make much better the Covenant relationship illustrated by God's familiarity with the man and the woman in the Garden of Eden.

Synodality is the large-scale blooming of this Covenant relation, provided that our human and ecclesial relations accomplish more than an esthetic representation of God's closeness. For *God walking with his people* is not a rhetorical formula, a beautiful, inspirational image, a popular representation with which to galvanize the crowds; it is the real presence of an immense and very concrete grace, a historical truth that is just as pregnant with meaning as the Incarnation

[6] See *LG*, no. 12.

of the Word and the outpouring of the Holy Spirit on Pentecost. Indeed, the synodal practice of the People of God, as a style of participating in the Trinitarian-ecclesial communion, cannot be reduced to the accomplishments of the human actors; it must give precedence to the Divine Actors who are engaged in history, and it must allow itself to be shaped by the personal mark of the Spirit of the Father and of the Son in the ecclesial traits of those who are baptized, consecrated, and sent by the Father so that the world might have life and have it in abundance. This kind of passage from an esthetic perspective to a dramatic perspective marks a turning point in our way of addressing synodality, since we start from God and from his manifestation in history, instead of starting from our aspirations and human representations, even if it means orienting them toward the Kingdom.

You may doubt that my change of perspective will succeed in providing a better foundation for synodal practice, because we are so immersed in an anthropocentric culture that any Trinitarian discourse runs the risk of appearing abstract, disconnected, and irrelevant to the furthering of ecclesial communion on promising paths. I speak about a change of perspective because thinking about synodality in terms of the Trinity, which is involved in the sacramentality of the Church, is notably different from a socio-anthropological approach in which one constructs a functional heuristic model, even if one does declare then that the Spirit suggested it. In practice, depending on the perspective that is adopted, the synodal process will be explained in terms of ideas to be spread and plans to be implemented—or else in terms of persons to love and poor people in real life to be consoled and uplifted thanks to the merciful charity of an immense Tenderness that precedes and envelops us. A perspective that is rooted in the communion of three Persons never abandons the concrete life of human persons who are loved for their own sake, whereas a perspective from below, starting from ideas that are generous but human, runs the risk of remaining partial solutions that do not give true life.

Allow me here to return to the constitution *Praedicate Evangelium* so as to reflect with you on the synodal revolution that it introduces in matters of government in the Roman Curia. From now on the dicasteries are not only authorized to include laypeople, men and women, among their members and their personnel, but they can also entrust to them the responsibility for heading certain dicasteries.

Some have described this inclusiveness as a Copernican revolution in matters of ecclesial government because, until now, everyone thought that the top management positions had to be reserved for bishops or ordained ministers by virtue of their power of jurisdiction founded on the Sacrament of Holy Orders. The new constitution relies on the synodal principle to justify this inclusiveness by virtue of the power of jurisdiction granted by the canonical mission that is given by the pope. The canonical explanation then emphasizes that all exercise of authority in the Roman Curia is based on the delegation of power granted by the Holy Father and not on the fact of being a bishop, priest, nun, or layperson. This explanation is canonically comprehensible, but to me it seems theologically lacking, and even contrary to synodality, inasmuch as the latter presupposes a baptized person endowed with a charism and not just a delegation of power that comes from above. The appointment of laymen or laywomen to positions of authority in the Roman Curia assumes a previous discernment by the pope of a charism or a particular competence that justifies his choice of integrating that religious or layperson into a position of great responsibility in the Curia. The authority that he delegates is his, and it makes all the difference, but it is not entirely without a basis in the chosen subject; it is conferred on a charismatic personality who is indeed capable of accomplishing the canonical mission received from the supreme pontiff.

What is at stake in this question about ecclesial governance entrusted to persons who do not have the power of Holy Orders is the recognition of charisms in the Church. It will take a lot more time before a change of our clerical mentality allows us to recognize that a charism bestowed by the Holy Spirit, duly acknowledged by the ecclesial authority, can be a source of authority and authentic governance. In this regard, our Catholic culture grants to bishops and priests an exclusive authority that struggles to discern and integrate forces to counterbalance their power; but such forces appear to be increasingly necessary for the growth and equilibrium of the ecclesial community. We know that this deficiency has led to abuses, and it is time to remedy them radically by putting an end to this pretense of exclusivity in which clericalism is rooted. On the juridical level, the apostolic constitution *Praedicate Evangelium* opens this door that has remained closed until now; this will make it possible to change the exclusively clerical face of the Roman Curia. The theological debate to justify this inclusiveness has scarcely been framed, and it must come to terms with a question that has been controversial for centuries: the relation between the power of orders and the power of jurisdiction. I will not go into this more for the moment, but I would like at least to mention a theological perspective that the Holy Father himself cited during the discussion about *Praedicate Evangelium*.

I mean the Marian principle to which he has often alluded since the start of his pontificate. He refers to it as context for the important place of women in positions of responsibility in the Church, without however conferring priestly ordination on them. Francis says that a woman is on the side of Mary, who is more fundamental than Peter. Indeed, two visible principles structure the ecclesial community: the Petrine principle and the Marian principle. We should ask ourselves whether the current synodal research has really taken the Marian principle into account. In Germany, for example, they speak about a division of powers in the Church according to a purely Petrine logic. This is why some call for revising the fact that the ordained ministry is reserved for men. How can we show that authentic synodality presupposes the integration of the Marian logic? This is the challenge faced by this plenary assembly of the Pontifical Commission for Latin America.

I do not claim to respond to this challenge at the outset, but I would like to mention in conclusion several questions that could recall the Marian logic of our Trinitarian approach to ecclesial communion. The Virgin Mary is the creature who was most intimately associated in communicating the Trinitarian communion to humanity. No one developed such explicit relations to each Divine Person as she did. The Holy Spirit overshadowed her, and the Word of the Father took flesh from her flesh so as to initiate with her a Covenant that was to define the salvific destiny of all humanity. How might we derive from her Trinitarian experience some practical guidelines for our synodal path in ecclesial communion? Her attitudes can enlighten us about the way to walk with God in the midst of his people. What relation to the Holy Spirit emanates from her witness? What fruit of her willingness can be discerned in the Gospel in relation to the growth of the primitive community of the Universal Church? What was Mary's way of participating in the debates of the Apostles? Under the impetus of the Holy Spirit, the Virgin Mary was empowered as the Immaculate Daughter of the Eternal Father, the fruitful Mother of the Incarnate Son of God, the Spouse of the Lamb who was slain; her divine maternity comprises all the moments of her intimacy with Jesus from his conception, his birth, his hidden and public life, his Passion, death, and Resurrection, all of it culminating in the paschal outpouring of the Holy Spirit, which gives her a universal fruitfulness as Mother of the Church and of humanity.

This peerless woman, this New Eve, walks with us; the holy People of God often know this better than their guides and ministers. Her maternal tenderness is reflected in the faces of her children as a source of light is refracted by a kaleidoscope. For the humble prayers of the People of God, in which they sincerely call on the Mother of mercy, obtain her help in their trials and perseverance on the road of salvation. Moreover, meditation on the mysteries of the Rosary infuses her virtues and her fullness of grace into souls, so that the Marian people of the Americas, from north to south and from east to west, walk in unity beneath her star in their hope for the Kingdom. They are a people made up of the poor who aspire to the glory of heaven more than to earthly glory, a people who suffer with dignity and give of their poverty by sharing especially a joy that comes from elsewhere. They are a people who evangelize by their spirit of solidarity and sharing, by their fidelity to the Word of God and to the breaking of the bread, a people who let themselves be guided by the Holy Spirit and the hierarchy of the Church, despite everything, because they know that the Mother of mercy covers all the weaknesses of her children in her great starry mantle, obtaining for them the courage to stand up again and the boldness to keeping going forward with the Successor of Peter on the paths of universal fraternity.

Dear friends, we are the witnesses to this heritage; we are all called to take up the challenge of a synodal Church in America, so that the testimony of the Holy Trinity might shine in the missionary communion of our communities. Let us humbly implore the Holy Spirit so that this synodal Church that we dream about with Francis may be Marian; otherwise, it will not exist.

Chapter 14

You Are the Light of the World

Dear recently appointed brother bishops,

We solemnly conclude our fraternal meeting in Rome with the Holy Eucharist in Saint Peter's Basilica, which will be followed by a dialogue with Pope Francis. These two powerful moments symbolize the grace of our calling and of our mission. The Lord chose us and empowered us to bring the light of his Gospel to the world. The Eucharist that we celebrate now and every day is the permanent source of this light; the meeting with the Successor of Peter is also a reminder that together with him, in our fraternal and sacramental communion with and under Peter, the light of Christ's love grows in us and shines in the sight of the whole world. Let us thank God for our entirely unmerited election and for the beauty of our mission!

Vos estis lux mundi—You are the light of the world. This is the title of the motu proprio by Pope Francis that since 2019 has looked after the accountability of the bishops in matters of sexual abuse. This powerful evangelical message presides in a way over the Church's vigilance concerning the moral integrity and pastoral prudence of her pastors. In this regard, Pope Francis is waging a decisive battle, following his predecessor Benedict XVI, to eradicate from the life of the clergy the scandalous abuses that have destroyed lives and dealt a serious blow to the Church's credibility. In becoming a bishop, which means watchman or overseer, each one of us, also, takes responsibility in this battle so as to assure that our communities have healthy, safe spaces where the light of Christ can shine with complete freedom. This vigilance is

This essay is based on a homily given during Mass at Saint Peter's Basilica at the conclusion of the initial formation session for new bishops, September 19, 2022.

not the essential element of our work, but without this vigilance, the essential work of our proclamation and witness would be compromised. May the grace of fortitude and courage be given to us to carry out this difficult and painful part of our mission.

Let us draw the grace and the strength that we need from the gift of the Spirit that we received by the imposition of hands at our ordination. The Holy Spirit indeed unites us, ontologically, to the Person of Jesus, so that we become his living instruments; it follows that by the grace of the sacrament he is the one who carries out his pastoral work through us. Let us never forget that the objective presence of Jesus in us, and not our own talent, makes the difference and makes possible our pastoral service to the People of God.

The contemporary requirement for clerics to commit themselves to celibacy meets with evermore criticism nowadays, and we see multiple suggestions for reforming or even abolishing this discipline. Human reason, sure of its scientific conquests, claims to arrive at this diagnosis, but nevertheless it seems incapable of recognizing the grace that dwells within us. Nowadays the campaign against priestly celibacy is louder than ever, but Pope Francis decided not to modify the discipline of the Latin Church. We have to thank him for not giving in to cultural pressures, for this witness of a dedicated life, following the example of Jesus, is an irreplaceable resource for evangelization.

When Jesus calls his Apostles to leave everything to follow him, his demand seems excessive and exorbitant to many who decline the invitation; those who accept it are touched by a permanent grace of faith in the mystery of Jesus, in his divine identity that alone justifies such a demand. As a result, the Yes to the Master's call to follow him in this way of life becomes a profession of faith in his Divine Person. This is why those men and women who follow Jesus for love of his Name evangelize by their choice of this state of life. Before any explicit apostolate on their part, their virginal state of life is a profession of faith that evangelizes. It is necessary to say this calmly and without any inferiority complex today, notwithstanding the failures and the mediocre members of the clergy or of religious institutes. The Latin Church respects the other ecclesial traditions, but it has good reasons for keeping this discipline, which goes back to the apostolic tradition and guarantees the fruitfulness of its missionary activity. Doesn't the light of the Word-made-flesh shine brilliantly in the sacred ministers who joyfully agree to be living signs of the Bridegroom of the Church?

The most excellent setting for the nuptials of Christ and the Church is the Eucharistic mystery. After the Last Supper of the Lord and his Passover, the Spirit of the Risen Lord put custody of this mystery into the hands of the Apostles and of their successors. When we pronounce Jesus' words "This is my body" (Mk 14:22) and "This is my blood" (Mk 14:24), these words are and always remain the Words of Christ uttered *once and for all*; these sacramental words always remain the same in every Eucharist celebrated since the origins. Only the Holy Spirit can unite in this way a Word, which is an act of eschatological love performed *once and for all*, with every particular celebration by the Church in all times and all places. This miracle is an unfathomable mystery of faith that is hidden beneath humble rituals. We are not the proprietors of this transcendent act of love that joins us in the sacrament in a specific and concrete way; the Holy Spirit is the One who possesses us and makes use of us to achieve his universal salvific ends. What astonishment and thanksgiving should accompany our contemplation of this mystery of communion in which Christ the Bridegroom gives himself to the Church, his Bride!

Dear friends, Vatican Council II declares that "the Most Blessed Eucharist contains the entire spiritual boon of the Church, that is, Christ himself, our Pasch and Living Bread, by the action of the Holy Spirit through his very flesh vital and vitalizing, giving life to men."[1] As bishops we have custody of this spiritual treasure of the Church for the purpose of distributing it widely to the pilgrim People of God, which has great need of this Viaticum, food for the journey. The bishop is assisted by his *presbyterium* in this work of salvation, conscious that Eucharistic communion is the source and the summit of ecclesial communion as well as the daily food of the sacramental fraternity of the ordained ministers.

In our offering on this day, let us bring all those men and women who are entrusted to our pastoral ministry; let us promise once again to be for all of them pastors after God's heart, ministers who are conscious of their limitations and faults yet confident that the divine

---

[1] Vatican Council II, Decree on the Ministry and Life of Priests *Presbyterorum Ordinis* (December 7, 1965), no. 5.

mercy touches in the first place our own misery so as to make us capable of living for others and for God.

Let us add however another intention that remains a priority regarding the portion of the People of God that is entrusted to you; I mean your membership in the College of Bishops, which associates you with the responsibility for the Universal Church, *cum et sub Petro*; this membership commits you to an episcopal collegiality that is both affective and effective; with regard to various currents of thought, it commits you to prudence and fidelity in your teaching in the name of the Church. Therefore, let us pray for the Holy Father and for the whole College of Bishops so that our personal and communal witness of charity and unity may be a light that is worthy of the One who said: "I am the light of the world" (Jn 8:12). Amen!

Chapter 15

Toward Ecclesial Governance More Open to the Holy Spirit

The whole sacramental economy of the Church is the pneumatological realization of the Incarnation: the Holy Spirit, therefore, comes to be considered by Tradition as the soul of the Church which is the Body of Christ. The action of God in history always implies the relationship between the Son and the Holy Spirit, who, in Irenaeus of Lyon's evocative words, are called "the two hands of the Father".[1]

—*Iuvenescit Ecclesia*, no. 11

The Permanent Heritage of the Movements and New Communities

This beautiful statement from the Letter *Iuvenescit Ecclesia* serves as a framework in which to reflect with you on the identity and the mission of the movements and the new communities that have developed in the Church following Vatican Council II. The postconciliar enthusiasm about these charismatic groups has gradually turned into a more serene and differentiated attitude, which also takes into account the possibility of ambiguous phenomena and deviances which, in some cases, cast shadows on persons and communities. On the other hand, these charismatic groups have matured; they have gone through crises that are often necessary in order to arrive at a more discreet,

This essay is based on a conference given during a meeting of ecclesial movements and new communities, June 20, 2022.

[1] *Iuvenescit Ecclesia* is quoting Irenaeus of Lyon, *Adversus Haereses* IV, 7, 4.

more fruitful ecclesial service, by benefiting from the test of time and from the discernment of the pastors who accompany the growth of the Kingdom of God in the world.

"The Church, 'like a stranger in a foreign land, presses forward amid the persecutions of the world and the consolations of God'", the Council says with Saint Augustine, "announcing the cross and death of the Lord until He comes (cf. 1 Cor 11:26)."[2] I would like therefore to propose several theological and pastoral considerations that contribute to our discernment of the presence of the Holy Spirit and of his charisms with the help of several criteria inspired by the reform that is under way, impelled by Pope Francis. It is true that our Heavenly Father promotes the realization of his Kingdom with the missions of the Incarnate Word and of the Spirit, his *two hands*, but the second hand has remained too much in the shadows in our Latin tradition; if we were more conscious of the presence and the resources of the Holy Spirit for the governance of the Church, it would enable us to overcome clericalism and other deviations. Let us try therefore to identify the signs of the Spirit at work in the present realities of the Church, as well as in the dialogue with the authorities for ecclesial discernment and recognition. We will proceed summarily by starting with the fruits of the Holy Spirit, so as to arrive at several criteria that can guide pastors in accompanying persons and communities endowed with charisms for the common good.

"The whole sacramental economy of the Church is the pneumatological realization of the Incarnation", says the document cited at the beginning of this conference. This means that not only the seven sacraments are concrete signs of the Incarnate Word, but the Church as such, in other words, as the Body of Christ, a mystery of communion, is the "pneumatological realization of the Incarnation". In developing this concept, we can say that the mystery of the Incarnation implies two fundamental realizations: The first is Christological; it gives us in Jesus the ineffable closeness of the Word of God made man. The second is pneumatological; it gives us in the Church, the Body of Christ, the invisible but concrete closeness of the Holy Spirit. This second pneumatological realization of the Incarnation constitutes the Church as sacrament, in other words, the People of God as "a sign and

[2] LG, no. 8, quoting Augustine, *The City of God*, XVIII, 51, 2 (PL 41, 614).

instrument both of a very closely knit union with God and of the unity of the whole human race".[3] The Council affirms that the sanctifying Spirit rejuvenates and continually renews the Church, inciting her to realize her identity as Bride with a view to bringing about the Kingdom of God in the unity of the Father, the Son, and the Holy Spirit.[4] Let us keep in mind this pneumatological horizon that sheds light on the mystery of faith and the hope of the People of God.

One of the providential tasks of the movements and new communities during the postconciliar crisis has been to make tangible the breath of the Holy Spirit, which animates the Church, leading her to move in a missionary direction and to manifest above all a visible, attractive identity as a body and a communion. The Council had opened the way to renewal in the Spirit with its major constitutions, the cornerstones of which are the Word of God, liturgical reform, and the new sacramental vision of the Church. However, in the postconciliar confusion, the charismatic movements, associations, and communities, particularly those formed at the initiative of the laity, are the ones that took more seriously the witness of faith and creative dialogue with the modern world, thus making an evangelizing contribution in environments that were sometimes indifferent, sometimes detrimental and hostile to the proclamation of the Gospel.

The charisms multiplied and diversified, finding expression sometimes through stable communitarian entities, thus becoming institutionalized and creating the conditions for transmitting the gifts of the Spirit to future generations through persons involved in the different communities and apostolates. The organic development of these ecclesial entities was accompanied closely by the hierarchical authority, which initiated institutional dialogues and encouraged the composition of appropriate statutes for these new entities, whose identity and mission often did not find their own juridical configuration in the Pio-Benedictine Code [1917 Code of Canon Law], and sometimes not even in the new 1983 Code.

Before addressing the juridical questions, however, I would like to point out a very important fruit of the postconciliar charismatic wave, a phase of self-proclaimed "charismatic movements", but also

---

[3] Ibid., no. 1.
[4] Ibid., no. 4.

a phase of a growing realization within the People of God that some fundamental institutions such as marriage, the family, consecrated life, associations of the faithful, apostolic movements, etc., belong to the charismatic sphere of the Church. This realization was followed up by the Magisterium of the Church and provoked a fundamental reflection on the *coessentiality* between "hierarchical gifts" and "charismatic gifts" in the Church, in the wake of the conciliar document *Lumen Gentium.*[5]

A Doctrinal Fruit: *Iuvenescit Ecclesia*

The letter *Iuvenescit Ecclesia,* published by the Congregation for the Doctrine of the Faith in 2016, is a postconciliar document that I consider very important for a more in-depth understanding of the pneumatological identity of the Church, the Body of Christ, and for finding a new equilibrium among the different grace-filled entities that make it up. It is well known that the charismatic dimension of the Church was redeployed by Vatican II after centuries of neglect, due to the underdevelopment of pneumatology.[6] The ecclesiology of the Council is a decisive pneumatological development, the reception of which is still ongoing. It promises new approaches with the current synodal research, which refers explicitly to the vital, active presence of the Holy Spirit in all baptized persons. *Iuvenescit Ecclesia* is an important doctrinal step in the process because, after a long and laborious gestation, it provides a theological and pastoral framework that opens new horizons for Church law and beyond, by facilitating the discernment and accompaniment of today's charismatic entities.

The principal merit of this document is its fundamental affirmation that hierarchical gifts and charismatic gifts in the Church are *coessential;* this *coessentiality* has been experienced for centuries, but it is explicitly acknowledged in this document, which compiles the teachings of Saint John Paul II and Benedict XVI. The hierarchical gifts are more easily identifiable in the ecclesial order, because they correspond

[5] Ibid.

[6] See Alberta Maria Putti, *Il difficile recupero dello Spirito: percorsi e luoghi teologici della Pneumatologia nella tradizione latina del secondo millennio* (Rome: Gregorian and Biblical Press, 2016).

to the degrees of the Sacrament of Holy Orders. The charismatic gifts are more widespread and diversified among the People of God *according to the distribution of the gifts of the Spirit* (1 Cor 12:28). They can be individual but also collective because "the charismatic gifts, when exercised, can generate affinities, closeness, and spiritual relationships. Through these the charismatic patrimony, originating in the person of the founder, is shared in and deepened, thereby giving life to true spiritual families."[7] This personal and community aspect is precisely what developed exponentially after the Council, giving rise to a great interest, but also to worries and questions about adequate discernment, for example, as far as new forms of consecrated life are concerned. This is why *Iuvenescit Ecclesia* formulates criteria for the discernment of charismatic gifts and insists on mutual reference between the charismatic groups and the authority of the pastors in the organization of the ecclesial communion.

For our topic, I recall the conclusion of *Iuvenescit Ecclesia*, which affirms the necessity of respecting two fundamental criteria in the relation between the hierarchical and charismatic gifts:

> a) respect for the particularity of individual charismatic groups, avoiding juridical straitjackets that deaden the novelty which is born from the specific experience ...; b) respect for the fundamental ecclesial *regimen*, this way favoring the effective insertion of the charismatic gifts into the life of both the particular and universal Church. Thus, any danger that the charismatic entities might be considered in some way as running parallel to the ecclesial life or not ordered in relation to the hierarchical gifts is avoided.[8]

Formulated in general terms, these criteria are easy to accept, and they provide a course of action for recognizing and accompanying charisms in the Church. We can refer to this document to find the theological and pastoral foundations that are authoritative in order to manage correctly the personal problems and institutional relations in and around charismatic groups in the Church. The charismatic sphere is appreciated in the same way as the hierarchical sphere, while

---

[7] *IE*, no. 16.
[8] Ibid., no. 23.

being subject to its discernment and accompaniment. Not only is pneumatology well integrated, but also the Trinitarian foundation of the ecclesial communion is made explicit and is articulated specifically insofar as the different gifts of the Spirit are concerned.

The Temptations That Hinder Ecclesial Discernment

However, in a concrete case of discernment and ecclesial recognition, other factors have to be taken into account that may affect or interfere with the relations between the ecclesiastical authorities and the various charismatic groups. In this regard, Pope Francis provided supplementary criteria that fall under the category of spiritual discernment and are the result of a historical-theological "diagnosis" elaborated in his papal plan for reform. I am referring to a recurrent theme in the pope's Magisterium: spiritual worldliness, inspired by the writings of Henri de Lubac, but refined personally in the papal analysis of the temptations that affect clerical and ecclesiastical milieus in a particularly subtle way: "One is the attraction of gnosticism, a purely subjective faith whose only interest is a certain experience or a set of ideas and bits of information which are meant to console and enlighten, but which ultimately keep one imprisoned in his or her own thoughts and feelings."[9] This Gnosticism is not exactly identical to the ancient forms of the phenomenon, but it certainly has points in common with the anthropocentrism, individualism, and immanentism of contemporary Western culture, which affect spiritual trends, as well as the development of individuals and communities. "The other is the self-absorbed promethean neopelagianism of those who ultimately trust only in their own powers and feel superior to others because they observe certain rules or remain intransigently faithful to a particular Catholic style from the past."[10] Here this neo-Pelagianism seems to be identified with a certain authoritarian conservatism that judges and controls instead of evangelizing; indeed, the temptation runs the full spectrum and concerns both conservatives and so-called "liberals" or "progressives". The pope adds: "In others,

[9] *EG*, no. 94.
[10] Ibid.

this spiritual worldliness lurks behind a fascination with social and political gain.... It can also lead to a business mentality, caught up with management, statistics, plans and evaluations whose principal beneficiary is not God's people but the Church as an institution."[11]

These two temptations are structural and atmospheric; they contaminate the spiritual ecology of Christianity and are found in all circles: laity, consecrated life, clergy, not to mention the Roman Curia and the diocesan curias. Thus, all discernment involving persons "in authority" and persons seeking help is conditioned by these pervasive temptations, the manifestations of which sometimes seriously hinder personal or institutional analyses and decisions. The Holy Father concludes: "This stifling worldliness can only be healed by breathing in the pure air of the Holy Spirit who frees us from self-centredness cloaked in an outward religiosity bereft of God."[12]

Toward Ecclesial Governance More Open to the Holy Spirit

Conscious of the temptations to worldliness that threaten ecclesial communion in general and the discernment of charisms in particular, I would like to address the juridical aspect, starting with the new apostolic constitution *Praedicate Evangelium*, which considerably modifies the approach of the governance of the Roman Curia. Article 5 of the constitution opens up the possibility for participation of baptized Catholics in roles of institutional responsibility in the various dicasteries, while respecting the competences that require the Sacrament of Holy Orders. The official canonical justification given is that all responsibility for governance in the Roman Curia is based on a delegation by the pontiff. This canonical explanation seems to me insufficient to account for the reform by Pope Francis, for it is based not only on the opinion of some canonists, but more profoundly on the role of the Holy Spirit in the governance of the Church. Indeed, the approach already initiated by the appointment of laypersons to positions of governance in the Curia presupposes that the delegation of authority was prepared

[11] Ibid., no. 95.
[12] Ibid., no. 97.

by the discernment of the charisms of the Holy Spirit that the ecclesial authority verifies before conferring a delegation.

I point out this "theological weakness" in the explanation of the constitution in order to emphasize that pneumatology is still absent from many processes of ecclesial discernment. The criteria at our disposal are often negative, in the sense that they aim to detect dangers and forms of deviance, but they often lack a search for the presence of the Holy Spirit, the concrete character of his gifts, the fervor and freedom that he gives to some believers, while some hierarchs tend to interpret these gifts in a way that is ideological and detrimental, or else through the distorting neo-Pelagian or Gnostic prism that we spoke about. Consequently, errors of judgment and abuses of power are not foreign to the curial offices of this world, including the Roman Curia. Sometimes forcing a matter juridically prevents the spirit of the evangelical counsels from flourishing and spreading the pure air of the Holy Spirit in families and communities. The Holy Spirit does not reign in the abstract realm of a disembodied spirituality but rather seeks the mud of our sins so as to absolve us, and his most moving *kenosis* consists of submerging himself in our limitations and sins so as to liberate us from within from all slavery.

Although on the one hand some charismatic experiences need to be tested and corrected, on the other hand excessive rigidity in applying norms can prevent the balanced development and the appropriate recognition of a charism, or imperil its realizations. We have in mind, for example, the approval of statutes, methods of governance, respect for founders and foundresses, the granting of necessary dispensations, the analysis of problematic cases that involve the failings of the superiors of charismatic groups. The latter are called to render an accounting for their members and to seek the support of the hierarchical authority in an authentic, trusting dialogue so as to resolve the abnormal situations. In the present context of synodal growth, the dialogue between "hierarchical gifts" and "charismatic gifts" has not yet reached a point of ecclesial maturity, in other words, has not recognized that the two kinds of gifts are *coessential*, because as a result of clericalism and the pneumatological deficiency that can still be noted, the balance leans too heavily in favor of those who make the final decision about the value and modalities of a charism. Today much courage, humility, and patience is needed to defend an authentic charism that the Holy Spirit inspires for the common good. It is as though an icy wind of suspicion had cast doubt on some precious realities that are indispensable for the Church's identity and mission. Let us hope for a new springtime of synodality, which will make it possible not only to preserve the heritage of the movements and new communities, but also to expand the awareness of charisms in all ecclesial communities.

In the Ignatian school of Pope Francis, we are gradually trained to appreciate the importance of discernment, a vital, complex exercise in which it is not enough to know doctrine or canon law well. It is necessary to learn also to discern the presence of the Holy Spirit at work in each situation, for he enlightens the person who prays attentively so that he may know instinctively how to apply norms appropriately and flexibly with regard to concrete moral or spiritual possibilities of persons and of communities. The temptation of *order at all costs* and of control must not prevail over the unexpected ways by which the Spirit wishes to lead some vocations and some charisms. In recent times we have been inundated with denunciations of ecclesiastics and religious who have gone astray; a certain pessimism becomes evident, and a mistrust has settled in with regard to founders and foundresses because of the bad publicity that is conveyed in a sometimes not very discreet manner by the authorities themselves. We must remember that a tree that falls does not eliminate the forest that remains standing and makes no noise.

To conclude: The great synodal movements throughout the Universal Church would not have been possible without the awakening impressed by the Holy Spirit on the postconciliar movements and communities, whose labors have contributed to the emergence of a synodal sensibility in the People of God as a whole. In *Evangelii Gaudium* Pope Francis had already shown to these movements and communities a path of integration and of service to the ordinary or extraordinary charisms present within the territory of each local Church. This opportune orientation was accepted, and we see its fruits in many synergies and forms of collaboration. Thanks to God and the many forms of his grace, we are all on a journey, pastors and faithful, in the Spirit of the Risen Lord, so as to arrive together at the goal, the Kingdom of God, while sowing the Gospel of love along the road in all our relations of ecclesial and missionary communion. Love makes us prodigal in our mission to all those who wait for the light of Christ through our witness of faith and hope. The particular gift of the Holy Spirit that each one has received for his mission fits into the evangelizing communion of the People of God for the benefit of all, sometimes at the cost of difficult sacrifices, but always in the joy of serving the greater love that enfolds us all.

EPILOGUE

For the reader who has skimmed through these chapters, perhaps some questions remain, or some perplexities, as a result of my Trinitarian, pneumatological, and nuptial approach: the Paschal Mystery as a Trinitarian exchange; the mystery of the Incarnation prolonged in the Church in a pneumatological sacramental modality; the centuries-old controversy between the power of orders and the power of jurisdiction, which is well on the way to a solution; and charisms raised to the state of a principle coessential to the structure of the Church—these, among others, are a few insights and materials offered for discussion with a view to a more synodal Church.

One might object that these considerations have little relevance to decentralization and the redistribution of powers in the Church, to the promotion of women, to the control of abuses of all sorts, and to adaptation to the democratic culture of our age. Consequently, the question arises of whether this ecclesiology in progress could have a real evangelizing impact, given the challenges of our secularized, pluralistic, hypereroticized, and technical-scientific societies. Time will tell; the future is in God's hands and in the hearts of those who believe in the power of the Holy Spirit.

It is true that the foregoing chapters give priority to dogmatic questions in comparison to moral and canonical questions—the problems of wielding authority, of organization, and of participation in making decisions that concern communities have not really been addressed in themselves. The option was taken to root these important sociological but secondary questions in a theology of communion. Otherwise, the plan for a synodal Church runs the risk of remaining at the level of the NGOs of this world.

The Eastern churches know that the archetype of synodality is the Holy Trinity—a mystery of love, a mystery of communion in which each Person constitutes the Three-in-One. By coming to walk with us in history, God manifests his being-love as infinite mercy. This is the testimony of Sacred Scripture. A synodal Church becomes in turn a witness to this, primarily by her theological virtues of faith, hope, and charity, before any other moral, functional, or organizational consideration.

These prolegomena for a synodal ecclesiology do not claim to do anything more than supply water for the mill of indispensable theological reflection. In the current state of the research, it is important to be "creative", but not without a compass, while making sure that our proposals come from the Holy Spirit and are in keeping with the Word of God, since the Spirit always acts in concert and perfectly in tune with Christ.

The provocative teachings of Pope Francis, which are the result of prayer, should be understood in the prophetic and missionary vein that characterizes his pontificate; he sometimes surprises practicing Catholics and the clergy, but he reaches a broader public that is less familiar to us. His merciful overtures to sinners must be understood not as dubious liberalizations of morality but as what they mean to express: God's closeness to every person and to every situation, whether or not living situations conform to the moral rule. Anyone who interprets him differently is encouraged to examine his own prejudices, unconscious pharisaism, or even ill will—judging at least by the Gospel in which Jesus was often criticized and persecuted because of his merciful overtures to sinners.

Remembering Mary Magdalene, the Apostle of the Apostles, let us leave the last word to the infinite mercy of the Father that bursts forth in the Resurrection of Christ, whose Holy Spirit makes us witnesses dazzled because we have dwelling within us him who gives us ineffable joy and a hope that does not disappoint.

INDEX